D0046463

Critical Acclaim for *The Learning Paradox*

"Every day the future keeps coming at us whether we like it or not. *The Learning Paradox* provides individuals and organizations with the keys to unlock the right attitude and the mechanism for developing the necessary skills to go out and meet the future with confidence."
— Kenneth Clarke, Chairman, Royal LePage

"*The Learning Paradox* allows us to internalize points and understand completely through meaningful, real-world anecdotes."
— Nick Truyens, Vice President, Finance, LEGO, USA

"Harris is one of the best speakers and authors I've ever been introduced to. His style is informative, topical and easy to understand. The paradigms presented have real-world application to a broad range of organizations."
— Bill Foster, Richard Chang Associates Inc., California

"A manual for today's business leaders — a template for future strategy and decisions. Continual learning should be the basis of every leader's agenda."
— Bill Williams, CEO, TEC (an international organization of CEOs)

"In an era of rapid change and uncertainty, job security has quickly become a thing of the past. *The Learning Paradox* is a must-read."
— Arthur R. Soler, President, Cadbury Chocolate Canada

"The paradigm discussion is both provocative and provoking — content rich and delivered with a human approach."
— Wynne Powell, Chief Operating Officer, London Drugs

"*The Learning Paradox* provided insight and focused on the future by teaching us that we are ultimately responsible for managing our careers."
— Mark Sheinfeld, Senior Vice President, SHL Systemhouse (an MCI Company)

"*The Learning Paradox* is one of the few books which addresses the importance of the individual's need to reflect on how they have to change their thinking and actions to support the organizational change.
— David Hardy, Senior Manager, Creativity & Innovation, Institute for Learning, Bank of Montreal

"The power of *The Learning Paradox* is in its breadth and conciseness. Mr. Harris has a strong grasp of the issues and the interplay of forces in today's business and working environment, and this is conveyed with clear language and effective examples."
— D'Arcy Mackenzie, Manager, National Education & Development, Ernst & Young

"*The Learning Paradox* forces you to think. Every leader and aspiring executive should read it."
— Rick Broadhead, Co-author, *Canadian Internet Handbook*

To my parents, Suzanne and Bob Harris,
whose love and support have encouraged me to pursue a life of learning.

To my brother and sister, Ian Harris and Cathy Harris,
with whom I have grown in love and life.

And to Aubie Graham and Thomas Berry,
my greatest teachers.

Strategic Advantage Mission Statement

We work to change the world
by changing ourselves and by helping our clients change.

Strategic Advantage is a learning and teaching organization. We study emerging trends and their potential impact on businesses. We are committed to advancing the understanding and practice of cutting-edge leadership and assist our clients—individuals and organizations—to achieve the greatest possible security within a dynamic and changing marketplace.

THE LEARNING PARADOX

Gaining Success and Security in a World of Change

JIM HARRIS

Learning is the key to joy & success in life!

MACMILLAN CANADA
TORONTO

Canadian Cataloguing in Publication Data

Harris, Jim (Jim R.M.)

The learning paradox: gaining success and security in a world or change. Includes bibliographical references and index.

ISBN 0-7715-7574-2

1. Organizational change.   2. Creative ability in business.   3. Organizational effectiveness

I. Title

HD58. H368 1998 658.4′063 C98-930425-6

1 2 3 4 5 TRI 02 01 00 99 98

The Learning Paradox is available on audio and video tape. See order form at the back of this book. Books and tapes are available in special quantity discounts for promotions and corporate training programs. See Volume Discount Schedule at the back of the book. Fax in your order or call 1-800-491-6000 or 1-800-561-3591. E-mail comments to: jimh@strategicadvantage.com

Cover photograph © copyright by James Gritz/Photonica

Macmillan Canada

A Division of Canada Publishing Corporation
Toronto, Ontario, Canada

Printed in Canada

Grateful acknowledgement is made for permission to reprint excerpts from the following works:

The Digital Economy: Promise and Peril in the Age of Networked Intelligence. Copyright © 1996 by Don Tapscott. Page 77. Reprinted by permission from McGraw Hill Companies.

Shifting Gears: Thriving in the New Economy. Copyright © 1992 by Nuala Beck. Reprinted by permission of HarperCollins Publishers. Published by HarperCollins Publishers.

Paradigm Shift: The New Promise of Information Technology. Copyright © 1993 by Don Tapscott and Art Caston. Page 129. Reprinted by permission of McGraw Hill Companies.

Moments of Truth. Copyright © 1987 by Jan Carlzon. Ballinger Publishing Company. Page 232-233. Reprinted with permission of Jan Carlzon and HarperCollins Publishers.

Diagrams on page 75, 76 and 88 from "Sustainable Enterprise," by Key Consulting Group in Calgary. Copyright © 1997. Reprinted with permission.

Microsoft Secrets: How the World's Most Powerful Software Company Creates Technology, by Michael A. Cusumano and Richard W. Selby. Copyright © 1995 by Michael Cusumano and Richard W. Selby. Page 146. Reprinted with permission of The Free Press, a Division of Simon & Schuster, Inc.

How to Succeed with People. Copyright © 1971 by Stephen R. Covey. Page 23. Reprinted with permission of Deseret Book Company.

Contents

Getting The Most Out of This Book

Right now, before you begin the book, I want you to rip out this page. Yes, you understood me correctly, I said rip out this page. If you are in a bookstore, please pay for the book first.

Go ahead. I give you permission to release all your inhibitions and rip this page right out of the book! If you have been raised to respect books and this is a horrible thought, you can do it secretively while no one is watching. That's okay. But just do it.

Making Your Mark

Now that you have ripped out the page, this book really belongs to you. Many readers are hesitant to mark books. They have been taught for years that it is evil and wrong. However, I encourage you to highlight the text, make notes in the margin and earmark the pages. I guarantee you will get more out of the book. You will have deeper insights and you will have a lasting reference of the points that you feel are of most value.[1]

Gaining Comfort from Discomfort

When I address conferences and seminars, I ask participants to write their names as fast as they can three times. Then I ask them to use their other hand and repeat the exercise.

At this point there is usually a lot of laughter. When I ask how it feels to write with the "other" hand, I get comments like, "Awkward!" "Frustrating!" "Clumsy!" One man said, "When I was writing the first time, I felt like a lawyer; the second time like a doctor."

Next I ask, "How would you feel if you were asked to write with your other hand for the entire first day back at the office?" Typical answers are, "I'd take the day off!" "Stressed!" "Anxious!"

Then I ask, "How about if you were told to write with the other hand for the entire next week?" Responses include, "I'd take holidays!" "Do you expect me to keep serving the same number of customers?" "I'd dictate!" "I'd delegate!" "I'd start typing!"

Finally I ask, "What if you were instructed to write with the other hand for the rest of your life?" People typically are resistant: "I can hardly wait to retire!" "What's in it for me?" "Why?" "Who are you to ask?" Some are accepting: "Well, I guess I'd learn how to use it!"

Most of us are addicted to feeling competent. We are uncomfortable when we feel incompetent. We like the feeling of knowing.

A new associate said to me one day, "I've been here three months and I still feel uncomfortable. I haven't quite mastered the job!"

My response was, "That's fantastic! It's great that you feel uncomfortable!" Naturally, she looked at me as if I was crazy, so I explained, "If you can become comfortable with the uncomfortable feelings you

> Give a man a fish and you feed him for a day; teach him how to fish and you feed him for a lifetime.
>
> Lao Tzu, philosopher

experience when learning new skills, and if you can become accustomed to the discomfort that change brings, then you will never have to worry about job security for the rest of your life!"

Individuals who go through the learning paradox over and over again develop greater comfort with ambiguity, uncertainty and not knowing. They no longer fear the unknown. They develop faith in their abilities to learn. The feelings of discomfort that learning and changing bring never go away but the tolerance for accepting them increases. And the excitement that learning and changing brings sure beats boredom and apathy!

In general, people are more excited when they are encouraged to fully engage their broad range of talents. As soon as they have mastered a task, completed a project or finished a training course, employees should be given a new challenge. Of course, no one deserves to be thrown into the deep end of the pool. Tasks should be carefully set in a series of stages to match abilities, and challenges should be based on the principle that people's reach should exceed their grasp.

[margin note: ? Throws org'n into chaos]

Our future will increasingly depend on our ability to learn and change. Yet what we fear most is the sense of discomfort we feel when learning and changing. At times, we lack the confidence that we will ever learn the new skill. Or we fear failing in front of colleagues. We are impatient with ourselves, expecting to learn a new skill the first time we try. Other times we are embarrassed to ask for help, or don't know whom to turn to. We try to figure it out ourselves and after repeated false starts or after it has taken too much time, we give up in frustration. If this is a recurrent pattern, we may eventually doubt our abilities. This is the learning paradox. The good news is that there are ways to overcome it. Becoming comfortable with being uncomfortable is at the root of the new security. This is the essence of learning-based security.

Questions, Not Answers, Create Security

This book is meant to challenge you to think differently. Today, many business-book readers are searching for solutions to the complex challenges their organizations face. Instead of looking for answers, I challenge you to wrestle with the questions that this book raises. The "answers" that work for one company, if applied in another, may create disastrous results. A strategy that creates exceptional success today may cause failure in the future.

[margin note: Good questions are better than good answers.[1] David Hurst, author]

Answers aren't the answer. Instead, we must question the questions. For example, imagine a ski chalet on a beautiful mountain. When an avalanche destroys the house, the owner is justifiably upset and demands that the government do something about avalanches. The owner is searching for a solution. However, it may be more fruitful to consider rebuilding the chalet in another location.

Instead of simply seeking solutions to perceived problems, successful individuals and organizations question the way they *see* problems. In other words, they question the questions. The way questions are posed predetermines the range of potential answers. By continually posing questions from different perspectives, successful individuals and organizations can more closely strike at the root cause of their problems.

In this book you will read many case studies that explain how the best organizations are continually reconfiguring their systems and structures to provide new value to customers by launching new products and services.

Dogma breeds blindness. Leaders of the most successful companies live amid the questions instead of believing that they have all the answers. When new answers don't mesh with their current perspective, they explore the new ideas rather than dismiss them.

> Taking an aspirin today won't eliminate my headaches tomorrow.[2]
> Stephen R. Covey, author

But in these rapidly changing times people are uneasy, uncertain about what will happen to their jobs, their departments or even their company. They are under stress at work and anxious about the future. They yearn for stability, security, peace and tranquillity—for simpler lives and jobs. I have experienced this strong desire myself. People have been beaten up by management theory and the latest fads. They are fatigued, burned out. They want "the magic bullet." People want prescription lists. "Don't talk about principles," they plead. "Just give us the 7 steps, the 42 critical success factors, the 17 fatal flaws, the 19 implementation techniques." What they are really saying is, "Help me." "Make the pain go away. Now!" "Tell me what to do." "Make it easy for me."

But formulaic, simple solutions are not only illusory but also dangerous. Don't accept any simple formula that a consultant suggests without testing and validating it from your experience and within your corporate culture.

Attempting to find answers without considering the differences between organizations—markets, capital intensity, maturity, competition, strategic direction—would be comparable to my taking medicine prescribed by your doctor for you. I may have some of the same symptoms, but the cause, the ailment itself or possibly my reaction to the medicine would likely be quite different.[3]

Albert Einstein was holding an exam for his university students when a teaching assistant rushed up to him and said, "Dr. Einstein, there's been a terrible mistake. This exam is exactly the same as last year's! All the questions are the same!"

"Don't worry!" replied Einstein. "This year the correct answers are all different."

The questions for business this year are the same, but the answers are different. How do we better serve our customers? Will we add more value by introducing new and better products and services? How can we increase margins? Increase customer delight? Increase employees' growth and development? Shorten cycle times? Better align stakeholder interests? Eliminate non-value-added activity? Create new products and services as new technology and practices enable new relationships with customers, suppliers and employees? Create, anticipate or at least respond quickly to new market trends as they emerge?

Even the best organizations cannot become complacent if they expect to remain market leaders. I predict that the courier industry's document volumes will fall 50 percent between 1995 and 2000. The exponential growth of electronic mail (e-mail) and the ability to send formatted documents over the Internet will kill this old market. The volume of e-mail in North America has for the first time ever surpassed the number of letters carried by the U.S. Postal Service.[4] In order to thrive in the Internet age, courier companies must refocus their business.

Microsoft was blind-sided by Netscape. Wal-Mart may one day be threatened by virtual retailing. In other words, even the most successful companies must remain eternally vigilant, continually questioning their assumptions. Furthermore, what works for one organization may not work for another.

Therefore, the examples in this book are intended to provoke you to think differently and create the strategies, systems and structures that are best for your customers, your employees, your department and your organization. People like the security of knowing the answers, but today we must live and work amid questions because everything is changing.

Do not swallow whole any theory set forth in this book. Think about it! Debate it! Challenge it! Ultimately, decide what will and won't work for your organization. (This book is written for people at every level in an organization. If you don't feel that you can change the organization, substitute division or department. Today everyone in an organization is required to assume responsibility for adding more value for customers.)

> If you can keep your head when all about you are losing theirs, it's just possible that you haven't grasped the situation.
>
> Jean Kerr, American playwright

> The road to success is always under construction.[5]
>
> Sam Geist, professional speaker

I believe that most organizations already have people with the talent, knowledge and skills required to solve all their problems. The challenge for organizations is how to draw out employees' full potential with an exciting, compelling vision of the future.

Reflection:
• What is the key learning/insight for me in this introduction?

CHAPTER 1

Shift from Satisfaction to Security

After co-authoring *The 100 Best Companies to Work For in Canada*, I began speaking at conferences and seminars on corporate strategies for survival and success. In 1990, participants most frequently asked, "What makes an organization one of the best companies to work for?" Today they want to know, "How can I gain a sense of control over my career and my life?" "How can I count on being able to support my family?" Executives are asking, "How can we encourage employees to constantly change?" "How can we create a culture where fear does not rule?" In short, everyone is looking for security.

Drawing on case studies of some of the best companies, including Microsoft, Wal-Mart, Intel, Federal Express, Hewitt Associates, Sun Microsystems and Progressive Insurance, this book outlines how organizations and employees can best guarantee their long-term security in an environment of rapid change. The determinants of success and security are not what they used to be.

A Job for Life

People have a deep yearning for meaningful, challenging work. Yet, it is staggering that 73 percent of North American employees report that they do not find their work exciting.[1] Given that we spend one-third of our adult lives at work, this is a terrible tragedy. Despite this yearning, the times are such that people today aren't concerned about having a good job. They consider themselves fortunate to have any job. Downsizing, rightsizing, reengineering and outsourcing have made people shift their concern from workplace satisfaction to workplace security.

The Old Rules

In her book *When Giants Learn to Dance*, Rosabeth Moss Kanter, the former editor of *Harvard Business Review*, says the old, unwritten social contract was based on loyalty in return for security. People worked for one company for most of their lives and at the end of their careers received a gold watch. The implicit message was: Work hard, do what you're told, don't question authority and in return, you will be secure. We all knew the rules of the game.

> There is no such thing as a secure job anymore. There are only secure people.
> Warner Woodley, CEO, Mainstream Access

What conditions created security in the past? What did you look for when deciding what company to work for? What indicators told you that you were secure? Typically, people suggest the following categories:

SIZE OF ORGANIZATION Security was a function of the size of the organization you worked for. If you landed a job with IBM or the government and worked hard, you never had to worry about the future.

SHARE OF MARKET If you worked for a corporate leader with dominant market share — Coca-Cola, Procter & Gamble or monopolies such as utility companies — you were more secure.

STABILITY OF INDUSTRY With a job in a stable industry such as insurance or banking, you had a job for life.

SALARY AND BENEFITS Many people worked for companies that offered good pay and benefits. If you were loyal, worked hard and didn't question authority, you could depend on regular salary increases. Upon retirement you could count on the company pension plan.

STATUS OF POSITION The higher up you were in the corporate hierarchy, the more secure you were.

SERVICE The longer you worked for a company, the more secure you were. After 40 years you could expect to retire with a gold watch awarded to you at the president's annual dinner.

SENIORITY Unions created security. Once you got into a closed shop, you were home free. The stronger the union, the more secure your job.

SPECIALIZED KNOWLEDGE If you had a PhD, MBA or specialized knowledge, you were more secure.

SPECIALIZED FUNCTION If you had a specialized function — mainframe guru, for example — you were more secure because the organization depended on you.

PLANTS A woman in a seminar once said, "Plants, green plants." When anyone got a plant in their office, it announced that they had "arrived." Plants represented security!

The New Rules

Almost everything that created security in the past—large company, market leadership, stable industry, senior title, long service, unionization, specialized knowledge or function—now creates insecurity. All the old guarantees have disappeared. The old rules no longer apply. In fact, the old rules have created the current problems that organizations are facing.

SIZE IBM once prided itself on offering employees lifetime security. But between 1989 and 1995, IBM laid off 200,000 people—half of its workforce. Announced layoffs have been dramatic:

Company	Date	Announced Layoffs[2]
General Motors	Dec. 1991	74,000
Sears, Roebuck & Co.	Jan. 1993	50,000
Boeing	Feb. 1993	28,000
IBM	July 1993	60,000
Delta Airlines	Apr. 1994	15,000
Digital Equipment	May 1994	20,000
AT&T	Jan. 1996	40,000

Loyalty is the absence of a better value alternative.
Dave Nichol, creator, President's Choice Products

General Motors, Coca-Cola, AT&T and many others have down-sized dramatically. Most of these job losses were due to changes within huge corporations that were once considered immune to market forces. Clearly, they aren't offering the security they used to.

SHARE In 1997, *Fortune* magazine proclaimed that Coca-Cola was America's most admired company and that "brands rule."[3] However, not even Coke has been immune to crushing market shifts. Coca-Cola has been hurt badly by private-label pop bottlers, most noticeably Cott. Wal-Mart annually sells over one billion 12-ounce cans of *Sam's Choice* pop produced by Cott. In Canada, Cott has cornered 23 percent of all supermarket pop sales.[4] Coke's profit has been so eroded that the company closed its Canadian head office and now runs the Canadian operations out of the United States. Despite *Fortune's*

By identifying the new learning with heresy, you make orthodoxy synonymous with ignorance.
Desiderius Erasmus, Dutch scholar

claims, any company that is selling one billion of anything is taking market share away from some other company. Private-label sales are putting brand loyalty to the test. Market share is less secure than ever. Competition is coming from unexpected sources and from small, cost-effective and highly focused companies.

STABILITY The less your industry has changed in the past 30 years, the more it is at risk of being blind-sided by competition from an unexpected sector. A study by Royal Dutch Shell found that between

1979 and 1994, 40 percent of Fortune 500 companies ceased to exist. Some were acquired or merged while others simply failed to keep up with the changing times and lost their leadership positions. Many people believe that a particular industry provides security. Consider the insurance field. Nothing really changed in insurance between 1960 and 1990. But all of a sudden, banks got into the business and everything changed. With technology enabling the birth of new businesses and making others obsolete overnight, the longer your industry has been stable, the sooner it is likely to suffer a shake-up.

SALARY AND BENEFITS As Judith Bardwick points out in *Danger in the Comfort Zone,* entitlement—the notion that salaries and annual raises are a right as a result of showing up for work, rather than rewards for productivity—is rapidly disappearing. Increasingly, compensation at all organizational levels is based on performance. Expectations about pensions are also changing. Many western governments are heavily in debt and employees are realizing that they must save for their own retirement. No longer can employees depend on the government or their employer to provide financial security in old age.

STATUS Downsizing, delayering, reorganization, restructuring and reengineering have undermined the security of having a title. Often, the more senior you are, the more insecure you are because of ever-increasing performance expectations. Apparently, the higher you go, the thinner the air gets.

SERVICE The longer you've been in your position without learning new skills or accepting new responsibilities, the more you risk relying on obsolete skills that will give you a false sense of security. In the past, people who worked for several companies or held many different positions were viewed with suspicion. They were considered unreliable, unable to hold a steady job. Now the opposite is true. If you stay at the same job all of your life, people will wonder what's wrong with you. Research shows that on average, today's workers will hold 10 different positions in three different fields over their work life.

SENIORITY The traditional union model of seniority no longer offers the job security that it once did. In fact, it creates insecurity! Unions must be challenged to change along with the organization. Who has the skills that will help the organization transform itself for the future? The 18-year-old who surfs the Web every night, or the 55-year-old union member who doesn't know how to turn on the computer? Based on seniority (last in, first out) in a downsizing situation, who will the union push out of the organization? The 18-year-old. In other words,

In 1993, large U.S. firms announced nearly 600,000 layoffs – 25 percent more than in 1992 and nearly 10 percent above 1991 levels.[6]

Gary Hamel and C.K. Prahalad, authors

seniority will increase organizational *insecurity* by shedding employees who possess the new skills necessary to help create a viable organization for the future. Traditional seniority over the long term increases the insecurity of all members because it does not ensure that members are continuously learning, undergoing cross-functional job training, rotating positions and hiring people from outside the company — bringing new skills and perspectives. Over time organizations that fail to keep up with change will perish, resulting in all employees losing their jobs.

Old-style unions typically oppose cross-functional job sharing and training. Which member is more secure — one who has only worked in a narrow job description for 25 years or one who has worked in four different positions over 8 years? In fact, I question the validity of job descriptions today. Products and services, markets and competitors are changing so rapidly that rigid, negotiated job descriptions only ensure that an organization will be unable to change rapidly, which over the long term will increase the likelihood of its demise.

New unions are embracing flexible work and new work arrangements, thereby creating greater security for their members.

SPECIALIZED KNOWLEDGE We are more educated than ever before. Knowledge has become a commodity in the global village – more widely available than ever. Why hire a North American graduate for $30,000 a year when an equivalently educated person in China is available for $1,200? Even specialized knowledge over time becomes a commodity. During the 1950s, 56 North American schools offered Master of Business Administration (MBA) degrees, turning out a few thousand graduates annually. Today, more than 650 colleges and universities graduate 70,000 MBAs every year.[7]

In times of rapid change, knowledge depreciates in value just as quickly as computers and software technologies. Knowledge counts, but the right attitude and a commitment to lifelong learning is more important. A PhD could simply mean you know a lot about old stuff. Stephen Covey, author of *The Seven Habits of Highly Effective People*, points out:

> Education's main value does not lie in getting knowledge, much of which will be obsolete sooner or later. It certainly doesn't lie in credits earned or degrees conferred. These may open doors of opportunity but only real competence will keep them open. In fact, in our rapidly changing world there is no "future," no economic security in any job or situation. The only real economic security lies within the person, in his competence and power to produce.

Education's main value lies in learning how to continually learn, how to think and to communicate, how to appreciate and to produce, how to adapt to changing realities without sacrificing changeless values. Result? An inner confidence in the basic ability to cope successfully with whatever life brings.[8]

SPECIALIZED FUNCTION Assembly-line workers, bank tellers, typesetters, telephone operators, receptionists and even mainframe programmers—every time you turn around, another job's existence is being threatened. If your job is being replaced by technology or restructuring, how can you feel secure? Specialized knowledge, while still important, no longer provides the long-term security it once did.

SOCIAL CONTRACT The old social contract of working hard and never questioning authority in return for security is dangerous. When markets were homogeneous and stable, consumers predictable and brand loyalty certain, the social contract could operate. Today, however, many of the best and brightest employees refuse to work 50, 60, 70, 80+ hours per week. People want "balanced" lives. Do we live to work or work to live? The social costs of workaholism are well documented. Working hard needs to be redefined as adding more value through creativity and innovation rather than as working longer hours. In many corporate cultures it is still a status symbol to work long hours. In the future, I predict it will be a status symbol to hold a significant position of leadership, serve well and work only 40 hours a week!

> The ability to learn faster than your competitors may be the only sustainable competitive advantage.[9]
> Aire de Geus, author

Finally, the old theory "Never question those in positions of authority" creates insecurity. To thrive today, organizations must promote open, honest and vigorous internal debate. Employees should be encouraged to challenge decisions they believe are wrong. None of us knows what the future holds. No individual has all the insight into which new products or services will be winners, or can say definitively how they should be designed, implemented and delivered. Creating new value for customers requires a corporate culture in which open, honest debate can occur and where employees can challenge management decisions without fear of recrimination. Serving the hierarchy must be subordinated to serving the customer. One executive coined the phrase "the egoless corporation" to emphasize how today no individual has a monopoly on insight. Organizations need to draw upon the full intellectual talents of all employees. The sign of an excellent place to work is one in which there is healthy, vigorous, open debate.

> Change is inevitable, except in a vending machine.
> Anonymous

SPEED Complacency kills. Even in rapidly expanding industries there is little job security. Let's look at the fastest-growing industry sector worldwide: computer software. This sector has grown by 30 percent in real terms, compounded annually between 1980 and 1995. Yet, even in this explosive industry there is no security. *Information Week* annually ranks the top 50 independent software companies in the world. More than half the companies on the 1990 list did not appear on the 1995 list! Some were sold, others fell behind and a few went belly-up. In short, even the vaunted software market is uncertain.[10]

Change: The Key Factor in Today's Economy

Companies in all industries are susceptible to complacency and arrogance. Of the top 100 U.S. retail discounters in business in 1976, only 24 existed in 1994! What happened to them? Wal-Mart happened! In 1983, Wal-Mart's 641 stores had sales of $4.8 billion.[11] By 1996, Wal-Mart had become the world's largest retailer with over 2,200 stores and sales of $95 billion. Old companies with complacent attitudes are easy prey for formidable giants like Wal-Mart.

Who or what brought all this dramatic and painful change upon us? We did! As consumers, we are driving the change. As consumers, we are more knowledgeable than ever, and we are exercising our freedom of choice.

"Value consciousness" is rapidly replacing brand loyalty as the driving force behind purchasing decisions. If you provide better value for your customers, you win their loyalty.

With consumers demanding value, and technology making it possible to serve needs faster and more economically, no wonder everything is in a state of flux! Every sector of our society is being affected — governments at all levels, health care, business, not-for-profit organizations, social programs, arts and culture. There are no exemptions. The change is sweeping and dramatic:

- In 1980, who could have predicted that a black political prisoner would become president of South Africa and end apartheid; or that the Cold War would end and the Soviet Union would dissolve; or that the Berlin Wall would crumble, broken apart by people with their bare hands?

- Who could have predicted in 1975 that the combined market value of Intel and Microsoft would exceed that of IBM by 1993; or that today, Microsoft would have greater market value than General Motors? How can a company that is less than one year old with sales of $16 million be valued at $2 billion on the first day of its initial public offering? The company is Netscape.

- In Canada, it is surprising to find that more people work in the computer industry (equipment, semiconductors and services) than in the auto, auto parts, steel, mining and petroleum refining industries combined!

- Why are companies such as Netscape, Microsoft, Intuit and Sun Microsystems investing a higher percentage of their revenue in developing on-line transaction software for banking than are the traditional banks? Why are some banks still busy building branches? Do they think that banks of the future will have more to do with bricks and mortar than keystrokes and mouse clicks? Who could have thought you would one day be able to get a checking account or a Visa card from your stockbroker? Charles Schwab's clients can also trade stocks, mutual funds and other financial products 24 hours a day from their personal computer. Why, as of January 1996, had none of Schwab's competitors caught on and delivered a competitive easy-to-use *Windows* product?
- Who could have guessed that Sony would produce a game system — *Playstation* — that delivers 200 million instructions per second (MIPS) for $200 in 1996, while personal computers that deliver an equivalent power cost $2,500?
- Who could have imagined that in the 1980s, General Electric would make more money from its financing operations than from making appliances in the 1990s; or that American Airlines' parent company, AMR, would make more money from its competitors through its Sabre reservation system than by flying its airplanes?

Creating Security in the Midst of Change
If work security no longer comes from traditional sources, how can individuals find fulfillment and peace of mind? In a sea of change, how can we create stability? I believe that there are three main sources of security today. They are:

- Our ability to learn continually.
- Our ability to change (personally and organizationally).
- Our ability to cope with uncertainty.

Paradoxically, these are what we fear most as adults.

Creating Security for the Future
Eighty percent of the technology we will use in our day-to-day lives in the next 10 years has yet to be invented! If you find this hard to believe, think about how quickly technology is changing. For instance, automatic teller machines (ATMs) were introduced in 1981. Would you deal with any bank today that was not connected to the Interac or CIRRUS network? I use a notebook computer that has the same raw power as a mainframe of 15 years ago, but notebook computers did not exist before 1988. Many people today wear a watch that has more raw power than the first lunar landing module (a bit of a worry for the first astronauts!)

So how can I take a course today that will prepare me for the future? I can't unless in the course I learn how to learn, think about how I think, become more creative about creativity and deepen my understanding of teamwork in order to become a better team player. This is "meta" learning — conscious learning about the underlying processes of learning, thinking, creativity and teamwork.

Security for individuals is based on becoming self-reflective and self-correcting. Similarly, security for organizations is based on putting in place processes that guarantee self-reflection and self-correction at the individual and organizational levels.

The Learning Paradox

A paradox is an apparent contradiction. This book will examine many paradoxes: To create security, we must accept the insecurity that uncertainty brings. To feel comfortable about our future, we must accept the discomfort of learning new skills. Stability of market share or peace of mind comes only from changing. The more tightly leaders cling to control, the more out of control their organizations will be. The more power leaders give away, the more power they will have.

The challenges we face in these dramatically changing times can be overwhelming. When an organization falls on tough times, employees need support and encouragement. Unfortunately, unless the leaders are exceptionally courageous, principled and centered, tough times are when people receive the least amount of help and support.

The things that once created security now create insecurity. Yet, paradoxically, we will only add to our burden of insecurity unless we overcome our fear of acquiring new skills and knowledge. The secret of creating a sense of security and stability lies in confronting the barriers in our minds that stop us from learning and changing. Fear and uncertainty stop us, not our ability to learn.

Individuals can create their own security on the road ahead by living a life of learning. Leaders are responsible for ensuring that processes are in place to guarantee organizational learning. Nothing is more important, rewarding, enriching and enjoyable than growing as a result of seeing and acting differently. Life is learning. Learning is life.

Reflection:

What is the key learning/insight for me in this chapter?

Action:

What one action shall I take tomorrow to move learning into action? And over time repeat, to move action into habit?

CHAPTER 2

The Learning Paradox

Imagine that you are the parent of a child who is learning to walk. She takes her first tentative step, wobbles and falls. You'd probably pick her up, give her a big hug, encourage her to try again and praise her. "Honey, grab the video camera! She walked! Call Granny!"

No parent would ever stand over the child, lean down and at the top of one's voice say, "I have seen many first steps in my time. That was the worst first step I've ever seen!" No parent would ridicule her for trying. Her setbacks would be treated with love and encouragement and enthusiasm.

No matter what our age, when we are learning and growing we will stumble and fall periodically. If we are always beating ourselves up or being beaten up by others for making mistakes, we will learn more slowly. Children who are punished every time they fall will grow up to be insecure. If we are perfectionists by nature, we often set unattainable goals and beat ourselves up when we fail to reach them. Even when we come close, we are not happy. Inwardly, we will always be punishing ourselves for making mistakes even though it is impossible to learn anything new without failures.

Rather than spurring us on to greater heights, perfectionism stunts growth and satisfaction. As a Chinese proverb states:

> *Wisdom comes from good judgment*
> *Good judgment comes from experience*
> *Experience comes from mistakes*
> *Mistakes come from bad judgment.*

True wisdom involves the head, the heart and the hand.

Thomas Berry, theologian

After reading this, a friend shared the following saying:

> *To live but not to learn is not to live*
> *To learn but not to understand is not to learn*
> *To understand but not to do is not to understand* [1]

A father once approached me after a presentation and said, "My son is learning to walk. He doesn't want to learn just for the sake of walking, he wants to learn to walk because it is the fastest way of getting from here to there. Walking is the only way he will be able to get toys for himself." This was a powerful insight. Is that not why we want to learn as adults? Because we want to get from here to there. We want to have richer relationships in our personal lives. We want our organizations to grow and gain market share, increase margins and add new value for customers. We are required to learn and change because we want to get from here to there.

Learning is Central to Life; Fear is Part of Learning

Martin Rutte is a consultant and speaker.[2] In his presentations he often talks about how he learned to dive. Rutte was in his 40s when he decided to take up diving. Before he knew it, he found himself standing at the end of a one-meter diving board with his instructor on the sideline.

One meter might not seem very high, but keep in mind that Martin's eyes are two meters above the board and when he looked down he didn't see the water but rather the bottom of the pool, another five meters below the surface. So, peering into the pool, Martin saw a drop of eight meters. He was frozen with fear. In fact, for such a period that a long line of little kids formed behind him. And their attitude was, "C'mon, mister, jump!" "We don't have all day!" "Just do it!" Rutte was terrified. He looked at the instructor and asked, "When does the fear go away?"

Her answer, "Never!"

When will the fear end? Never.

When Rutte became comfortable with jumping off the one-meter board, his instructor pushed him back into his discomfort zone, challenging him to learn how to dive. Once he mastered diving, she challenged him to learn a forward flip. Then a one-and-a-half flip. Once he mastered every dive on the one-meter board, where did she send him? To the three-meter board. And then the terror really set in! There will always be new dives and higher diving boards to awaken your fear. If you are always learning and growing as a human being, if organizations are committed to always providing new value for their customers, always pushing the envelope, the fear will never disappear.

The fear abates once you have mastered a new skill. But we human beings soon become bored and need to challenge ourselves again. As we go through the process of facing fear and overcoming it time and time again, we increase our tolerance for discomfort, ambiguity and uncertainty. We develop courage and faith in our abilities to face and overcome the unknown.

Fear of failure is a part of learning and growing. Once you accept that, you will get better at dealing with and overcoming it.

We need to treat ourselves as we would treat a child who is learning to walk. Similarly, we must treat other people who are learning with patience and understanding. If we beat up others when they fail, we justify their resistance to change and reinforce their fears.

But just because we are respectful of ourselves and others doesn't mean we should ignore the need for results and tough decisions. It is the difference between acceptance and complacency. I am complacent when I know a problem exists but am either too frightened or lazy to act or ask for help. By contrast, I need acceptance once I have honestly done everything in my power to correct a situation.

A man told a story that had a powerful effect on me. His son was born with deformed legs. Every week for the first year of his child's life, the man took him to the hospital where doctors would twist the child's legs and set them in a temporary cast. The little boy would scream in pain. The father had to witness his son's torment. He worried terribly, "What is my son thinking of me? What kind of father does he think I am?" But the man didn't relent and every week took his son back to the hospital. Eventually the child began to fear driving in the car because he knew it meant going to these appointments, but the father's resolve didn't waver.

Today, the boy can walk and run as well as any healthy child because his father set aside his own feelings to do what had to be done. Compassion and love were at the core of his actions.

> A man's reach should exceed his grasp.
> Robert Browning, poet

At times, managers must be demanding to get results. But whatever actions are required, they must be undertaken with care. We must always look to the work culture in which we are asking people to function before we point fingers, make demands or take disciplinary action. Is the culture built on blame, or does it accept that stumbling and falling are part of learning? Are people given the freedom they need to be accountable? Are they given the necessary training and education to help them overcome the challenges they are expected to overcome? Unless employees are treated fairly in the first place, it is almost impossible to solve long-term problems.

Many once-sound organizations are undergoing the wrenching pain of reengineering. The term was first popularized by Michael Hammer in the 1990 *Harvard Business Review* article "Reengineering Work: Don't Automate, Obliterate,"[3] in which he celebrated Ford Motor's decision to cut 75 percent of its 400-person accounts payable staff. Ford's internal processes had become inefficient, overstaffed and unnecessarily expensive. By comparison, Mazda's accounts payable staff totaled five. Why the huge disparity?

Organizations that must reengineer typically have not kept pace with the times. Consequently their competitors, their customers and the whole market have passed them by. In a desperate effort to catch up, they cut the duplication and fat from the system. Ironically, unwillingness to change, develop options and question operating systems had caused the costly build-up in the first place.

Michael Hammer is confused by resistance to reengineering. For instance, in a *Fortune* article he is quoted as saying, "Human beings' innate resistance to change is the most perplexing, annoying, distressing and confusing part of reengineering."[4] What is hard to understand? Imagine that I arrive at your organization and say, "I have a wonderful new management theory. It simply requires you to terminate three out of four colleagues and may require you to fire yourself." It would be natural for people to oppose it. Hammer uses terms such as "nuke" and "obliterate," and refers to "breaking legs." Does this language tend to increase or decrease fear? Does Hammer's theory show a sensitivity to people? And, lest we forget, it is people who make organizations work.

A rigid management style that stifles learning, creativity and change is like a cancer-causing habit. After smoking two packs of cigarettes a day for 40 years, a smoker gets cancer and then goes to a specialist to be cured. Reengineering is the supposed surgical cure to intervene and "fix" the company. But often it's too late to deal with the root problem.

By contrast, Peter Senge, in his book *Fifth Discipline: The Art & Practice of the Learning Organization*, advocates preventive medicine by creating "learning organizations." Like adopting a healthy lifestyle, lifelong learning creates personal and corporate security. This path may sound simple, but it is not easy. Everyone knows exercise is good, but too few people work out regularly. Knowledge (theory) is one thing, application (practice) is another.

More books have been written on management and leadership in the last two decades than in the last century combined. Do we really need more knowledge? Or do we need to better practice what we already know? I believe we need to focus on application.

We live in the information age. In fact, far more information is available today than an individual can assimilate in a lifetime. What we need is wisdom. Below are four definitions:

STATISTICS are data. For a shoe store, data would be daily sales figures, the average sale, the sales of different kind of shoes. But statistics have little value. We are drowning in data.

INFORMATION gives meaning to data by explaining its relevance, thus allowing for interpretation and determining of importance. Patterns in data are recognized.

KNOWLEDGE is the assembly of information, often from disparate sources to create new understandings.

WISDOM is the application of knowledge to create new value.

For instance, imagine that in 1980 an airline examined its passenger records. Millions of records (data) were analyzed. Patterns (information) became apparent. For example, certain passengers were flying frequently. Further study revealed that these frequent fliers were the most profitable customer segment (information). This led an analyst to ask, "How can we ensure the loyalty of this small segment that comprises the bulk of our profits?" (knowledge) How can we better understand the behavior and profile of customers in this segment? (knowledge) What program can we implement to guarantee the loyalty of this segment, which is the most profitable? (knowledge)

Airlines designed frequent flier programs to ensure that their most frequent fliers remained loyal. (wisdom) American Airlines was the first airline to co-brand a credit card giving one frequent flier air mile for every dollar a customer spent on the card. (wisdom) This program was based on the insight that frequent fliers have high disposable incomes and therefore are a good target market for a prestige credit card.

This example shows how knowledge combines disparate pieces of information to create new understandings of customers or markets. Finally, wisdom is having the courage to act on the knowledge and implement the programs. Because the programs will not be implemented perfectly on the first attempt, patience and courage are required to venture through the uncertainty and persevere until new value is created and the market responds.

Knowledge is not even enough today. I could be a world authority on balance, having read all the books on the subject and even having

> I can't read my way into physical fitness.
>
> Jim Harris, author

taught a course at Harvard on the workings of the inner ear, but if I can't ride a bicycle while a seven-year-old can, who has more wisdom? Knowledge without application is worthless.

While knowledge can be acquired by reading and reflection, wisdom is only acquired through practice, self-reflection and self-correction. Some companies are very open to sharing their strategic plan with suppliers and customers and are seemingly unafraid that this information could get into the hands of competitors. Knowledge of competitors' plans gives little strategic advantage. The key is in execution. Intel, I am certain, plans to design and produce faster, more powerful generations of computer chips. As Intel's competitors already know, this knowledge isn't much help.

It is better to have a B-grade plan and an A-grade execution than to have an A-grade plan and a B-grade execution. The key to all wisdom is execution. It is not enough to know what we should do, the key is to have the courage and stamina to carry it out.

Learning as Play; Life as Challenge

Many children today play video games. Parents describe their kids as "intense," "challenged," "excited" and "obsessed" when they receive a new game. A mother once commented that her son was "deaf" while a father said, "Unable to mow the lawn!"

Do kids read the manual before they begin? As one mother put it, "I'm the one who reads the manual." Children show no fear while learning.

Have you seen or heard of any courses such as Sega Genesis for Advanced Users or Nintendo 101? Or have you seen that bestseller *Sega for Dummies?* Of course not. So how do kids learn? By doing. By trial and error. How many times are kids willing to make mistakes? As many as it takes to learn.

To play a video game, a child must develop certain competencies at Level One. Once mastered, the child moves on to Level Two, where new challenges require the development of new skills. As soon as these are acquired, the child progresses to Level Three, which presents more complex challenges requiring even higher levels of skill. To keep a child's attention, game designers make each level more difficult. One tactic is to require players to develop skills that are the opposite of those needed at a lower level. That is, the very moves that allowed them to escape the challenges of Level One cause their character to die at Level Three. Unless they can *unlearn* what made them successful at Level One and learn new skills, they will not progress. As much as we need to learn, we also have to unlearn.

Each time a new challenge is overcome, a new problem presents itself. At every stage the child is challenged to learn new skills. At seminars, I ask the audience, "What happens once the child has mastered all six levels?" They answer, "They show all their friends." Then I ask, "And then what?" Usually I hear answers like, "They stop playing." "They chuck the game." "They trade it or sell it."

This reveals a simple but powerful insight: Challenge is one of the greatest human motivators. This is the second aspect of the learning paradox. The first aspect is that our future security is based on what we fear most—learning, changing and accepting uncertainty. The second is that facing our fear also provides our deepest sense of satisfaction.

I challenge you to think of some time in your life when you were most proud. I am sure that upon reflection you will find it was when you undertook some challenge you didn't know how to overcome. But through hard work, trial and error, perseverance and networking with colleagues you whipped it. You got the "YES!" high-five feeling that kids get when they master all levels of the video game.

Learning a video game is a powerful metaphor for developing a business. Whether new or established, organizations require progressively different competencies. At every stage of growth, new problems are encountered that will limit development unless they are overcome.

With a new business, capital is often the first limiting factor. So the entrepreneur works out of his basement, puts in sweat equity, buys second-hand furniture and equipment and generally keeps costs to the bone. As cash flow increases, hiring personnel may be the next hurdle. But the entrepreneur hires people with little experience because he can't afford high wages. That may give rise to the need for training. So the entrepreneur invests in training, increasing employees' marketability, and then the company experiences high turnover. Eventually the entrepreneur must pay market wages as well as invest in training. After that, it may be necessary to focus on marketing. From the founder's basement, the company may be forced to lease office space, hire more staff, introduce benefit programs, acquire more equipment and so on and so on. Every level of development presents a new set of challenges.

Imagine, for example, that a manufacturer launches a new product with an aggressive advertising campaign in an effort to increase market share. The campaign is so successful that demand exceeds the company's production capacity. This results in long delivery delays for customers. The company must increase production capacity, maintain sufficient inventory levels and more accurately forecast market demand.

> The chief object of education is not to learn things but to unlearn things.
> G.K. Chesterton, English novelist

> In the middle of difficulty lies opportunity.
> Albert Einstein, physicist

As soon as one limiting factor is addressed, a new one will arise. Suppose the company responds to increasing demand by hastily building new production facilities and rushing products to market before all the manufacturing problems are solved. As a result, product quality suffers and customer loyalty declines. Quality is now the limiting factor.

To confront the quality problem, a total quality management (TQM) program is implemented. Statistical measurement and process control systems are introduced and the quality problem is licked. After spending $500,000 on TQM, the company may have to respond by lowering prices in an attempt to win back disgruntled customers.

Our aim must be to make our successive mistakes as quickly as possible.
Karl Popper, Australian philosopher

But now there is a new problem. When the new production line was built, the company required additional volume to cover costs. Rather than have the line sit idle, sales reps were given incentives to increase volume, even with low-margin business, thereby amortizing the cost of the new line. This strategy lowered the per-unit cost of production. Compensation systems were designed to reward sales reps based on volume. The results were so successful that after a few years the company experienced another capacity crunch. Peak volumes were again losing the company business.

The solution to one problem has now become a new problem. Now that the line is at full capacity, the company needs a new strategy: drop the high-volume, low-margin business and concentrate on the lower-volume, niche markets with high margins.

As the business booms and profit margins rise, the sector becomes more attractive to competitors. Competition may become the primary problem. As soon as this problem is addressed, another one will crop up, guaranteed.

Once any limiting factor is overcome, a new limiting factor will arise. Put another way, solving any problem will, over time, create a new problem in any business. The problems will not necessarily be linked, but they will always emerge. There will always be problems and challenges in business.

As in the video game, as businesses graduate to higher and higher levels, the problems become more and more complex. The problems challenge us to think in new ways—ways that were not previously required and that may in fact be the opposite of those that worked at lower levels. The interaction of the various forces may also be less apparent.

At the very start of a business, the entrepreneur is involved in every decision. That's what created success (Level One). But now that the company has grown to 100 people (Level Three), the entrepreneur's involvement in every decision is the problem. In other words, what made the company thrive at Level One could cause the company to fail at Level Three. So, as much as we need to create learning organizations, we also need to foster unlearning organizations. To progress and develop, we must also be prepared to unlearn or let go of practices that may have been key to our past success!

To grow and change, an entrepreneur must accept that his or her greatest strengths from yesterday could become his or her greatest weaknesses today. When a snake sheds its skin, it gives up its tough, old armor for a soft but flexible covering. The old skin wasn't working but the new skin isn't working either. The snake must live through the vulnerable time—similar to writing with the other hand. Even in our personal lives, we must be prepared to evaluate old attitudes and replace them, if necessary, with ones that work better in the present. This will ultimately make our lives happier and more fulfilling.

The business "video game" ends only if the company ends. As a company continues to grow, the systems and structures become more elaborate, more complex and more cumbersome. Sometimes, these systems prevent the organization from being able to respond effectively to change—bureaucracy chokes the lifeblood out of the organization. The company has come full circle. It needs to be more entrepreneurial, not in the old style when the entrepreneur did the accounting on the back of envelopes, but in a way that focuses on the customer and strategic growth, and allows for flexibility with enough checks and balances to avoid fatal mistakes.

> The art of progress is to preserve order amid change and change amid order.
> A.N. Whitehead, English mathematician

Life is Difficult

I often encounter a disturbing assumption in my consulting work. Clients will say, "If we just do this reengineering or this quality thing or this customer focus approach, then all our problems will be resolved."

The assumption is that we just need to solve this one thing and everything will be all right. What a dangerous notion! As we have seen, no sooner is one bottleneck overcome than another presents itself. Will any business ever be easy and problem free? Never! When will the challenge end? Never!

M. Scott Peck begins *The Road Less Traveled* with the first of the four noble truths of Buddhism:

> Life is difficult. This is a great truth, one of the greatest
> truths. It is a great truth because once we truly see this truth,
> we transcend it. Once we truly know that life is difficult—

once we truly understand and accept it—then life is no longer difficult. Because once accepted, the fact that life is difficult no longer matters.[5]

Corporate life is difficult. The search for simple solutions to problems is futile. Not only does the belief in a single, simple solution lead to continual disappointment and more problems, it limits our vision and confines our thinking. We need to rise above the problem/solution dynamic if we are to see the larger world of possibilities. No consultant or program can "save" us.

Bottlenecks are always at the top of the bottle.[6]
Lou Pritchett, author

In reference to total quality management (TQM), I often hear, "Quality is not working!" According to reports, three-quarters of quality initiatives in North America fail. *Information Week* reports that two-thirds of reengineering initiatives fail. According to Arthur D. Little Inc., only 16 percent of companies are satisfied with the results.[7] That's like saying 70 percent of all screwdrivers are failing. To blame the tools is to miss the point. It is how tools are used that determines how successful they are at solving problems. Quality, reengineering and customer focus are just tools. They are processes, not the answers. The way in which these programs are *implemented* over the long term determines their success or failure.

The truth is, problems are central to the human condition. We need to increase our tolerance for the discomfort, ambiguity and failure that learning and changing bring. Only by facing up to what we fear most will we be able to learn, grow and make our work rewarding, stimulating and secure.

Learning as a Child

Like other business people, I have been influenced by such thinkers as Peter Senge and Stephen Covey, whose work provides powerful tools for analyzing and implementing change. Yet in my work with executives over the years, I have been constantly amazed at how few companies are able to make necessary changes, even with so much theory, so many examples and good suggestions at their disposal. We often know what needs to be done, but we still aren't able to do enough. What forces are holding us back?

Let's get back to the child who is learning to walk. We would be surprised if, after falling a few times, she suddenly gave up as if she thought, "Hey, this walking stuff is just too painful. I'm going to give up right now and save myself from more bumps and bruises." That sounds ridiculous and yet how many times do adults give up too quickly? We must get back that childlike love of learning, letting go of our insecurities and ego that hold us back through fear of stumbling and falling.

The best companies have a high tolerance for mistakes. Why? Without risk, innovation is impossible. Risk-taking and mistakes go hand in hand. Corporations that get results take extra pains to create environments that encourage ideas, risks and mistakes.

Once we truly accept the need for change and undertake to create a working environment where change is encouraged, risk-taking rewarded and mistakes expected, learning becomes fun, joyous and exciting.

Think again about kids with their video games. What emotional state are children in when they open a new game? They are thrilled, engaged. They have mastered four levels before breakfast and are already asking for the next version. It's pure fun. Yet it's challenging, and parents hear enough groans to know that mistakes are being made.

If you have a daughter, think back to when she was two years old. Whenever you come home she runs up to you and throws her arms around your legs. You call her "my Princess," and she thinks you are wonderful. She makes your heart melt. But two-year-olds are a real challenge. It has been difficult for you. You have had to learn to be firm and yet compassionate. You can't negotiate with a two-year-old or she will run your life. So you have worked hard to develop this fantastic relationship with her. However, you remain frozen in time. You don't change as a parent, and two years pass. She is now four but you treat her the same as when she was two. After all, you had perfected the relationship and it worked. How is the relationship going—is it stronger or weaker? Someone once said, "She has you wrapped around her little finger."

She is now 10 years old and you treat her exactly as you did when she was four. How is the relationship now—happy or tense? Your daughter is now 16 and you treat her as you did when she was 10. What's your relationship like? I get answers like, "What relationship?" "She isn't talking to me." "She has left home."

This is very difficult for both of you. You are both continually venturing into the future, uncertain of how to behave, uncertain of how to create a meaningful relationship. When raising your first daughter, you never had a two-year-old before. You don't know how to treat her. You were always questioning yourself, "Is she getting to bed at the right time? Is she spending enough time with other kids? Is she watching too much TV? Are my expectations too high? Am I too permissive?

> Nothing in life is to be feared. It is only to be understood.
>
> Marie Curie, inventor

> In this world nothing can be said to be certain, except death and taxes.
>
> Benjamin Franklin, inventor

What is the right balance?" You are learning at every stage of the child's development. And no sooner do you start to feel that everything is under control because you have perfected the relationship at a certain age, than she grows and new challenges arise. The relationship is characterized by periods of stability and then instability when you feel out of control again. At every stage of this growing relationship you must continually question yourself and work through the dynamics of the evolving, uncertain future. You must continually learn, change and accept uncertainty. When she is going through adolescence is a particularly difficult time. After all, we have all read those national surveys that show that kids today are having sex at 13 and 14—but not your Princess!

It is equally difficult for your daughter. She is facing new situations, too. She has new peer pressure, she is starting to date and her parents are acting strange. Everyone is struggling, learning and changing together. Everyone must accept the uncertainty that the future brings.

Life is funny. It tends to be circular. Despite your discomfort with her emerging sexuality, you have to begin modifying the parent-child relationship to a peer-to-peer relationship. The success of the relationship will depend on how well you make that transition. And the degree of compassion and understanding that you show her in this difficult time is likely the degree of compassion she will show you when the roles are reversed and you become the child at 80 with Alzheimer's, and she the parent.

Security is not in doing what you did well in the past. Your security lies in letting go of the past and creating new relationships. All of life is learning.

If you married your childhood sweetheart when you were both 19 and your relationship is still the same 30 years later, what is your relationship like? We all intuitively know that learning and changing offer us security, yet we resist them. Ultimately, we have to accept the uncertainty that life brings because we cannot know the future.

A grandfather told me of spending time with his grandson as he learned to ride a bicycle. It was his first day without the training wheels and he fell, scraping his knees. Crying, the grandson came back saying, "I don't want to ride a bike ever again."

It broke the grandfather's heart. He would have gladly taken the fall and the pain for his grandson but he couldn't. Pain is part of the process of learning.

"Yes, you do, son. Only you just don't know it. The day I learned to ride my bike was one of the most exciting days for me. Instead of

> Everything is in a constant state of change. Nothing ever stays the same.
> Heracleitus, Greek philosopher

just walking a few blocks from my house, all of a sudden I could ride 15 miles from home! It opened a whole new world to me."

When we stop learning we limit our horizons. Too often we focus on the scraped knee and not the excitement, the wonder, the new worlds that await us on the other side of learning.

The consequences of our mistakes become more serious as we grow older. The child learning to walk will only fall about a foot. When learning to ride a bike, knees can be scraped at 10 miles an hour. CEOs are in the same boat. When a company is entering a new market, everyone is on a learning curve. However, the stakes are higher and the consequences of an error could cost 500 people their jobs. The fear never goes away. Continual growth in the context of the learning paradox requires that we increase our emotional muscle, our ability to accept uncertainty and discomfort. We must increase such character strengths as patience, compassion and courage. There must be a tolerance for, and acceptance of, learning and the mistakes that it, by definition, brings. Leaders work to ensure that the mistakes are non-fatal.

Corporations can create and benefit from cultures that encourage the joy of learning and change. Only by rising to the challenges of our changing times and working through the learning paradox will we gain security and prosperity.

To Summarize:
- Security today depends on the ability to learn and change.

- We become better at overcoming fears associated with the unknown by continually taking on new challenges.

- Mistakes are part of the learning process. We must accept that we and others will make mistakes.

- Security lies in change. Changing will ensure an organization remains viable and that people remain employed.

Reflection:
- What is the key learning/insight for me in this chapter?

Action:
- What one action shall I take tomorrow to move learning into action? And over time repeat, to move action into habit?

CHAPTER 3

The Business of Paradigms

The word "paradigm" has become something of a cliché and is often misused. As a result, many people don't understand the power or importance of paradigms. What exactly is a paradigm? A simple story illustrates the concept. Imagine yourself in the following situation adapted from a story in *The More Than Complete Hitchhiker's Guide to the Galaxy.*

You have a stopover at Heathrow International Airport in London, England, and you're very hungry because you weren't served breakfast on your morning flight. You go to one of the airport shops, buy a package of Walker's shortbread cookies and put them into your carry-on bag.

You venture back into the airport, which is very noisy and crowded. Exhausted, you finally find a seat. After a minute of your stomach growling, you reach down into your bag and pull out your package of cookies.

What is unnerving about the situation is that the man next to you is literally staring at the cookies—his eyes are riveted on the package! As you open the package and take out the first cookie, his eyes follow your hand to your mouth. Then, without saying a word, he reaches for the package and grabs a cookie!

The eye cannot see itself.
Anonymous

You are shocked! You are speechless. You are in England, so you think, "How would the English react?" The answer comes to you, "Keep a stiff upper lip, pretend the situation is not happening and say nothing." Not knowing how to react, you impulsively go for another cookie. He grabs another. And so it goes.

How would you describe this man to your spouse or to a colleague at work? "What an aggressive jerk!" "Maybe they didn't serve breakfast on his flight, either." Once, an audience member said, "He's obviously with the government—he's used to taking 50 percent!"

What would you do? The best answer I've ever heard is, "I'd lick all the cookies." A woman once said, "I'd shoot him."

With all the reserve of a Brit, you continue to ignore the situation and do nothing. You take a cookie. He grabs the next.

Finally, it's down to one cookie. He reaches over, grabs the last cookie, breaks it in half, gives you half and eats half himself.

In a great indignant huff, you gather up your belongings and forfeit your seat, anything to get away from this cookie snatcher.

You're terribly upset. Your stomach is churning. You decide to go back to the shop to get some Alka-Seltzer and more cookies.

You pay for your new purchases and open your carry-on bag to drop them in. And what do you see? Your unopened package of cookies! Suddenly you realize that you accidentally reached down into his luggage and were eating his package of cookies! You were the cookie thief!

> We do not see the world as it is, we see it as we are.
> Stephen R. Covey, author

Now, how would you describe this man to your spouse or to a colleague at work? The person you branded a villain just a moment ago suddenly becomes a saint—so tolerant, so generous. Your perceptions shift instantly. You have experienced a paradigm shift.

A paradigm is the way we see a situation. It's a mental model, a map. Paradigms encompass all our beliefs, values and attitudes towards life and people. All our thoughts, all our actions flow from our paradigms. It's like a pair of glasses that alter our perception of what we see.

Getting back to the cookie debacle, imagine that you hadn't experienced the paradigm shift when you purchased another package of cookies. While walking through the airport, your original package of cookies had jiggled its way to the bottom of your bag. When you opened the bag at the shop, you didn't see your original package of cookies and put the new package on top, unaware that you now had two packages of cookies in your carry-on luggage. So now you can get back into the frame of mind that this jerk was eating your cookies. Reinvest yourself emotionally. Now, I don't know about you, but for me there is nothing more enjoyable than self-righteous, indignant, justified anger!

You board your plane, and can you believe who they've seated beside you? The cookie snatcher, of all people!

They are about to serve lunch. What's your attitude towards him? "You come near my lunch, and I'll stab you!"

Look at how the paradigm colors our interpretations. If he is smiling when they're serving lunch, how would you read his behavior? "You're smiling because you stole my cookies, you think it's funny and you're plotting to steal my lunch." What if he is frowning? How would you interpret that? "Bloody well right, you should feel guilty for eating my cookies!"

You see, whatever the man does, we will find evidence in his behavior to justify our paradigm. The frightening thing about paradigms is that we are not conscious of them. We assume we know the truth. We assume we are objective. Only by changing our paradigms can we profoundly change.

If we want to transform our organizations, reinvent government, create a new society or make our own lives happier, we must change ourselves first by questioning our own belief systems, our own paradigms. Paradigms are primary. Notice how your behavior and attitude changed instantly when the paradigm shifted in the airport. Changing the way we see ourselves, our organizations and our world offers the greatest hope for personal and professional success.

In Christopher Columbus' day, most people believed that the earth was flat and that if you sailed too far, you would fall off the edge. People who held this view never sailed far out into the ocean; they always kept land in sight. Their actions were entirely logical given their paradigm.

But Columbus saw the world differently. He saw it as being round and believed that by sailing West he could get East to India. His actions flowed out of his paradigm.

The interesting thing to note is that reality remained constant. The world didn't change. The earth remained as it had been for five billion years. What changed history was the way Columbus saw the world. As a result of seeing the world differently, he behaved differently. As a result of behaving differently, he achieved different results.

A paradigm is like a map. Why? Because it is not the actual territory, it is a mental model, a visual representation of the underlying territory. The paradigm is primary. Working with a better map will make more difference than working harder and longer hours with a bad map.

Today, individuals and organizations can create their future by "seeing" new products and services that do not exist and then working to bring them to market. Creating value where none exists today requires an active paradigm shift, which makes real that which exists only in our imaginations. For instance, our need for the telephone existed before Alexander Graham Bell discovered it. It's just that consumers of his time didn't know they had a need for this device. Similarly, the principles of physics required to enable the invention of the phone existed before Bell stumbled upon them. Bell had to actively uncover them.

By contrast, creating a more accurate map of what already exists is a passive paradigm shift, because the underlying territory is already visible. So Columbus' confirmation of the world being round was a passive paradigm shift.

Our imagination and the creation of new value shape the future. Customers will overwhelmingly respond when businesses delight them by meeting and exceeding their needs. The most successful organizations work to meet needs that their customers may not even be aware that they have. The challenge for businesses is to uncover these needs or anticipate them and then work to meet them. Businesses must constantly revise and update their maps in a dynamic, ever-changing business environment.

In *Paradigms: The Business of Discovering the Future*, Joel Arthur Barker relates what has become the classic business paradigm shift.[1] In 1968, the Swiss had more than 65 percent of the worldwide market share of watch sales and over 80 percent of the profits. By 1981, their sales had collapsed to a 10 percent share and profits fell to less than a 20 percent share. A staggering 50,000 of the 62,000 Swiss watchmakers lost their jobs in two years. What happened? The world changed because of a paradigm shift in the way watches work.

The crisis was entirely preventable. In 1967, researchers at the Swiss industry research center in Neuchâtel, Switzerland, invented the electronic quartz movement. This revolutionary watch had no mainspring, didn't need bearings, had no gears and was electronic and battery powered. Swiss manufacturers rejected it outright because it did not fit their paradigm of what a watch was. They believed the discovery was so worthless that they let their researchers show the invention at the 1967 World Watch Congress. Seiko took one look and the rest is history. Seiko and other Japanese companies now have about 33 percent of worldwide watch sales and an equivalent share of profits.

> One does not discover new lands without consenting to lose sight of the shore for a very long time.
> André Gide, French novelist

When we are most successful we are most at risk of becoming complacent and ignoring the potential risks and benefits of paradigm shifts. The watch story is fascinating, not only because it highlights how precarious market share is, but also because it demonstrates the enormous potential power contained within new ways of perceiving the world. The Japanese conquest of the international watch industry began when they recognized a paradigm shift. From that point on, competitors could only play catch-up; the world market had already changed its preference. As the Japanese expression goes: there are only three things that matter: market share, market share, market share.

Remember the simple observation that 80 percent of the technology we will use in our day-to-day lives in just 10 years has yet to be invented! Think about how quickly technology is changing and how much it's affecting our lives. By the year 2005 most people will not deal with a bank that does not offer its customers on-line access to their accounts. This will have wider implications than the shift to 24-hour ATM banking. Each technological change can dramatically alter our lives. Each innovation brings a future vision into the present.

Gordon Moore, co-founder of Intel, devised Moore's Law.[2] It states that the computing power of microchips will double every 18 months while staying at roughly the same price point. Moore's prediction has held true, even though it was made in 1965.

This compounded annual growth in microprocessor power has forced high-tech companies to adopt non-traditional management methods and structures because the rate of change in the industry is so fast. High-tech leaders such as Sun Microsystems live on the "bleeding edge." Ninety-five percent of Sun's revenues come from products introduced in the last 18 months![3]

These facts have profound implications for all organizations. To begin with, the policies and procedures that made companies successful in the past may produce failure in the future. Many historical practices and structures run counter to the new reality.

For instance, businesses used to have five-year plans. The speed at which change is occurring within markets has rendered such planning obsolete. IBM's 1989 five-year plan was off by 200,000 employees! Between 1989 and 1995, "Big Blue," which once prided itself on life-time job security, laid off half of its workforce. Long-term strategic planning as we knew it is dead. Strategic planning in the past assumed that things would basically be the same as they were in the past, but with a 10 percent annual growth in sales. This can no longer be the case. Now, strategic planning must assume that the future will look radically different than the present and past.

In these turbulent times, how can we cope? How can individuals and organizations create security? Only by serving as paradigm innovators, continually questioning personal and organizational paradigms. Amid the dramatic and sudden shifts that characterize our modern world, how can we plan for the future? Only by creating it!

This is at the core of the learning paradox. Security can come only by accepting the uncertainty of an unfolding future.

TO SHIFT OR NOT TO SHIFT . . . THAT IS THE QUESTION Imagine that you are appointed vice president of marketing and sales for a company that is a market leader. Here is the chart of your annual sales in your new position after just two years:

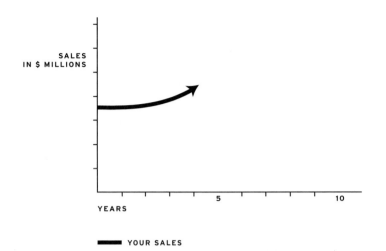

SALES
IN $ MILLIONS

YEARS
5   10

■ YOUR SALES

You are justifiably proud of your record. After just a few years in the position you look back on your sales and see how they have been growing 10 to 15 percent a year! Your product enjoys 75 percent of the market share. That's dominance! You are at the peak of your career and are featured on the cover of *Marketing* magazine as executive of the year.

After a few years, a small competitor introduces a product that is panned by the media. Customers also view it as a flop and sales of the product go nowhere. Do you pay any attention to it? Probably not. In hindsight, your decision is justified because your sales rise to the highest levels ever while your competitor's sales languish:

Planning by its very nature defines and preserves categories. Creativity by its very nature creates categories or rearranges established ones. That is why strategic planning can neither provide creativity, nor deal with it when it emerges by other means.[4]

Henry Mintzberg, author

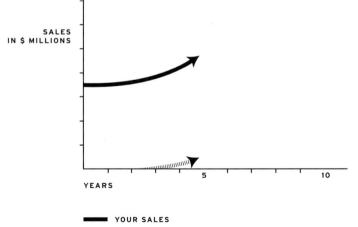

SALES
IN $ MILLIONS

YEARS
5   10

■ YOUR SALES
IIIIIIII YOUR COMPETITOR'S SALES

A couple of years later, the competitor introduces an updated version of the product and again it receives bad reviews. Customers don't really respond. The competitor's sales increase but only marginally. Why worry: 10 percent growth on top of nothing is still nothing. Would you focus on this product? Most say they would ignore it. Your sales continue rising, reaching record-breaking heights. Visions of the value of your stock options dance in your head. Your company and the industry have never seen such growth. You now enjoy 75 percent of worldwide market share! That's dominance. You are at the top of your game.

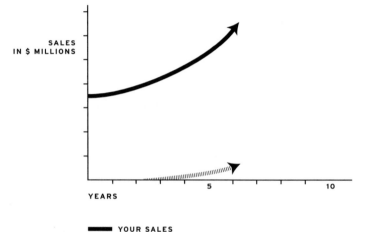

The competitor introduces a new version of the product and this is what happens:

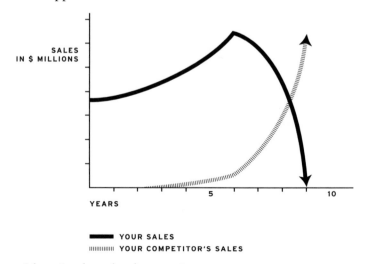

I hate it when that happens!

This is an actual case study. You were the vice president of marketing and sales for *Lotus 1-2-3* for *DOS*. You enjoyed 75 percent of market share. In November 1983, a tiny company, Microsoft, announced that it would develop a new graphical user interface (GUI — pronounced "gooey"). Working with *DOS* was difficult initially; you had to use long, hard-to-remember commands. For instance, to copy a file to a diskette you would have to type in copy C:\windows\business\ marketing\reports\ 021261. doc A:report.doc. If you misspelled anything, the system would not execute the command. The system was "user-vicious,"[5] counter-intuitive and difficult to learn. The Macintosh, by contrast, uses visual symbols called icons. Most people remember visual and spatial relationships easily. For instance, you always know that your letter opener is in the top right drawer of your desk. Using this principle, Macintosh computers kept files and programs as pictures on the screen of your computer. Apple did not invent this graphical user interface. Steven Jobs was exposed to the concept at a demonstration at the Xerox PARC research facility in Palo Alto.

> Faced with the choice between changing one's mind and proving that there is no need to do so, almost everybody gets busy on the proof.
>
> John Kenneth Galbraith, economist

In November 1985, Microsoft released *Windows* Version 1.01. It was awkward, sluggish and user-vicious. Version 1.01 was widely seen as a marketing flop and taken up only by computer programmers and "techies." Microsoft stood behind its initiative, continuing to develop *Windows*. Version 2.0 was released in November 1987 with improved features and sales increased slightly.

With the continued success of *MS-DOS* (Microsoft Disk Operating System, the operating system for 90 percent of the world's personal computers in the 1980s and early 1990s), Microsoft was able to fund the development of *Windows*.

Microsoft had faith in the eventual success of *Windows* and during the early years was the only vendor developing and offering a wide number of applications for this new environment: a word processor, a graphics package and a spreadsheet. Because market analysts and software makers were pessimistic about the future of *Windows*, very few of Microsoft's competitors developed any *Windows* products.

Following the release of Version 2.0, Microsoft again invested the revenues in improving *Windows*. Version 3.0 was released in May 1990 and took off, with sales exceeding even Microsoft's wildest projections. As the only major software vendor with a variety of *Windows* applications, Microsoft was well positioned to reap the long-awaited benefits. Microsoft's early lead and the quality of its products have given the company dominant market share in most of the major mass-market business applications, including the large spreadsheet and word processing categories.

Bill Gates, CEO of Microsoft, noted in October 1993:

> At the time that *Windows* came out, our competitors in applications paused. And in doing that, it took them a long time to come out with their first *Windows* version that many people would have deemed adequate. And it's only recently that they either have come out with or are about to come out with decent *Windows* versions. So we've had all that time to continue to move ahead and lengthen our lead."[6]

Microsoft smoothed out many of the bugs in Version 3.0 with the release of Version 3.1 in April 1992. By then, *Windows* was recognized as a major force in the computer world, but just how powerful no one could have predicted. The upgrade immediately began selling 1.5 million copies a month and by the end of 1994 was selling more than two million copies a month — 66,000 copies a day! With the corresponding revenue flowing into Microsoft, the company began stretching its tentacles into every software market imaginable. By the end of 1995, *Windows* was installed on more than 100 million computers worldwide!

In 1993, sales of *Windows* applications such as word processors, spreadsheets and graphics programs surpassed *DOS* software sales. The personal computer (PC) world had undergone a fundamental paradigm shift.

DOS ruled the PC world from 1981 to 1993. Only a handful of companies challenged the widely used *DOS* applications. Lotus became synonymous with spreadsheets. In the *DOS* world, *Lotus 1-2-3* enjoyed a market share of over 75 percent! As vice president of marketing and sales for *Lotus 1-2-3* for *DOS*, would you invest millions to develop spreadsheets for a new environment — *Windows* — that was experiencing little success?[7]

> **Lord grant that we may always be right, for thou knowest we will never change our minds.**
> Scottish proverb

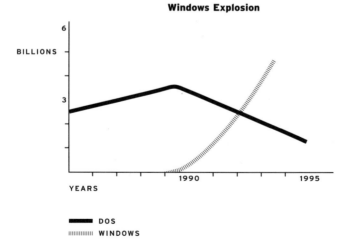

Windows Explosion

BILLIONS

YEARS

▬▬ DOS
‖‖‖‖ WINDOWS

From 1985 on, you knew about this terrible operating system called *Windows*. You felt that Microsoft had no chance of ever becoming a successful spreadsheet competitor. After all, your sales had been steadily increasing. But all of a sudden in 1990, *Windows* became a sales phenomenon. Still, you didn't really worry. After all, standard *DOS* sales had been steadily increasing for the past few years and projections showed a rosy future!

But your concern grew as *Windows 3.0* continued to sell at a terrific rate. You had no *Windows* products and you knew it would take two and a half years to develop a proper application for this new operating system. What to do?

Lotus began developing the two-and-a-half year development cycle to bring out *Lotus 1-2-3 for Windows*. By 1993, Microsoft had captured 56 percent of the spreadsheet market, dominated by *Windows* application sales. *Windows* had become the dominant operating system for personal computers.

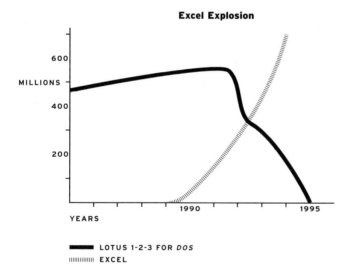

Excel Explosion

As VP for Lotus your stock options were plummeting in value. You felt ill whenever you saw Bill Gates on the cover of a magazine. If only you could have seen the future, it would have been different. However, you could now rest easy—at least your *Windows* spreadsheet was out on the market.

Not just Lotus was blind to the shift. Almost all *DOS* software developers missed the boat, including *WordPerfect*, the program that had the dominant market share in the word processing category. Most successful *Windows* software developers—companies that have sold more than one million copies of their programs—began developing software after 1990! In other words, they saw the opportunity because they were new to software development, they were not entrenched in the old *DOS* paradigm.[8]

The *DOS*-to-*Windows* shift did not happen overnight; it emerged slowly over more than four years, from the release of Version 1.01 until Version 3.0 became the best-selling operating system.

The success of *Windows* reminds me of Chinese bamboo. You plant Chinese bamboo and in the first year it produces a one-inch shoot. A year later the shoot is still only one inch tall. You begin to worry, "Does it have enough sunshine? Has there been enough rain?" In the third year, the shoot is still only one inch tall. The fourth year it's the same! You wonder, "Did I buy a genetically deficient bamboo?"

In the fifth year the bamboo grows 90 feet in just six weeks. The question is, did the Chinese bamboo take six weeks or five years to grow 90 feet? The answer is five years. Most of the time was spent laying the root system that would support the stunning growth. The same is true in this Microsoft example.

Microsoft had less than 10 percent of the spreadsheet market before the introduction of *Windows 3.0* in 1990. By 1993 it had soared to 56 percent! But Microsoft was still not complacent. The company began bundling its *Windows* applications—*Word* (word processor), *Excel* (spreadsheet), *PowerPoint* (graphic presentation), *Mail* (e-mail client) and *Access* (database)—as an application "suite" called *Office*. Microsoft priced *Office* at slightly more than the price of one stand-alone application. Suites integrate the stand-alone applications. Instead of each application having its own spellchecker, they share common code.

Just when Microsoft's competitors were releasing good *Windows* applications, the ground rules changed again. Now they had to make word processing, spreadsheet and database software, and then integrate and sell them at roughly the price point of a single application! Applications suites, for both technical and pricing reasons, have virtually eliminated the sale of individual applications. Microsoft now dominates the suite category with over 80 percent of market share. So from 1990–1997 Microsoft went from less than 10 percent market share of all spreadsheet sales to over 80 percent through the sale of Microsoft *Office!* As Chris Peters, vice president of *Office*, notes:

> Everything we've ever done won't matter three years from
> now. In terms of products, the amount of computing power
> that will become available in the next five years will be equal

Take care of what is difficult while it is easy and deal with what will become big while it is still small.

Lao Tzu, philosopher

to all the computing power ever made before. What it basically means is that you always have to be jumping well ahead. If you internalize that exponential growth, everyone else thinks that the thing will be like last year only a little different, which of course is true for a very short period of time. When you look at the industry in a two-year chunk, it does look very linear and you have to step back and find out that it's always exponentially growing. And then, when you do that, you do make bigger bets and a little bit different kind of bets.

I think it's the underlying principle for Microsoft. I think it's something that Bill Gates always understood and internalized, that you [must] radically change things and really have big plans. A classic example is that, *DOS* was doing great. [We could have said,] 'Let's just come out with this new version of *DOS*. Why make *Windows?*' And, 'Well, *Windows* takes up so much more hardware and computing power.' In a sense, [though, an innovation like] *Office* makes the individual apps obsolete. Just when our competitors are trying to be good in *Windows* [applications], now they have to make a good word processor and a good spreadsheet and a good database. You have to be that kind of software company now.[9]

In planning for the future, Microsoft looks at the exponential change in the computer industry and makes non-linear assumptions. For instance, what will an average PC look like in five years? Where you feel the market is moving will profoundly influence the bets you place today. Microsoft assumes that the size of the average hard disk of a new personal computer today will be the amount of RAM (random access memory) of an average new computer in five years! In 1997 the average size for the hard disk of a new computer was 2.3 gigabytes or gigs (2,300 megabytes).[10] Imagine 2.3 gigs of RAM on a new PC by 2002! All sorts of new applications become possible. Powerful voice-recognition applications, such as dictating letters to your computer, become feasible. Full-motion videoconferencing becomes possible.

> In times of rapid change, experience could be your worst enemy.
> J. Paul Getty, U.S. oil billionaire

By 2002, applications will look fundamentally different than they do in 1997. Therefore, strategic planning needs to be radically different than it is today. It needs to assume the future will bring radical discontinuity.

The *DOS*-to-*Windows* shift will, I predict, repeat itself with *Windows NT*. *Windows NT* is Microsoft's high-end operating system. It is more robust than *Windows 95* and it allows inexpensive microprocessors such as Pentiums to be harnessed together like a team of workhorses to deliver significantly more power. Microsoft has been investing a great deal of revenue in *Windows NT* over the years.

Harnessing the power of multiple processors is the wave of the future. If, as a result of *Windows NT*, fewer companies buy mainframes, hasn't a software maker become the main competition to mainframe vendors?

The first version of *NT* did not sell as well as Bill Gates boasted, which led a number of analysts to pan it. But Microsoft is not in any market it enters for the short run. The company continued to invest in improvements, and the second release—Version 3.5, launched in 1994—gained wider acceptance, passing the one-million mark in sales in 1995. *Windows NT 4.0*, released in August 1996, brought the total sales of *Windows NT* to eight million copies in 1997.

Windows NT will, over time, dramatically change the high-end operating system market, threatening *Unix* and *Novell-Netware*, just as the shift occurred to *Windows* from *DOS*. The pattern is a predictably slow initial adoption, with Microsoft continually investing in the new operating system. Eventually, a critical mass of sales will be established and then the product will take off. This doesn't mean that *Unix* and *Netware* are dead, it's just they will not experience the growth they would have had, had Microsoft not entered the market.

As Joel Arthur Barker says, "When a paradigm shifts, everyone goes back to zero." In other words, success in the old paradigm will not guarantee success in the new. In fact, success in the past actually tends to inhibit success in the future because organizations seem to be inherently incapable of seeing things in new ways. If leaders in an organization cannot see the market differently, they will not seize emerging opportunities and avoid potential problems. They will not create any urgency around the need to change. Organizations that are slow to change will lose market share to more agile competitors that can quickly seize opportunities. Organizations that are incapable of seeing new paradigms as they emerge become victims of paradigm rigor mortis.

> **Success has ruined many a man.**
>
> Benjamin Franklin, inventor and statesman

Shifts from Slow to Swift

Imagine a pond that starts with one lily pad and the number of plants doubles every day until the pond would be entirely covered by lilies after 30 days.

However, one day before the entire pond is covered, half the water would still be open. On Day 28, two days before the lilies completely cover the pond, three-quarters of the pond would be open water. On Day 27, a full seven-eighths of the water would be open. And on Day 26, more than 90 percent of the water would be open.

By Day 26, you have noticed the arithmetical progression. You have studied the situation, become alarmed and begin to go around yelling, "Beware, beware, the pond is about to be covered over with lilies." But people look at you as if you're crazy. "What are you talking about?" they ask. "Can't you see that 94 percent of the water is open?"

It is hard to be a paradigm shifter. The shift from *DOS* to *Windows* is like the pond being overtaken by lilies. *Lotus 1-2-3* and *WordPerfect* were overrun.

Imagine that you are a programmer at Lotus and see the emerging pattern of Microsoft *Windows* growth. You start making noises. You want to develop *Windows*-based products. But at the time, 1989, Lotus is making significant net profits of almost $68 million, principally from sales of *DOS*-based *Lotus 1-2-3*. *Windows* Version 2.0 is a dog. So a few more lilies appear on the water's surface. You yell a bit louder and people still think you're being an alarmist. By the time people finally wake up, the pond has been overgrown with lilies.

> **History is the ability to select from the many lies that which most closely resembles the truth.**
>
> Herodotus, Greek historian

The more successful a company is, the more is at stake. Today, the longevity of successful companies is surprisingly low. The average life span of large companies is less than 40 years. In more recent studies the trend has been shown to continue. In 1994, a staggering 40 percent of the Fortune 500 of 1979 had ceased to exist. To succeed in the long term, organizations must continually reinvent themselves.

In the next chapter we'll see that in a learning-based organization it is everyone's business to question and challenge the paradigms that are shaping their work. The leaders, though, are ultimately responsible for creating an environment where innovation and change are possible, valued and encouraged.

To Summarize:

- Paradigms are ways of perceiving. They govern our attitudes and actions.

- In today's business world, paradigms are constantly shifting. Sometimes, the change is imperceptibly slow, but more often the shifts are sudden.

- The only secure individuals and organizations are those with the ability to anticipate and discern paradigm shifts.

- Paradigm shifters are market makers.

- Leaders create their own paradigms consistent with their vision, and shift existing paradigms to keep their organizations in a leadership position.

Reflection:
- What are the paradigms in my department, organization, industry and even my own responsibilities that I don't question.

Action:
- What one action shall I take tomorrow to move learning into action? And over time repeat, to move action into habit?

CHAPTER 4

Leaders are Paradigm Innovators

As we prepare to enter a new millennium, the greatest challenge has become problem-seeing, not problem-solving. Business leaders and managers are generally excellent problem solvers. But we have to become more adept at anticipating problems and perceiving opportunities to stay ahead of the competition and exceed customer expectations.

To create new products and services, executives and others in organizations must perceive opportunities. The highest margins lie in creating as yet unrealized value for the customer.

If we are all apple vendors in a small town, what price can we get for our apples? What is the nature of the market? In such a market, how do you win market share?

A leader is a dealer in hope.
Napoleon Bonaparte, French emperor

It's a dog-eat-dog, price-driven, commodity market. What the competition does affects us powerfully. To survive we might differentiate ourselves by polishing the apples or by spending more on advertising. While important, these approaches add to our cost. Unless we can raise our prices, we are squeezing our own margins.

In commodity markets, competitors who offer the lowest price win. This is Wal-Mart's strategy—always striving to increase operational efficiency and lower prices. Wal-Mart wants to maintain the perception that it offers the lowest prices.

Price-sensitive market share is the easiest to win, but also the easiest to lose. If your competitors lower their prices tomorrow, you instantly lose customers.

Back to our story of fruit vendors in the small town. If only one vendor sells oranges, what price can be commanded? Whatever the market will bear. Margins are high. The orange vendor isn't concerned about what competitors are doing with apples because of the monopoly on oranges.

Leaders who continually question business paradigms and create new value for their customers create *effective monopolies* for a period in which they can enjoy high margins. As competitors catch up, the market leader must be prepared to introduce new products and services that will make their original product obsolete. This keeps them at the front of the market.

At a seminar a CEO observed, "What you're saying is, if we were our own competitors, knowing what we know about our own weaknesses and strengths, we must always be trying to beat ourselves." He was right. Organizations must continuously compete against themselves and reinvent themselves to remain market leaders.

The Changing Nature of Leadership

How we perceive leadership is changing significantly. A marching band is the perfect metaphor for the way organizations used to be. There was one leader and everyone else marched in lock-step conformity. As products and services became more complex, specialization was required. An orchestra became a better metaphor. A series of specialists and a conductor selected the music, assigned the solos and controlled the tempo. The new model is more like a jazz band. A group of highly specialized, talented players improvise together. No one individual is in charge. Leadership "flows" from one player to the next. They celebrate one another's successes. They play best when they let each other shine in the spotlight for some time. And no one individual controls the play. In this scenario, leadership is demonstrated in the bringing together of the jazz players, ensuring that the group works well together, and perhaps managing the finances and logistical challenges facing the group so that the players can do what they do best — play.

In today's dynamic, changing market, strategic planning is a bit like trying to fly a plane while building it.

Future Challenge

Think about what your industry will be like in five years. Do you think competition will have increased or decreased? Will customers be more, or less sophisticated? Will competition in high-margin niches be increasing or decreasing? Will price-based competition be increasing or decreasing? Will competitors be coming from non-traditional areas, or will you be competing against the same competitors you have faced for ages? How about people? Will the best and the brightest employees be easier or harder to retain? Will there be increased or decreased pressure to integrate more tightly with suppliers to shorten cycle times? Will you be able to do exactly what you are doing now, only work a little bit harder or longer or with a more positive attitude and gain market share, increase customer satisfaction and create higher margins? We all know that our organizations must change. Change is inevitable; either organizations change or their market share will.

The Challenge of Leadership

People often envy leaders. I was speaking with a group of 200 managers from a large national bank. They were complaining about all the problems they faced, including how unresponsive the organization was to their needs. So I asked them, "The higher you rise in an organization, do more or fewer people bring you problems? Are the problems harder or easier to deal with? Does the weight of responsibility grow or diminish? Are the timelines for implementing solutions longer or shorter? Are the consequences of decisions more, or less difficult to anticipate? Are the factors affecting the decisions more, or less numerous? Are the solutions more, or less complex? Do the problems require deeper or simpler analysis? In working with people who bring you problems, do you require more, or less patience?"

> Maturity is the ability to delay gratification.
> M. Scott Peck, author

The higher you rise in an organization, the greater your tolerance for challenge, pain and complexity must be. The higher you go, the greater the weight you carry; therefore, the deeper your analytical abilities and the greater your patience and perseverance must be. And yet many people equate leadership with perks and prestige. Remember, the higher you go, the thinner the air gets. So at the end of this line of questioning to the group of 200 managers I said, "Remember, you chose to be leaders."

How Do Leaders Stay Ahead?

Leaders must continually question the viability of their products and services to ensure that their organization is not succumbing to complacency and, over time, mediocrity. Complacency kills. It's the only corporate disease that prevents you from knowing that you have it. Continually questioning helps individuals and organizations to deepen their understanding of potential market shifts, helping the organization to formulate and embrace new paradigms. Here are some examples:

Who does the work? I was in Florida to give a talk and discovered that I had forgotten to take any U.S. currency. There I was in the sunshine state with only Canadian cash, which my American friends call *Monopoly* money. I went to a bank I have never heard of — the First Third Bank of Florida (apparently it was a merger); stuck my bank card into the automatic banking machine (ATM) and on a Sunday night withdrew U.S. dollars from my Canadian account. Now think about what banking used to be like in 1980: Monday to Friday, 10:00 a.m. to 3:00 p.m., only at my local branch. Today, banking is anywhere, anytime and in any currency. The technology has dissolved what were once barriers to banking, enabling a radically different relationship between banks and customers. It's not about efficiency but radically new relationships.

Who does the work? I, the customer, am doing the work, not a teller. Not only that, but I paid one dollar for the honor and privilege of doing the work myself. And I was profoundly grateful to the bank for allowing me the opportunity. Now that's a paradigm shift!

If we limit ourselves to seeing only our employees doing work, then self-serve gas stations and banking machines would be impossible to imagine. We must look beyond traditional employee-driven workplaces and consider introducing new technologies and perhaps outsourcing some functions to the customer so we can remain focused on what we do best.

Federal Express introduced *PowerShip* in 1987, giving its 1,000 largest customers a free terminal to automatically fill in waybills and keep track of packages, courier costs and shipping volumes. Before 1987, people had to write out the waybills by hand, then call the courier to order the pick-up. The courier took the packages and waybills. Back at Federal Express someone had to key in the information, occasionally entering errors. You would receive the bill in the mail, catch the error, call Federal Express and another invoice would be issued. You would approve it, send it to accounts payable where the information was keyed in to your system and payment was sent through the mail.

PowerShip software automates the whole process. The software automatically fills in your shipping information. And when you have keyed in a customer once, they are on a quick-pick list. So the software eliminates most of the time it used to take to complete the waybill. The system orders the pick-up on-line, FedEx's system generates an invoice that interfaces with your on-line accounts payable system and through electronic funds transfer sends payment back to FedEx. The whole process is instantaneous.

These 1,000 largest clients represented 30 percent of FedEx's total package volume. The program was so successful that FedEx launched a spin-off program called *FedEx Ship* in 1995. Now businesses of any size that have the software can order on-line pick-ups. Over 550,000 FedEx customers use these two systems daily.[1] Finally, FedEx allows

You can't dig a hole in a new place by digging the same hole deeper.

Edward de Bono, author

customers to log on to its World Wide Web page, key in their waybill number and find out in real time exactly where their package is. As a result of these three initiatives, FedEx has not had to hire an additional 20,000 staff or to sort and file over two billion pieces of paper a year![2] More than 600,000 inquiries a day are answered on-line by customers themselves, twice as many as are answered by FedEx's own customer service agents over the phone. And who is doing the work? The customers. And the customers are profoundly grateful because from their perspective it eliminates unnecessary administrative work, too.

What business are we in? Any business that defines itself in terms of its product or service is ultimately doomed because products and services are constantly becoming outdated. During the late 1800s and early 1900s in the northern part of North America we kept our food cold in ice boxes. Numerous companies went out to the rivers and streams in the winter. Using saws, teams of men cut large blocks out of the ice, leveraged them up onto the horse-drawn sleighs and dragged them to barns where they were insulated in hay. During the summer, small blocks of ice were chipped off and delivered door-to-door using horse-drawn carriages.

Think about the core competencies required for the ice-block company: working with saws, working with horses, first aid would probably be good, there would be a barn acquisition department, a door-to-door sales force and an accounting department. And how would the company spend its research and development (R&D) budget? Most likely on trying to find better ways of cutting ice, insulating materials and breeding horses that work better in cold weather.

> There are three kinds of organizations: those that run into brick walls; those that see the brick walls coming and swerve to avoid them; and those that are out in front and are busy building walls for their competitors.[3]
>
> James Champy, author

But when refrigeration came along none of the companies that survived in the ice age made it in the refrigeration paradigm. Why? Well, look at the core competencies required in the new paradigm: handling Freon gas, manufacturing and servicing compression motors, mass manufacturing, and retail and wholesale distribution. The only competency that would remain would be accounting.

Why is it so difficult for organizations to change? Because in the ice-box paradigm, if you were a good saw handler you became head of the saw department, the employee who handled horses best became head of horses, the best barn buyer became head of barn acquisition. However, none of these skills was required in the new paradigm. In other words, the strengths of the organization—its people, its R&D—were the weaknesses in the new paradigm.

We need to separate *form* from *function.* Banking is essential but banks are not. The function of banking is essential but the current form is not. The way you will travel to your bank in the future is through software programs produced by Intuit, Netscape, Microsoft and Sun Microsystems. And over time you may come to associate banking more with these names than the traditional bank names we are accustomed to.

An organization focused on meeting its customers' underlying needs in the best way possible is more likely to have the courage and freedom needed to continuously reinvent itself, its products and its services. Ultimately, all organizations should exist to serve the needs of their customers. Many needs of customers will remain unarticulated until an innovative individual or organization discovers them and creates products and services to meet those as yet unrealized needs.

But don't throw the baby out with the bath water. Paradigm shifts happen over time. Organizations should not stop what they are doing and focus exclusively on a new way of doing business. Instead, they must make the transition from old paradigm to new one gradually as demand for the new product or service grows. For example, we still have radios. It is just that radios no longer occupy the dominant position in providing family entertainment at home. So a radio manufacturer in the 1930s would not give up radio production. But to create security in the future, it would have to be constantly searching for new applications for radios; for example, car radios and portable radios (such as the Walkman invented decades later by Sony). As television emerged as a new and growing medium, the company's long-term security would be guaranteed by making the move to manufacturing televisions.

Where do we serve the customer? Traditional wisdom in retailing teaches that only three things matter — location, location, location. But when I order a shirt from Land's End or L.L. Bean, I don't know if I am talking to a customer service representative in Texas, Florida or Michigan. When the shirt arrives by FedEx the next day, I don't know where the manufacturer or warehouse is located. Similarly, banking can be done with ease wherever there is an ATM.

If the owners of a mechanic's garage were to define their business in terms of physical location, then it would be impossible for them to conceive of 24-hour, roadside service anywhere in North America, dispatched from an entrepreneur's basement to tow-truck contractors across the continent. Technology has redefined the workplace.

Similarly, where does work occur? One physical location? Or any location where employees and associates are working?

When do we serve our customers? Who in 1980 could have predicted 24-hour banking available through ATMs, or 24-hour shopping centers, or software support from Dell Computer Corporation 24 hours a day, 7 days a week, 365 days a year?

When is it best for people to work? Most organizations have a nine-to-five mentality. People are expected to be physically present at work during those hours. Why? Because our work paradigm comes from the textile mills in England in the 1700s. People were called "hands" to the industrial process. Employees had to be physically present on the production line during their shift because production was physical. But today, what are we interested in—people's brawn or their brains?

Many computer programmers and other creative people often do their best work late at night. If their organization demands their presence from nine to five, they grudgingly show up by 9:00 in the morning, but they probably aren't productive until 11:30 or so—after they've had 15 cups of coffee—because they were up until 3:00 a.m. working on their pet programming project. In such cases, where does energy, enthusiasm and creativity go—into day jobs or late-night, pet projects?

If organizations want creativity, they must give employees the latitude to work under the special set of conditions that most foster creativity for them. Some people may be most creative listening to music, while others may be late-night workers.

Why shouldn't computer programmers do most of their work during the hours when they are most creative? I am often asked, "If employees worked at home, how would we know that they were working?" New information technology (IT) systems allow us to overcome barriers of time and distance. If the issue is trust and a company wants to have time clocks, log-on and log-off times can be recorded and keyboard activity measured. But I would ask in return, "How do you know how hard your employees work during office hours?" More important than measuring log-on and log-off times or the number of keystrokes is measuring results. Manage by results, not methods. Organizations want new, high-margin products and services, increased sales, higher productivity, shorter cycle times, higher quality and increased customer satisfaction and retention. If you can achieve these things, it doesn't matter where or when employees do the work.

How do we serve our customers? Do we serve them based on our rules, policies and procedures that are designed for our benefit? Or do we design policies from customers' perspectives?

An insurance firm studied its internal processes and discovered that, on average, it took eight weeks from the time one of its clients suffered an accident until they received their claim payment in the mail. Imagine that you suffered a car accident. You would call your insurance broker (IB), who would call the insurance company (IC). A case manager (CM) would be assigned to your file. The file would then go to the claims adjuster (CA), who would talk to your garage mechanic (GM). Then the file would come back to the case manager (CM), who would have to receive the police report (PR) before finally approving the file and sending it off to accounts payable (AP) until, finally, you receive your payment (Ya!)

Paper-based, Time-intensive Process

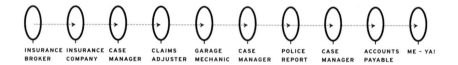

| INSURANCE BROKER | INSURANCE COMPANY | CASE MANAGER | CLAIMS ADJUSTER | GARAGE MECHANIC | CASE MANAGER | POLICE REPORT | CASE MANAGER | ACCOUNTS PAYABLE | ME - YA! |

The company found that, throughout this time-intensive, paper-bound, linear process, the amount of time actually spent working on the average case by all staff totaled only eight hours! The rest of the time, the file was either in someone's in-box or out-box, or in transit between boxes.

Here is how one insurance company reengineered. The claims service objective of Progressive Insurance's Immediate Response is to provide policyholders with fast, fair, caring and personal service when they need it.

Progressive reengineered its processes in 1992 because of CEO Peter Lewis' vision of reducing the human trauma and economic costs of auto accidents. Lewis believes insurance companies abuse customers: "They get dealt with adversarially and slowly. I said, 'Why don't we just stop that? Why don't we start dealing with them nicely?' It would be a revolution in the business."[4]

Lewis wanted to restructure insurance processes so that Progressive could help customers when they need it most—when they're in accidents.

The first problem was that people are so flustered when they get into an accident they can't remember the name of their insurance company, let alone the phone number. Focus group studies show that people will carry "Gold Cards" in their wallets. So Progressive gave all its policyholders a "Gold Card" with a toll-free, 1-800 number that is staffed 24 hours a day, seven days a week. With the prevalence of cellular phones today, policyholders are now calling from the scene of the accident. Progressive staff work to help in any way they can. Company claims representatives don't sit in the office, they rove around North America in marked company vehicles. The operator can dispatch the nearest available claims representative to the accident scene. At times they have arrived before 911-dispatched vehicles! The claims reps are focused on assisting you. They have a cellular phone that you can use to call your family or friends to let them know you will be late. They interview witnesses and take photos in case the accident ends up in court.

From the scene of the accident, the rep will arrange for your car to be towed and repaired. Progressive pays for the services up front rather than you paying for it and then trying to claim for it. The rep will also arrange for a rental car and will drive you over to pick it up. Or, if you prefer, they will drive you to where you need to go and have the rental car dropped off at your home.

Some clients prefer the cash to fixing their vehicle. Using specialized software and a notebook computer, the claims rep can estimate the damage and issue payment to the policyholder on the spot.

Progressive representatives now make contact with 80 percent of all accident victims less than nine hours after learning of the accident. Adjusters inspect 70 percent of damaged vehicles within one day and wrap up most collision damage claims within one week.

The benefits for the policyholder are obvious: the insurance company becomes a personal valet, a problem solver during the time of greatest need and stress. Progressive becomes an ally. It's one-stop shopping. It's help when the client needs help.

From Progressive's point of view the benefits are also obvious: faster claims processing, less paperwork, fewer people involved, significantly higher customer satisfaction and strategic advantage in the marketplace. The company knows that when people are dealt with quickly and fairly it reduces the involvement of lawyers, and of the overall amount paid out by the company, more goes to policyholders rather than to pay legal fees.

Progressive has been one of the fastest-growing insurance companies, going from the forty-third largest U.S. insurer of private passenger autos in 1980 to the seventh largest in 1996. It has also been very profitable, with a 24.3 percent annual compounded rate of return between 1971 and 1995 (the comparable Standard & Poor's 500 rate was 7.6 percent in the same period). Progressive is able to insure risky drivers that no other insurance firm will accept because its overheads are so low.

Best of the Bad

Progressive looked at the database of drivers who are typically thought of as bad risks by insurance companies — drivers with bad records such as driving while under the influence of alcohol, reckless driving charges or numerous accidents. If the average driver pays a premium of X, all insurance companies charged this group of bad drivers 4X premiums. Progressive's analysts who set the rate for premiums began to ask, "What possible changes in lifestyle would lead us to assess these drivers' risk profiles differently, despite their past bad records?" The analysts decided that if you had your first child it would likely change your sense of responsibility and therefore your driving pattern. So Progressive went into the database, found all new parents who were bad drivers and offered them a premium of 3X, which was better than any other insurer in the market. By looking differently at these customers they skimmed a very lucrative category of customer.

How could Progressive continue to challenge existing paradigms? Imagine that the company places a small microchip/transmitter under the hood of insured cars that would emit a radio signal if a car was in a collision at over 15 miles an hour. The signal would be picked up through a land-based cellular or radio network and relayed to an orbiting satellite. Using geographic location software, the satellite would determine the location of the accident, call the client on a cellular phone and, if necessary, dispatch the nearest claims adjuster. If the impact occurred at greater than, say 45 miles per hour, the system could be designed to call 911 services. Imagine a near-fatal crash on a little-traveled road late at night. You swerve to avoid a deer, roll your car and crash into a telephone pole. You are unconscious, and without immediate medical help will die, but your insurance firm saves your life! Sound too far off? New Lincoln Continental cars come with such a system:

> ... Our roadside service ... goes 10,000 miles into space with a satellite. It's the Remote Emergency Satellite Cellular Unit we call RESCU. Simply push a button and global positioning satellites will determine your location. Your position is then relayed to the Lincoln Security Response Center, which will dispatch assistance and keep you informed via your hands-free cellular phone. Both of these systems are part of Lincoln Continental's Personal Security Package with RESCU.[5]

It's not just reengineering an old process, it's radically redefining the relationship between the company and the customer.

As a policyholder, which insurance firm would you choose—one that pays in eight weeks but has given the customer service agents training, teaching them to smile while talking to customers over the phone because their happiness is conveyed through their voice, or one that is capable of paying on the spot?

How we deliver products or services to our customers is significant. For example, how is corporate training delivered? Until 1995 it was usually delivered in person. I used to organize executive development conferences that cost $1,000 per person for two days. Executives, who came from across North America, would easily spend another $1,500 on flights, hotel rooms and meals. The travel cost more than the course!

In 1997, Tom Peters charged $100,000 per day to speak. Few companies or seminar promoters can afford this fee. Today it's possible to participate in a live Tom Peters seminar in the comfort of your boardroom or auditorium by satellite or PictureTel videoconferencing system for just $2,500!

When I turn up to see Tom Peters or Stephen Covey live, I am usually in the audience with 1,000 other people. From the back of the room I'm not watching the speaker, I'm watching a projected image on a large screen. So if I'm watching Peters or Covey on TV at the live site, I find little difference in watching them at a remote location by satellite or videoconferencing. Instead of paying $350 to $500 for registration, I pay as little as $50! Any participant at any remote location can pose questions by telephone and interact with the presenter.

Business education no longer has to be expensive and exclusive to executives. It can be made available to thousands of employees, allowing for consistency of training and the development of a common language across a whole organization. You can afford to have the world's leading business thinkers—Tom Peters, Edward de Bono, Stephen Covey, Joel Arthur Barker and many others—presenting live in your boardroom! [6]

Individuals and organizations must question how they conduct business. Companies must not define themselves by their policies or procedures.

Why are we in business? Over the years the primary purpose of business has shifted. In the past, the purpose was to produce the best possible profit or dividends per share. In other words, the purpose of business was to serve the shareholder(s). In the 1980s the popular focus turned to customer satisfaction, the theory being that if you take care of your customer the bottom line will take care of itself. Taking this progression one step further, my research into the best companies showed that success is also dependent upon having excited, satisfied employees (internal customers) who, in turn, are motivated to serve the (external) customer. We need to continue expanding our concept of why we are in business. It is ultimately to serve the needs of all stakeholders. Stephen Covey has a simple definition of stakeholder. He asks, "Who would be hurt if your business failed?" Anyone who would be hurt is a stakeholder. Ultimately, the most successful businesses follow an inspiring mission to serve all stakeholders.

Paradigm shifts in the past happened slowly over a long period of time. For instance, the shift from horse-drawn carriage to car took two decades. This was due to the time it took Ford to develop and refine the assembly line, but more importantly the lack of infrastructure to support and promote car sales. On unpaved roads car travel was bumpy and slow. Paving happened slowly as automobile travel became more common and drivers demanded better roads from governments. The shift from *DOS* to *Windows*, by contrast, took eight years, primarily due to the time it took to refine the software. Today, however, with easy-to-use software and powerful microprocessors, the information technology infrastructure is in place to enable fast-and-furious paradigm shifts. For instance, new technology allows PC users to make long-distance phone calls over the Internet without paying long-distance charges. VocalTec, Lucent and NorTel (Northern Telecom) are all selling equipment to facilitate this. In 1997 only 0.2 percent of all phone traffic in North America is carried over data lines, but by 2002 one analyst predicts this figure will rise to 18.5 percent![7] How will this affect phone companies that rely on long-distance charges to supply most of their profit? To date, phone companies have downplayed the significance of this technology, ignoring its potential threat.

A journey of a thousand miles begins with a single step.
Lao Tzu, philosopher

Paradigm Shifting Differs from Reengineering
Reengineering has been the hot management theory in North America from 1991 to 1996. Reengineering focuses on how to make existing processes more efficient, but does not create new products, services or markets. Reengineering is necessary but insufficient to ensure thriving in the future. Businesses can better their bottom line by increasing revenue (numerator) and/or cutting costs (denominator). As Hamel and Prahalad point out:[8]

> ROI [Return on Investment] or RONA [Return on Net Assets] . . . has two components, a numerator — net income —

and a denominator—investment, net assets, or capital employed. (In a service industry a more appropriate denominator may be headcount). Managers know that raising net income is likely to be a harder slog than cutting assets and headcount. To grow the numerator, top management must have a point of view about where the new opportunities lie, must be able to anticipate changing customer needs, must have invested preemptively in building new competencies and so on. So under intense pressure for a quick ROI improvement, executives reach for the lever that will bring the quickest, surest improvements in ROI—the denominator. To cut the denominator, management doesn't need much more than a red pencil. Thus the obsession with denominators.

In fact, the United States and Britain have produced an entire generation of denominator managers. They can downsize, declutter, delayer and divest better than any managers in the world.

Adding to the numerator creates greater long-term security because inventing new, high-margin goods and services creates new markets and distances the competition. Cutting costs is the focus for mature industries and commodity, price-driven businesses, where competition is fierce and markets are limited. Few people can see the future—focusing on the top line requires creativity, ingenuity and innovation. It requires trial-and-error testing to discover or uncover new value that customers may not even be able to articulate. The numerator mindset focuses on what everyone (including competitors) can already see. It's not an *either/or*; business must focus on *both*. To summarize:

$$\frac{N}{D} = \frac{+\text{VALUE}}{-\text{COSTS}} = \frac{\text{SLOW}}{\text{QUICK}} = \frac{\text{HARDER}}{\text{EASIER}} = \frac{\text{LONG TERM SECURITY}}{\text{SHORT TERM SECURITY}} = \frac{\text{EFFECTIVE}}{\text{EFFICIENT}} = \frac{\text{INVISIBLE}}{\text{VISIBLE}} = \frac{\text{ANTICIPATE}}{\text{CONTROL}}$$

Paradigm Shifts Are Not Black or White

People often see issues as black or white. Paradigm shifts often take time to become apparent. For instance, the *DOS*-to-*Windows* shift occurred from 1985 to 1993. In hindsight the shift would seem sudden. Looking back from 1992 or 1993 it would seem that the market would have shifted in just a year or two. However, the early warning signals of the impending shift were there for years before. These subtle early warning signals are often imperceptible to leaders. Not only are the indications small but, more important, they are outside their realm of experience.

This blindness plagues even the best companies. How did Netscape initially blind-side Microsoft? Bill Gates is supposedly the brightest guy in the computer industry. How could he have initially missed the trend to the Internet and the World Wide Web? No one is immune to missing the paradigm shifts.

Billions of electronic mail messages are now being sent daily. In fact, e-mails now exceed the number of letters carried by the U.S. Postal Service! (Chapter 11). This along with the exponential growth of the World Wide Web has dramatically eroded the anticipated growth in the courier market for letters and documents. Does this mean that the Internet is killing FedEx's markets? Yes, in some ways it is. But FedEx is thriving because it is reconfiguring its operation to take advantage of the new opportunities the Web provides.

Paradigm shifts simultaneously offer peril and promise. While FedEx has not experienced the anticipated growth in documents, it has significantly saved administrative expenses by integrating the Web into all of its business as discussed above. However, to use new technologies only to cut costs is to miss half the equation. FedEx is adding new value for customers. FedEx has introduced a new service, *VirtualOrder*, which is aimed at small businesses. FedEx will develop and maintain an electronic catalog for a business on the Web. FedEx takes customer orders, ships products, accepts payments and remits funds to the business. This allows a small business to have a large presence on the Web and access to world-class logistics and fulfillment. Does this mean that FedEx is now in the business of Web page design? Product fulfillment? Virtual warehousing? Yes. Yes. Yes.

Every company will be blind-sided at some point. The real challenge is whether:

1. An organization can anticipate shifts and reconfigure its operations to provide new goods or services.
2. An organization that does not proactively create shifts recognizes and responds to them as they are occurring, taking advantage of the new opportunities.
3. When an organization has missed a shift, executives have the humility to admit it and then the courage to re-orient the corporate strategy to the new reality.

When these shifts occur, the new way may not eliminate the old. Some people dismiss these "paradigm shifts" as being unrealistic. Some have challenged me, saying, "The Internet will not completely eliminate branch banking." I agree. ATMs haven't eliminated tellers. For some transactions customers will use a teller, some an ATM, and

I can't tell you what the future will look like, but I can tell you it won't look like the present or the past.

Jim Harris

for others the Internet. Some customers will never use the Internet to bank. But over time, more and more customers will use the new media.

New ways of looking at business require leaders to question every aspect of their operations. The policies, systems, structures, products and services that produced success in the past may produce failure in the future. Leaders at all levels of an organization have to unlearn what made them successful in the past in order to learn what will make them successful in the future. Leaders have to learn, change and accept uncertainty. This is the essence of the learning paradox.

What are the early warning signs of an impending shift? Customers' classic frustrations are a good predictor of potential shifts. For instance, the *DOS*-to-*Windows* shift could have been predicted because of the difficulty in learning *DOS*. People who had never owned a computer before were able to boot up a Mac, open a word processor, type and print off a letter all within the first five minutes of owning the computer. But the same process was painful and user-vicious for IBM-compatible PC owners in the *DOS* era. It wasn't until the introduction of *Windows 3.0* that PCs began to approach the user-friendliness of Macs.

I can tell when there has been a power failure in someone's home because the VCR will be flashing "12:00." Resetting the time is a major project for most people. The manual must be found, the instructions read and numerous attempts must be made before the consumer emerges victorious. It seems that you need to have a PhD in engineering before you can figure out how to program your VCR. This is an early warning signal that a software company needs to develop an easier-to-use, faster-to-learn, more intuitive interface, thereby creating a paradigm shift in the VCR market.

Leadership Begins with Humility[9]
"An amazing invention, but who would ever want to use one?"
— *U.S. President Rutherford Hayes, after participating in a trial telephone call between Washington and Philadelphia in 1876.*

"Everything that can be invented has been invented."
— *Charles H. Duell, Commissioner, U.S. Office of Patents, urging President William McKinley to abolish his office, 1899.*

"Sensible and responsible women do not want to vote."
— *U.S. President Grover Cleveland, 1905.*

"Horses are here to stay. The automobile is only a novelty, a fad."
— *President, Michigan Savings Bank, 1903, advising Ford's lawyer not to invest in Ford Motor. Disregarding the advice, he invested $5,000 and later sold the stock for $12.5 million.*

"There is no likelihood man can ever tap the power of the atom."
— *Robert Millikan, Nobel Prize winner in physics, 1920.*

"Who the hell wants to hear actors talk?"
— *Harry Warner, Warner Brothers, 1927.*

"I think there is a world market for about five computers."
— *Thomas J. Watson, Chairman, IBM, 1943.*

"Television won't hold on to any market it captures after the first six months. People will soon tire of staring at a box every night."
— *Darryl F. Zanuck, head of 20th Century Fox, commenting on the effect television would have on the film industry in 1946.*

"640K is enough for anyone."
— *Bill Gates, Chairman, Microsoft, 1981.*

"There is no reason for any individual to have a computer in their home."
— *Ken Olsen, president, Digital Equipment, 1977. In 1997, annual world-wide sales of new computers surpassed 80 million. The majority of North American sales were to home users.*

Execute Within Paradigms — Innovate Beyond Them

Stephen Covey highlights the difference between leadership and management in a simple story.[11] Imagine trying to cut a swath through the Amazon rain forest. Management would be working with the front-line machete wielders, putting on motivational seminars, providing training in sharpening and machete-wielding techniques, holding scheduling optimization courses for production managers and conflict resolution classes for angry machete wielders — a dangerous vocation at the best of times.

But what would leadership involve? Climbing to the top of the highest tree in the forest, judging the lay of the land, getting the big picture and asking questions like, "Are we heading in the right direction? Are we even in the right forest?" Leadership might involve having to yell down, "We're in the wrong forest!"

What might be management's response? "Shut up, we're making progress!"

At times leadership is dangerous, especially if management, in its enthusiasm for progress, accidentally cuts down the tree the leader has climbed!

Leadership deals with vision, direction—the big picture—and requires ongoing evaluation of existing paradigms. It focuses on effectiveness. Management, on the other hand, deals with execution and focuses on efficiency. Managers deal with existing problems. Leaders work to identify new problems and opportunities.

In *Managing in Turbulent Times*, Peter Drucker says that in periods of change and upheaval the most important managerial skill is the ability to anticipate. Unfortunately, most organizations and professions are deeply into management (efficiency) without ever questioning whether they're even in the right forest (effectiveness).

Imagine you are working for a company that is making horse-drawn buggies in 1900. The company launches a total quality management (TQM) program so that its products meet quality standards of six defects per million buggies. It has also embarked on a continuous improvement program to reward employees for productivity-enhancing suggestions so that, over time, production costs fall, allowing the company to lower the price of buggies. Furthermore, the company takes the executive team through an outdoor team-building exercise in which they have to fall backwards off a wall into the arms of their colleagues, which succeeds in increasing trust within the organization.

Perhaps the company has also embarked on a new focus on customers, asking past buyers whether they prefer blue leather seats or black leather seats and which would influence their buying decision? It has involved staff in customer service training that stresses the need for a pleasant approach. And the marketing department is busily thinking up such slogans as, "Buy a buggy—get a whip free."

> I never go to where the puck is, I go to where it is going to be.
> Wayne Gretzky, hockey player

These sound like good management strategies. The company is clearly working to increase the efficiency of existing processes. But none of these efforts will be effective because the industry is doomed by the automotive industry. By 1910 an irreversible paradigm shift will become apparent and it will be too late for a business without strong leadership to survive. Most of the buggy companies will go bankrupt. Paradigms are primary, efficiency is secondary.

Leadership, Vision and Mission

Imagine that you win the lottery and decide to build your dream home. What's the first thing you'll do? People in my seminars have answered, "Buy the land." "Hire an architect." "Pinch myself to make sure it really happened." "Deposit the money in the bank."

"Why hire an architect?" I ask. Answers include, "To structure our concepts." "So that we take an idea of what a dream home is and make it a reality, really plan it out." "So that we can measure the progress during construction."

A woman once answered, "So I won't get divorced!" She meant that while she had one concept of a dream home, her husband had another. An architect would act as a referee and make sure the overall concept and the details of the design had been agreed to before construction.

Leaders are the architects of business. In the world of shifting paradigms, leadership has become more complex and more necessary. But unlike a house whose blueprints are static, businesses are involved in a dynamic, ever-changing environment. While the mission (Why are we in business?) will tend to remain constant, the vision or direction (Where are we going?), will be continually changing over time. Therefore, everyone in the organization needs to be involved in creating the corporate blueprints of where the organization is headed.

Blueprints allow the clients, builders, trades workers and architect to visualize the end goal before construction begins.

Imagine arriving on the job site with no blueprints and saying to the workers, "Hey, you guys, I'm not paying you to stand around here drinking coffee and smoking cigarettes. Get cracking, build this baby!" How effective would that be?

How many people on the job site should have access to the blueprints? Everyone! Imagine that the master architect would not let anyone see the blueprints and only verbally told the supervisor what the various wings of the dream home looked like. What kind of dream home would you have? Visitors would likely comment, "My, what eclectic taste you have. This wing is Tudor in style, that one is Japanese and the one over there is distinctly Spanish."

Without seeing the blueprints, every supervisor would assume a common vision while in fact working toward an individual goal. The result would be nobody's dream home!

One of the exciting promises of new technology is that you will be able to visit an architect's office and strap on a helmet and visor connected to a computer. Using virtual reality, you will be able to tour conceptual houses. A three-dimensional blueprint will allow you to experience your dream home in every detail. As a result, the final blueprint will be a closer reflection of your ideas, needs and desires.

Designing a building is not only a top-down process. It's also bottom-up. There is one master set of blueprints and then subsets of the master plan. For instance, the plumber has plumbing blueprints and the electricians have electrical wiring diagrams. Multiple blueprints can exist as long as they are in harmony or alignment. In the planning process, the plumber could go to the master architect and suggest moving the bathroom on the ground floor from one location to another to install the plumbing more easily, thus saving thousands of dollars. The architect would then have to check with the owners and redesign the plan.

Plans are not static. They can and must evolve with everyone's input. By encouraging input, you create an empowered work team in which individual ideas matter and everyone is encouraged to question and challenge assumptions. Paradoxically, a house that people have spent more time planning will meet high standards and will take less time to build because it has fewer mistakes and needs less rework. Worker satisfaction on the job site will definitely be higher, too.

Empowering employees is not a one-shot deal. Some people have a negative view of empowerment that stems from the experience of being given carte-blanche responsibility and then being criticized or fired for not meeting expectations. Empowerment is not abdication. Leaders must create an environment in which people are willing to take risks and act with autonomy. Individuals earn autonomy over time as their competence increases. This brings us back to the learning paradox. By definition, people will make mistakes while they are learning, yet many organizations that demand innovation don't tolerate mistakes. Leaders must ensure that the mistakes are not fatal; first, by including everyone in planning so there is ownership and understanding of the mission, and second, by monitoring progress. The goal is to create a learning environment. Of course, the company shouldn't bet its whole future on just one product or service. During times of rapid change, security is actually achieved through a diversity of strategies. For instance, Microsoft has *MS-DOS, Windows 3.x,*[12] *Windows 95, Windows 98, Windows NT, Back Office,* single applications, *Microsoft Office,* a small business bundle, *Microsoft Network, Encarta,* games and home applications divisions, Internet products and developer tools, and Microsoft and NBC have created MSNBC. The company is constantly innovating and working to find new opportunities.

Credibility

Many leaders believe that they will lose credibility if they make a mistake or make a decision and then don't stick with it. They see changing their mind as a sign of weakness. The unspoken assumption that this is based on is that leaders are in control. They are all-knowing.

Imagine the president of a company standing in front of employees and saying, "I am baffled by the market. The change is so fast and furious that time and time again I find myself caught off guard. I am continually having to adjust my ideas of where we are going. I don't have all the answers, in fact I am not absolutely certain where we are going.

I often feel I don't know what I am doing—and isn't it exciting!!" Does this inspire faith? Is this reassuring? Is this what people want to hear?

The president could easily add, "But what I do know is that if we work together as a team, we will ultimately be successful."

But it is the truth. The environment is changing so quickly that no leader can have all the answers. Bill Gates' Microsoft was blind-sided by Netscape. The emperor has no clothes. Leaders are only human. A healthy, creative environment is one in which everyone, including the leader, is allowed to make mistakes, take responsibility for them, learn as quickly as possible and move on. Leaders who have the humility to recognize when they are wrong and the courage to admit it engender loyalty and respect from employees and create greater organizational security.

Leaders Stay on Course

It is inevitable that any project or organization will stray from its course, even with excellent leadership. How should we feel when we deviate from our mission? Imagine you are sailing on the ocean in the middle of thick fog. How often do you look at the compass? Constantly.

The average airplane is off course 98 percent of the time. Changing wind currents are always altering the flight path. As a result, the pilot or autopilot is constantly making small corrections to bring the plane back on course. There's no sense of guilt or shame involved. The pilot doesn't say, "I've been off course for Cincinnati 98 percent of the time. I'm a bad, bad pilot. I feel so guilty. In fact, I feel so bad that I've decided to give up the course and head for Buffalo instead! Besides, I like chicken wings."

I am off course with my personal mission much of the time. I shouldn't, however, beat myself up and give up the goal.

We need to adopt the same attitude when discussing a corporate mission. Rather than blaming, how do we come back to the mission? What should we do from first principles, given this situation? Leadership requires tremendous patience, especially when listening to criticism about the company's direction from employees.

Listening is the first step to converting criticism into constructive suggestions, fresh ideas and renewed creativity. Listening is essential for creating and fostering a positive environment.

I am often asked, "What is the one thing that all the best companies to work for have in common?" In a word, I would say, "respect." The best companies respect people as individuals. This means that people have faith that if they have a problem they will be able to raise it and find a solution. Having a culture that is open and honest is essential if an organization is to auto-correct when it is off course. Only by listening to new ideas — some of which may initially sound crazy — can an organization create new products, services and markets. Sometimes it is only when we are lost that we discover new places.

Imagine the pilot, after noticing that he is far off course, begins to feel terrifically guilty. Eventually his depression is so great that he begins to take Prozac so he won't feel bad. Or he covers up the compass so he won't have to look at it. When I get depressed about something, usually my conscience — my personal compass — communicates with me to let me know that I am off course. But I shouldn't kill the messenger by medicating the symptom. I need to search for the deeper root cause.

The key to success for both individuals and organizations is to practice self-reflection and self-correction, for we are all blind when it comes to the future. Whenever I am in a hall with a tall ceiling, I ask the audience, "Imagine a pillar stretching from the floor to the ceiling that represents all knowledge in the universe. Both knowledge that we have uncovered as a human race and knowledge we have yet to discover. Where would all collective human knowledge fall as a percentage of all knowledge, close to the top of the pillar, close to the bottom or in the middle?" Inevitably people respond, "Close to the bottom."

"Okay, let's take all human knowledge, that little section close to the bottom and stretch it out until it represents a pillar from floor to ceiling. Where would my knowledge or your knowledge as an individual fall as a percentage of all human knowledge, close to the top, the bottom or in the middle?" Most people answer, "Close to the bottom."

I only know a tiny fraction of a tiny fraction. Am I not, therefore, a child of the universe? I need to have the same compassion for myself as I would for a child learning to walk. I must practice compassion and tolerance with myself because by definition I will make many mistakes — both personally and in business — if I am trying to add new value for my family or my customers. Because I will make mistakes I need to practice self-reflection and self-correction.

> People like the security of knowing the answers. What you're really saying is that today we have to live and work amid questions — because everything is changing.
>
> Barbara Marshall, human resource professional

> Sometimes the best places are discovered when one is lost.
>
> Judy Bell, labor relations consultant

Leaders Work on Context

Leaders work on the quality of relationships. It is the relationship that governs, organizes, entices and excites performance. The gardener doesn't grow the plant, the plant grows itself. The gardener (the business leader) works on the context — tilling the soil, planting the seeds, weeding and watering. As in a classic Zen paradox, the leader does nothing but is responsible for everything.

In *Leadership and the New Science: Learning About Organization from an Orderly Universe*, Margaret Wheatley uses quantum physics as a metaphor for organizational leadership. Among the atomic particles, which ones are in charge? None, they are governed by laws of physics, organizing principles. The electrons, neutrons, photons and other particles naturally fall into their respective patterns. It is the same with an organization. If there is a strong, commonly shared mission and vision, it will organize the activities.

Every business is founded on relationships—relationships with customers, employees, suppliers, shareholders and the community. Businesses operate within a web of relationships. Shifts in the nature of these relationships change the nature of business. Business leaders must be careful to foster relationships that will benefit their organization.

Old-style union management relations often operate within a win-lose paradigm and are characteristic of a low-trust corporate culture. Imagine that two criminals jump ship at night while being taken to an island prison such as Alcatraz. But there's a catch: they're handcuffed together. In order to get a breath of air, Convict A pushes the other's head under the water so he can hold his head high and take a huge breath. That's a win-lose situation (A wins; B loses). On surfacing, Convict B, sputtering and gasping, knows that he needs a good, deep breath so he pushes Convict A's head under. That's a lose-win situation (A loses; B wins). This goes back and forth until one of them is too tired to keep going and drowns. As Convict B begins sinking, Convict A is dragged down with him. This is the ultimate lose-lose situation!

In interdependent relationships, only win-win agreements are sustainable. Win-win relationships take a great deal of time to cultivate.

Unionized organizations wanting to remain viable in an increasingly competitive international marketplace have no alternative but to alter the win-lose paradigm. No union wants to see its members out of work. When historically adversarial union-management opponents get together to discuss new security, their objectives are basically the same. Both groups want to ensure the longevity of the organization. Both want satisfied, empowered and challenged employees. Both want greater financial security. Reaching these objectives requires an entirely new approach, an entirely new relationship.

Think about a marriage. When the relationship is strong, is the marriage contract what keeps you together? No. If the relationship is poor, will the contract keep you together? No. So what is more important, the relationship or the contract?

This raises a simple philosophy that has stood me well over time:

The sage is like a little child... so return to the beginning, become a child again.
Lao Tzu, philosopher

The universe is full of magical things patiently waiting for our wits to grow sharper.
Eden Phillpots, Victorian poet

Never get married on the first date. I know it's old-fashioned, but I'm just not that kind of guy. I never get married on the first date.

Long-term success requires a commitment to continually question the prevailing industry wisdom, and a long-term focus on developing strong relationships based on mutual gain. Using the gardening metaphor: in the absence of a gardener the weeds will grow the fastest, but they are easy to pull out, they have no strong, deep, sustaining root systems. By contrast, trees—or Chinese bamboo—take many years to show growth but once rooted are very difficult to remove. Gardening is an active, not passive, experience. So it is with corporate leadership. In any organization, without active leadership bad practices will cause dissatisfaction and tension (weeds in a garden). Leadership by definition is active and requires creating organizational systems and structures that proactively work to bring out the best in all employees.

> It takes a long time to grow young.
> Pablo Picasso, artist

Leaders Optimize the Whole

The leader's role is to optimize the whole organization. At times this will require "sub-optimizing" certain departments. On the surface this seems counter-intuitive. Within any organization this leads to tension because the natural inclination of people is to optimize their departmental function.

For instance, the accountants buy the best accounting software to address their needs, the marketers buy the best marketing software, the MIS (management information system) team buys the best MIS software, the executives get the best executive information system and the shipping department buys the best logistical software. Each department is fully optimized, but the company ends up with many islands of information technology that may not be able to communicate with one another. Information can't flow seamlessly through the organization and as a result customers' needs can't be dealt with quickly. The organization cannot respond adequately in a dynamic, changing environment. But the costs of poor performance—for example, loss of market share to more nimble competitors—do not show up as any one department's fault. Instead, how the organization works as a whole is the responsibility of the leader.

> A man can know even less about God, than an ant can know of the contents of the British Museum.[13]
> Carl Jung, psychologist

Each department must keep in mind that it exists to serve the organization as a whole. Departmental decisions must be made within the context of what is best for the whole organization.

In the above example, the company should standardize using one software package that meets 80 percent of the accounting department's needs, 80 percent of the marketing department's needs, 80 percent of the MIS department's needs and 80 percent of the executives' needs.

Each department can then customize the software to obtain the remaining 20 percent of its required functionality, still allowing data to flow seamlessly through the organization. The leader should ensure that the entire organization is optimized first, and then the departments can further optimize their functions within the new systems and structures.

If the purchasing manager receives a bonus based on how low a price is paid for goods and services, the organization is optimizing one departmental function at the expense of other departments. A purchasing manager who buys cheaper equipment is rewarded, but when that equipment breaks down and the company can't ship product, the shipping department is blamed. The savings accruing to purchasing may be small compared with the costs for the shipping department, the MIS team or the training professionals. The root of the problem, as we will see in the next chapter, is a faulty system. In this case it is a compensation system that rewards the purchasing manager for attaining the lowest possible purchase price for computers. However, the hard cost of the computer is like the tip of the iceberg, representing 18 percent of the total cost of ownership. The vast balance is training, ensuring system compatibility, software, repairs, maintenance and ease of use.

Often individual departments, in their quest for quality in their particular field, lose sight of the fact that the real goal is the quality of the ultimate product. Software developers have many competing goals to balance: as few bugs as possible, increased functionality, ease of use, speed of the software, simple code and getting to market before the competition. Many of these are opposing goals. The more features developers include, the longer the software takes to reach the market and the greater the chance of being beaten by the competition; the more features (more code), the more bugs; the more code, the slower the software runs—but if there are not enough new, compelling features, few users will upgrade. The tricky part of leadership is to find a balance that results in the most marketable, timely product that users desire.

Paradigm Shifts Equal Growth

Today, powerful forces are at work fundamentally changing the way every organization operates. Relationships on all levels are changing—business-customer relationships, employer-employee relationships and even the nature of competition. Both individuals and organizations need the tools and skills to meet new challenges and create paradigm shifts. Leaders who work to understand and accept the nature and

Human relationships are the key to all commerce.
Robyn Allan, management consultant

effect of these forces and who change accordingly stand an excellent chance of advancing the success of their organizations. The financial rewards that stem from acting proactively in all these areas are astonishing, as we will see in case study after case study. By bringing an enterprise into alignment with these shifts, the organization can benefit from the changes and experience growth.

Growth and success in any organization is only achieved through teams. The switch from a hierarchy to a team-based organization can be painful for everyone, but once teams are established and begin to function, a natural balance is found, barriers to decision-making are removed and the whole organization begins to focus on the big picture.

The next chapter discusses the changing nature of leadership. Leaders work to change organizational systems and structures to create greater alignment and to enable the organization's vision to come to fruition. Chapter 6 outlines a process for creating a common vision, where employees across the organization not only understand the vision, but are committed to and excited by it. The process involves, excites and galvanizes employees, drawing out their best ideas and greatest commitment from people.

Nothing inspires genius like a tight budget.[14]
Sign at the California State Finance Dept

To Summarize:

- Leaders must continually assess their organization's direction and question personal, organizational and industrial paradigms.

- A "blueprint" is essential. All parties involved with a project should have input into its development.

- Leaders cultivate win-win relationships, both inside and outside the organization.

Reflection:

- When was the last time that I questioned the industry wisdom, the "way we have always done it," or how I see problems?

- Do I distinguish between what I assume to be true and what I know to be true?

Action:

- What one action shall I take tomorrow to move learning into action? And over time repeat, to move action into habit?

CHAPTER 5

Creating Sustainable Enterprises

Each organization—its systems, structures and the results it experiences—is a product of individual interactions. A business is nothing more than a web of relationships between the business and its customers, employees, suppliers, shareholders, the community and governments.

Change Begins with Self

I attend over 70 conferences a year and everywhere I go I hear people talking about how we need to change. Individuals need to change, organizations need to change, society as a whole needs to change. With so much discussion, why then is there so little change relative to the rhetoric? And why does change take so long to implement?

These questions haunted me and prompted me to search for answers. Despite powerful and growing literature on change, what is holding us back?

Organizations are nothing more than a collection of individuals. If the individuals in the organization are incapable of changing, the organization as a whole will not change. So fundamentally, change begins with the individual.

We can't change the world if we can't change ourselves. If we can't change ourselves, we will not be able to bring about change on a grander scale. Many people want to save the planet, end poverty or fix government, but few want to wash the dishes after dinner. If we make the world a better place, the best thing we can do is make ourselves better people. The Serenity Prayer reads:

God grant me the serenity
To accept the things I cannot change,
The courage to change the things I can
And the wisdom to know the difference.[1]

First, it is important to determine what we have the power to change, both individually and organizationally. For instance, I can't change the government's pattern of deficit spending, but I can change my own pattern of credit-card usage. I can't change my partner's habits, but I can change my reactions, thereby contributing more positively to our relationship. I can't change the government's tax credit system for research and development, but I can influence how my organization focuses its R&D efforts.

Second, we need to identify the changes we would like to make to ourselves, and then set out on the long and winding road to find the answers and support needed to change.

There Is No Objective Reality

Werner Heisenberg (1901–1976), the nuclear physicist, noticed that in laboratory experiments atomic particles often behaved differently than he predicted. This led him to postulate the Uncertainty Principle, which shattered the notion of objective reality and the relationship between observer and observed. Heisenberg discovered that the very act of observing the atomic particle influenced its behavior. Until Heisenberg, cause and effect had been thought of as a linear, one-way street:

CAUSE ·········▶ **EFFECT**

Instead, Heisenberg discovered that the relationship is circular — effect influences cause just as cause influences effect:

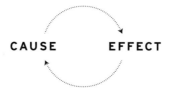

CAUSE   **EFFECT**

Cause and Effect

When scientists observe an atomic particle, they change its behavior.

How we see determines *what* we see. In other words, as our perceptions — or our paradigms — change, the object we observe changes. As you will recall, in the cookie story (Chapter 3), our beliefs led us to assume that the strange man in the airport was stealing our cookies. Initially, we saw the other person as a thief, but by the end of the story, the man had become a generous and charitable chap.

What We Focus on Tends to Improve

An experiment conducted by Elton Mayo in 1927 at the Western Electric's Hawthorne plant in Illinois examined working conditions and their effect on factory personnel. Before the experiment began, the workers were introduced to the concept and informed that their productivity would be measured in relation to various factors. A base level for the workers' performance was determined. The lights in the factory were turned up and productivity increased. The lights were turned up further and production increased again. A pattern was emerging. Mayo then turned the lights down, but to his surprise production continued to increase.

Known as the Hawthorne Effect, the experiment revealed that what we focus on will tend to improve. Nobody had ever paid attention to the factory personnel before. The researcher's attention influenced the workers' performance.

Cause and effect are interrelated. How we see a situation determines what we do. What we do determines the results we get. We need to focus on the way we see situations. Some of the most powerful breakthroughs in science, medicine and management have come from individuals who were willing to assume that their preconceived notions were wrong.

We need to question the way we do things (who, what, where, when, how and why). The interrelated nature of cause and effect underpins the "Be–Do–Have" principle. Who we are as people — our paradigms, our values (be) — determines what we see in the world and how we interpret it. Who we are and what we believe determines what actions we will take (do). Our actions determine the results we experience (have). Being is the foundation of Be–Do–Have.

BE ⸱⸱⸱⸱⸱⸱⸱⸱▸ DO ⸱⸱⸱⸱⸱⸱⸱⸱▸ HAVE

In North America, happiness for many people is a function of what they have or do. Many people think, "If I win the lottery, I will be happy." In other words, by winning I will have a million dollars and be able to afford a Mercedes-Benz and expensive vacations. Because of my power, property and prestige, I will attract a perfect partner. Then I will be happy. My internal state of being (happiness, security, self-esteem and sense of fulfillment) is a function of external circumstances — doing and having.

This outside-in approach inherently creates insecurity. If my security comes from people, places or things, and circumstances change, I lose my security. At a luncheon once, a woman at my table, when asked how she was feeling, replied, "Not too well, I just had a double mastectomy." Her answer took me aback and forced me to ask myself, "Who am I? Am I more than my body?"

If I derive my security from external factors and these are taken away from me (I don't get the promotion, I lose my job, my spouse dies or the house burns down), then I lose my security, happiness and sense of self-worth. Grieving loss is human, but using it to define our existence is dangerous. Lasting security, stability and happiness can only be a function of being—who I am, what values I believe in. Expanding this model, we can apply it to organizations.

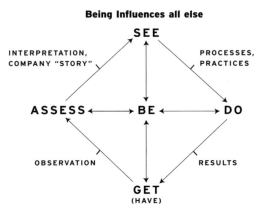

From "Sustainable Enterprise" copyright © 1997 by Key Consulting Group, Calgary.

Our sense of *being* influences everything. It shapes what we see, what we do and, indirectly, the results we get. Finally, it determines how we assess our results.

Let's say we see employees as being untrustworthy (be and see). Unconsciously, we will tend to set up policies and procedures that send clear messages to staff members that they're not trusted (do). A lack of trust and respect undermines people's motivation and breeds contempt and subversive behavior (get). Our view is confirmed by the mediocre performance of our unhappy employees (assess). We then create belief systems that reinforce our paradigm (be). (See above.)

How can we break the typical self-fulfilling cycle? If we really want to create change, we need to work at the level of our personal paradigms, exercising our freedom to think and see in new ways.

Learning organizations and the executives leading them are continually working at the level of being. Focusing on the marketplace, they work to perceive and anticipate emerging opportunities, potential problems and new competitors. Leaders are always assessing how they see their results. Just because the company had its most profitable year is no reason to become complacent. In fact, the more profitable the company, the more competition it will attract. Therefore, the more successful, the more vigilant its leaders must become about small but potentially major problems and opportunities. They must become sensitive to designing systems and structures that encourage people to always work to intuit the classic frustrations of customers and create products or services to solve them.

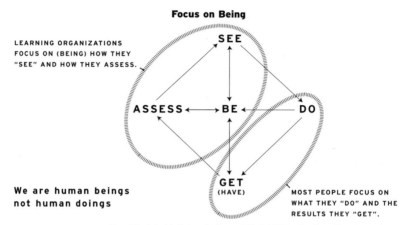

From "Sustainable Enterprise" copyright © 1997 by Key Consulting Group, Calgary.

Rationalizing the Present

Most organizations are locked into paradigms of the past. Too much time is spent explaining and rationalizing why we do things the way we do. In fact, most policies and procedures exist for this purpose. We use rules to explain to customers why we can't serve them the way they want to be served. We limit the freedom and decision-making ability of employees.

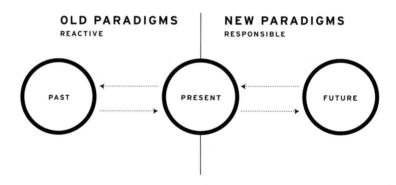

The Future is Our Reason for Being

What we need to do is to spend more time looking to the future. We need to delight customers by providing for needs that they have not yet articulated (Chapter 9). By working with the future in mind, we can take a more objective look at how we're functioning in the present.

We can ensure that we are setting the stage for future success. This is a proactive approach.

The past gives us a sense of our history. The present is our opportunity to act. The future, however, gives us inspiration and vision. As the expression goes, "If we do not dream, we have no power to act."

Inevitably, organizations that are locked into old thinking eventually perish. The definition of insanity is: "doing the same thing over and over again and expecting different results," as Alcoholics Anonymous points out. And yet, most organizations are caught in this trap. Their efforts, rather than being focused on the future, are rooted in the past and present. They are focused entirely on doing, not on being. They lack the self-reflection and self-correction required to bring themselves to think differently.

Anticipating the future is transformational. We can get a glimpse of destiny, both on an individual and an organizational level. Western culture tends to place too much emphasis on doing; otherwise, why would there be such demand for time management? We are all trying to do more with less. But too much focus on doing and not enough on dreaming negates the power of the future. As you will recall, the real value of any manager, states Peter Drucker, is being able to anticipate. Leaders who anticipate trends are able to conceive a future different from the current reality. Then they work to change their organizations.

> If a ship misses the harbor it is seldom the harbor's fault.[11]
> Dr. Janet Lapp, professional speaker

Leveraged Activity

Pareto's Law states that 80 percent of results come from 20 percent of effort, and the remaining 20 percent of results come from the remaining 80 percent of effort.[2] The goal in organizations, then, is to focus on high-leverage activities. In North America we work at a frenetic pace, often losing sight of what are the most important issues. What is most important is not always apparent.

A supertanker that is three football fields long is moving at 35 miles per hour through the ocean carrying hundreds of thousands of tons of cargo. Think of the momentum.

If the captain of the ship decides to turn the ship 180 degrees, who has the most control — the captain who gives the order, the helmsman who turns the wheel or the engineer in the boiler room who runs the engines? It's a trick question. The answer is, "The architect who designed the ship!"

The efforts of the seaman, engineer and even the captain all focus on doing. But the designer's efforts alone focus on being. What the captain, seaman or engineer can do is constrained by the limitations imposed by the designer. They all work within the existing systems and structures of the supertanker, unaware that these constrain their ability to act.

Would a supertanker with hundreds of thousands of tons of cargo be able to turn around quickly, or would it take a great distance?

100,000 TONS OF MOMENTUM

Now imagine a different structure. Instead of one supertanker carrying 100,000 tons, the cargo is divided among 100 smaller ships, each carrying 1,000 tons, working as a fleet.

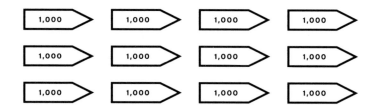

The supertanker is a metaphor for the command-and-control structure of many old organizations. This model emerged from the military and the church. Organizations based on it are hierarchical, top-down, inflexible and bureaucratic. These characteristics make them constitutionally incapable of responding rapidly to a dynamic, changing environment. Such organizations are based on the unspoken assumption that one person or an elite group at the top does all the important thinking and everyone else carries out orders. How many people have power in the supertanker model? One (the captain), perhaps two or three others (the first mate and second mate).

By contrast, the fleet is a metaphor for the new organization, where employees captain their own ships. I do not believe that leadership is the purview of one individual or an elite group of individuals. We are all called upon to be leaders—in our families, in our communities, in our society and in the workplace. In the new paradigm, the organization needs and calls upon the full intellectual power of all people.

W. Edwards Deming, recognized as the founder of the quality movement, believed that systems and structures determine the performance of an organization. The organizational architect determines the performance of an organization. Deming believed that 90 percent of problems in organizations are due to bad systems and structures,

> If you fail to plan, you plan to fail.
>
> Anonymous

> Organizations will have to be flexible, fast, focused and friendly to succeed in the future.
>
> Rosabeth Moss Kanter, former editor, *Harvard Business Review*

not bad people. People are basically good and have good intentions. The systems and structures generate unproductive actions. Even the way an organization hires people is a system and structure.

Rosabeth Moss Kanter, former editor of the *Harvard Business Review*, said, "To be successful in the future, organizations will have to focus on the four Fs: fast, focused, flexible and friendly." Applying the four Fs to the supertanker and the fleet highlights significant differences between the two structures:

FAST Which structure, the supertanker or the fleet, can get up to speed faster? Which can slow down sooner? Which can turn more swiftly?

After the audience had answered "the fleet" to all three questions, a man yelled out, "Assuming they all turn at the same time!" "And in the same direction!" added a woman.

> Power isn't given, it is taken.
> Pat Robinson, health care professional[3]

Yes, we need empowerment, but empowerment without alignment is downright dangerous. Alignment, the ability to coordinate the activities of motivated, empowered, knowledgeable and competent individuals captaining their own ships, is the responsibility of the senior leaders of an organization.

FOCUSED Which of the two structures, supertanker or fleet, is more focused? This is a trick question. People invariably answer that the supertanker is more focused. Yes, at first it appears more focused. But it is mono focus. Which structure can have more foci?

In nature, security is diversity. There are thousands of varieties of wheat. It is only modern farming techniques that have focused on having a single strain of wheat that is susceptible to blight and therefore requires large inputs of insecticides. Nature's more elegant solution is to have a number of varieties, each with different properties. If there is ever a blight, not all strains will be affected.

> Don't ask a barber if you need a haircut.
> Daniel Greenberg, author

In business, diverse strategies within the same set of core competencies will have a greater chance of creating lasting success. Microsoft doesn't have one strategy—there is *DOS, Windows 3.x, Windows 95, Windows 98, Windows NT*, single applications, Microsoft *Office, Microsoft Network (MSN), MSNBC*, an alliance with *America Online*, home products division, products such as Microsoft *Mouse* and *Natural* keyboard, games, *Encarta*. There is not just a single monolithic focus, there are many foci.

Edward de Bono—the world's leading thinker on creativity—cites the case of a species of hawk with excellent eyesight that only preys upon mice. Another type of hawk has bad eyesight and can't distinguish between mice and other small creatures. This species will prey upon mice, baby rabbits, small gophers and so on. If the mice population is devastated by a disease, which hawk species is better off? Who has perfect eyesight when it comes to the future?

If the supertanker hits an iceberg, ripping a hole in the first three panels of the bow, what happens to the ship? By contrast, if the fleet hits an iceberg, what happens? The first three ships sink, but as they do they radio back to the fleet and warn of the impending danger. Then a few ships stop and pick up their comrades while the rest of the fleet navigates around the iceberg.

The issue of focus also applies to the creation of strategy and tactics. At a conference, Gary Hamel, co-author of *Competing for the Future*, related an experience of consulting to a large multinational firm. He was working with a group of the top 20 executives. He asked them, "How many of you have worked for the company more than 20 years?" Everyone raised their hand. "How many of you came up through sales and marketing?" All but two raised their hand. It was a very market-driven company. "How many of you have worked for five years or more outside of North America?" Only two people had any significant international experience, and it was a transnational firm. You know what used to happen in the 16th century when there was too much inbreeding in royalty!

Hamel's point is that organizations need genetic diversity. Mono focus, having only one way of thinking, creates insecurity when the future is unfolding rapidly. Organizations tend to weed out genetic diversity, as people often feel uncomfortable facing sustained challenges to their assumptions.

FLEXIBLE Which of the two structures has more flexibility? There can be only one direction, one strategy and one set of tactics with the supertanker. But the fleet can apply a variety of directions, strategies and tactics. A few ships can be sent on a strategic sortie to explore a new market, develop new products and return. If the venture is successful, the organization can dedicate more resources to the new direction. This type of exploration is essential to create new value for customers and to ensure long-term security for an organization. Microsoft's success was due to its sales of *MS-DOS* and *DOS* applications, but the company now receives less than five percent of its revenues from these sources. In a rapidly shifting marketplace, organizations need to be continually exploring new, high-margin markets that in some cases may eliminate the need for their current core products and services.

Search behavior is more important than brilliance. Dave Nichol, when he worked at Loblaw to create President's Choice products, spent

What most companies want is homogeneity. They want 150 trumpets playing in unison. But homogeneous teams have blind spots; they move like a herd and often in the wrong direction. What's needed instead is complexity, the team as a jazz band that both harmonizes and improvises.
Dave Marsing, vice president, Intel

his time travelling around the world eating at the best restaurants and visiting the best retailers. Sam Walton, the founder of Wal-Mart, was infamous for always carrying a notebook to jot down ideas when he visited competing stores.

FRIENDLY Which of the two structures is more friendly? Would you prefer to be a hired hand on the supertanker, always being told what to do, or the captain of your own ship? Remember, 73 percent of North American employees report that they do not find their work exciting.[4] This is because organizations generally underutilize employees' talents.

Many people feel that power is zero-sum gain. That is, if one person in an organization has more power, others by definition will have less, because power, like a pie, is fixed in size. Power is only limited by an organization's systems and structures.

How many people have power on the supertanker? One, perhaps a few. How many people have power in the fleet? At least 100. The captain of the supertanker becomes an admiral in the new structure. Promotion or demotion? The structure of the fleet unleashes over 100 times more power than the supertanker.

In the old command-and-control paradigm, only one leader had to have full knowledge of the organization's mission, vision, strategy and tactics. In the new model, all 100 captains must know the fleet's overall mission, vision, strategy and tactics. When power increases exponentially, so must communication. The fleet doesn't require twice as much communication but 100 times more! Everyone needs to know where the fleet is going, what its purpose is and how to contribute to its overall goals.

Effective communication has never been more important than today. In an empowered organization, everyone has a role to play in creating an exciting and compelling vision of the future.

In most organizations, if there is loss of market share, what is the typical response? Downsize. Using the analogy of the supertanker, this would be equivalent to firing all the engineers on the ship. The organization still has the same problem but fewer people to cope with the workload. The structures and systems remain the same. If losses continue, what happens next? More layoffs. In the short term, productivity may increase as the crew, fearful of losing their jobs, scramble to get in and out of port as quickly as possible. But over time they will tire, burn out or quit and productivity will nosedive. Often, the response is to cut even deeper. The crew is smaller, but the ship has not changed. Downsizing in many organizations is like amputation before diagnosis.

Such downsizing is futile when it does not question an organization's design at its most fundamental levels. We need to rethink the organization. This is what looking to the future rather than to the past is all about. We need to be drawn to what we and our organizations can become rather than focusing on where we have been or where we are now. Unfortunately, most organizations need to experience acute pain before they are willing to rethink their structures. They behave like an individual stoically suffering through a toothache for years rather than facing a visit to the dentist.

Only when the pain of staying the same is greater than the perceived pain of changing do many organizations begin to take actions required for change.

Creating a Sustainable Enterprise

Leaders must continually ask, "Are we taking responsibility for creating the future? How will we thrive in the future?" Organizations need to meet the challenges of today while constantly enhancing their capacity to meet future challenges. In the *New Webster's Dictionary*, enterprise is simply defined as, "a firm or business." For our purposes, enterprise includes public and not-for-profit organizations as well as private companies. Elements of the enterprise can be seen in teams, departments and project groups.

An organization is influenced by many stakeholders whose individual perspectives all count. Sustainability for any organization means striking a dynamic balance among all the individual and collective interests involved.

Shareholders, customers and suppliers are all influenced by the actions of business, and we must not underestimate our responsibility to all involved. Remember Covey's definition of stakeholders: if a business fails, anyone who is hurt is a stakeholder.

Other stakeholders include the community and industry in which a business operates, the natural environment, the families of employees, the government to whom the company pays taxes that support social programs and researchers at universities who support the advancement of knowledge in the field.

There are no guarantees that an organization will last forever. Change is constant. Stakeholders, however, are united by a common interest in seeing the business thrive and generate value and opportunity. Harnessing their interdependent power can produce extraordinary and sustained results.

If you would hit the mark, you must aim a little above it.
Henry Wadsworth Longfellow, poet

"Outside-In" Diagnosis

Every enterprise operates within a unique environment. The challenges presented by paradigm shifts that we will discuss in Chapters 7 to 12 (the new economy, the role of people, keeping customers, information technology, the Internet and the environment) are increasingly complex. More than ever, organizations must be prepared to continuously redefine their products and services, and rethink their internal practices. Doing this involves:

- identifying the organization's key stakeholders
- defining and delivering value that will delight stakeholders
- anticipating and responding effectively to challenges and opportunities presented as the business environment changes
- taking responsibility for designing aligned systems and structures, thereby contributing to the development of conditions in which business can prosper

"Outside-in" thinking takes into consideration the bigger picture and how the organization can create a brighter and more fulfilling future. Service quality, economic success, satisfying work life and societal responsibility are all important elements of outside-in thinking. This chapter ends with a diagram. I will explain every component of the diagram first and then tie together all the pieces.

> In an age of perpetual change, it's no longer just the big who devour the small, but rather the quick who eat the slow.
>
> Richard Searns, president, Key Resource Group

Service Quality

Successful businesses anticipate and exceed the needs of their customers. These organizations focus on customer delight. Customer retention rates are high. These companies are always developing products and services that deliver more value to customers than those in the past (Chapter 9). Other indicators of sustainability are sales revenue compared with revenues of competitors and market valuation relative to the total market valuation of the industry segment.

> Even if you're on the right track, you'll get run over if you just sit there.
>
> Mark Twain, author

Economic Success

The fundamentals of accountability—expense, cash flow, profitability, productivity of assets and return on investment—have always been hallmarks of business. Now, such words have crept into the language of government and not-for-profit organizations. To be accountable is to be responsible, to prove that organizations can thrive within specific limits.

If we are to become captains of our own ships, we must understand such basic rules of business as the need to maintain a positive cash flow. Most bankruptcies are caused by poor cash flow. Even an organization with a large net worth can go bankrupt if a positive cash flow is not sustained.

But very few companies go to the effort of ensuring that all employees understand how the business works. How can employees help increase the bottom line if they don't know how the company makes money, what the cost structures are and how one department's actions influence another's? Companies benefit when every employee, on a rudimentary level, knows how to read a quarterly report and understand cash flow, operating and capital expenses. Organizations with profit sharing, gain sharing and employee stock-ownership plans generate great interest in understanding the bottom line.

Complex concepts are best understood through simple stories, that people can relate to in their personal lives. For instance, cash flow is more important than equity (the value of the business). Say you buy a house for $300,000. After several years of paying the monthly mortgage, you own 50 percent of the house ($150,000). In other words, you have 50 percent equity. You now miss six mortgage payments in a row. What happens to the house? The bank repossesses it. In this case, cash flow is more important than equity. You may get some money back from the bank, but you have lost control of your house and have to find another place to live. This is a simple business principle, but does everyone in your organization understand why cash flow is crucial?

The bottom line is important but it is not everything. Too many organizations experience the consequences of making economic gains while service levels and workforce loyalty have suffered. What is needed for sustainability is a holistic view of management, a recognition that every part is essential to the health of the whole. With creativity and an openness to new possibilities, improved production in one area does not have to come at the expense of another.

Satisfying Work Life

Sustainable organizations seek to benefit from the capability, creativity and common sense that every member brings to work each day. Job satisfaction and productivity are inextricably linked. What determines satisfaction varies from person to person.

A simple thing as recognition — taking note of employees' contributions — has a tremendous impact on satisfaction. Dale Carnegie in *How to Win Friends and Influence People* notes that parents who do not feed their children for six days will be charged with criminal negligence. Yet how many of us go for six days without praising our children, our spouses, our colleagues or our bosses, even though praise is food for the soul!

Sustainable organizations pay attention to such things as employee attitude surveys, turnover rates, competitive compensation surveys, job security, atmosphere, communication and personal development—in other words, the degree to which an organization develops its people, and ensures that they are challenged and happy.

Societal Responsibility

An organization exists within many communities: local, national, global, ethnic and sectoral. Communities at large are protected by laws and enforcement agencies. There is plenty of room for organizations and individuals to maneuver within the laws of the land and we all have the choice to be a positive or negative influence. Being a socially responsible corporate citizen brings many rewards, including customer loyalty, greater political influence, a more relaxed regulatory environment and improved community relations.

> Too many executives are quick to hire and slow to fire.
>
> Peter Buchanan, management consultant

Sustainability is greatly enhanced when every employee and stakeholder is aware of a company's strong sense of community responsibility and is encouraged to make an individual contribution on behalf of the organization.

Measuring Your Sustainable Capacity

Accepting that an organization is like an ecosystem, composed of a complex web of relationships, helps to further explore levels of development that can help keep your company's system connected and functioning effectively.

Individual Capacity

Individual capacity is at the heart of organizational sustainability. The responsibilities that individuals are given in organizations should match their abilities.

Many organizations have concerns about the philosophy of empowerment. Empowerment is not abdication. No one would build their dream home by telling a contractor to go ahead without planning the design. If I did, I would be disappointed with the result. Empowerment is not the problem. Empowerment works only when both parties are disciplined in developing a clear, mutually understood vision of the end result and criteria. This may come back to requiring more patience or courage on the part of both parties.

Or problems with empowerment may involve delegating tasks to people not suited to the work. In assigning responsibilities, managers should always help their staff reach beyond their grasp. When organizations continually challenge people, leaders must ensure that people have the necessary support to succeed. Leaders are responsible for ensuring that all the enabling factors are in place. Is there sufficient training and education? Do we hire the best and brightest people? Do we provide them with the equipment they need? Do our systems and structures ensure that managers will challenge people (being demanding on results) while being compassionate (empathetic with people)? Do we assign tasks to individuals and teams so that they are challenged (stretched) but not overwhelmed? Do we spend enough time in self-reflection and self-correction? On a personal level? In teams? As managers and leaders? As an organization as a whole? Do we have systems and structures in place to share the learning throughout the organization? Are all systems and structures in alignment with our mission and vision?

People are Programmers; Systems and Structures are Programs

People are the "programmers" of the organization, all the other elements are the "programs." A commitment to learn and grow, to serve, to be fiscally responsible, to reach for higher standards or to be good community members is an individual decision. Organizations comprising individuals who see the "big picture" and want to contribute to making it better should be sought and valued. Organizational behavior is rooted in individual behavior. For instance, the type of hiring system that is established will determine what kind of people will work in the organization. Microsoft, for example, hires only two to three percent of all its applicants. The rigorous screening process (up to seven interviews) means that the company can attract the best and the brightest minds.

External change requires the organization to respond, which in turn requires people in the organization to change. Sustainability depends on individuals who are willing to accept opportunities to develop their competence as new technologies, processes and practices are introduced. Sustainability also depends on their commitment through the periods of uncertainty and turmoil that change often brings.

Trust in Relationships

We live in an interdependent reality. None of us can do our best work without some reliance on the efforts of others. Before we can do anything, we rely on others and the work of others to help us. Trust is the glue that holds the sustainable organization together. In the workplace, trust comes from understanding the strengths and limitations of individuals, from providing them with a clear understanding of expectations but still allowing them to make decisions and exercise their creativity.

Without trust and respect, communication is strained, small problems fester into large ones and attempts to work together are sabotaged by apprehension, conflict and self-protection. Mistrust produces breakdowns, draining productivity away from production. In short, where trust is lost, truth is obscured.

Trust provides the foundation for collaboration and coordination at the work level so that joint efforts can be maximized. Trust is also an essential ingredient in sustaining leadership and influencing others.

Work as Stewardship

An organization's capacity to perform is enhanced when people, individually and in teams, act out of a sense of ownership and accountability for their work. Traditionally, organizations have emphasized control and management of performance. This has typically produced compliance, dependence and indifference toward organizational results on the part of employees. These strategies are expensive, drain energy from workers, stifle creativity and innovation, and directly contribute to low levels of morale and productivity when organizations can no longer offer secure employment. These conditions are not sustainable.

For stewardship to exist, leaders must commit to help employees understand how they can benefit personally by upholding the company's mission and by meeting performance expectations. In a culture of trust, capable people will feel a sense of ownership and will come to believe that their contribution matters.

The creation of a thousand forests is in one acorn.

Ralph Waldo Emerson, philosopher

Aligning Form and Function

A company's strategies, structure and systems must be aligned in order to sustain the organization's vision. Strategy is the action plan for achieving the vision. It defines the connection intended between organizational capacity and the reality of the environment. Structure and systems are designed to support strategy and each other. As environmental forces change, infrastructure must also change. When people don't understand the changes going on around them and don't identify with the vision, they hold on to old strategies, structures and systems. They resist change, ultimately at their own expense.

Sustainability demands that the organization's efforts be focused by the realities of the environment and the shared vision of the future. Development at each level (see diagram on page 88) is necessary but insufficient. Efforts for change that are targeted at only one level will be hindered or undone by the resistance of forces at the neglected levels. Building sustainable organizations requires a comprehensive and coordinated approach to change.

At one seminar a CEO asked why CEOs are compensated on quarterly stock performance when organizations and investors are ultimately interested in long-term performance. Why not award CEO bonuses based on a five-year rolling average of the stock price? It was a brilliant insight. Systems and structures determine performance. Why are most organizations focused on quarterly performance? Look no further than the incentive system.

The Role of Leaders

Sustainable organizations require individuals from all levels to step up to the challenge of leadership. These leaders will play two critical roles — pathfinding and empowering.

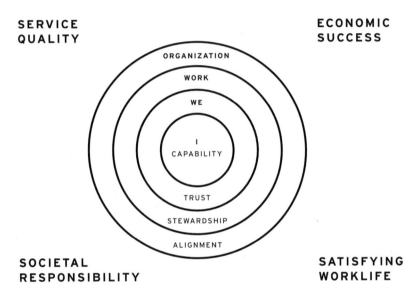

SERVICE QUALITY

ECONOMIC SUCCESS

ORGANIZATION

WORK

WE

I
CAPABILITY

TRUST

STEWARDSHIP

ALIGNMENT

SOCIETAL RESPONSIBILITY

SATISFYING WORKLIFE

From "Sustainable Enterprise" copyright © 1997 by Key Consulting Group, Calgary.

Pathfinding

Pathfinding involves "outside-in" thinking. It begins by examining the environment the organization must respond to, understanding its nature and dynamics, and forecasting the challenges and opportunities it will present. Second, pathfinding requires raising the consciousness of environmental realities throughout the organization. Finally, pathfinding leaders invest in building the commitment of people in the organization toward a shared, positive vision of the organization's future.

Empowering

Empowering leaders nurture the conditions in which every member can and will make a unique contribution to sustain the organization. This is an "inside-out" process, an upward spiral of growth rooted in individual capability and progressing through the other levels of the organization. The empowering leader's first challenge is improving him- or herself to become an effective model of what is required of everyone else to be sustainable. The second challenge is to serve others, enabling everyone to contribute fully to a shared vision of the future.

Creating Common Vision

The next chapter will present a process to create a common, compelling vision of the future.

To Summarize:

- Successful leaders always work to sharpen their perception of the future, and anticipate opportunities and competitive threats. They focus on the future, not the past.

- Systems and structure determine performance; leaders are the architects of their organizations and create appropriate systems and structures.

- Empowerment without alignment creates chaos.

- Creating an empowered, aligned culture unleashes exponentially more power in the organization, but requires exponentially more communication.

Reflection:

- What is the key learning/insight for me in this chapter?

Action:

- What one action shall I take tomorrow to move learning into action? And over time repeat, to move action into habit?

CHAPTER 6

Creating Value

Leaders are responsible for creating the environment in which employees work. Creating a positive, motivating work environment is challenging. How do leaders:

- Build a positive, motivating vision of the future while experiencing the wrenching, demoralizing effect of reorganization or cutbacks?

- Focus people on the challenges facing the organization when they are so focused on their personal concerns?

- Align people with a strategy when they seem so cynical and lacking in trust toward those who developed it?

- Create, innovate and continuously improve while maintaining the atmosphere of stability and security that people need?

- Maintain control, yet allow people the freedom to do what they need to be effective and satisfied in their work?

- Be "hard" (demanding, insistent, challenging) on performance while being "soft" (empathetic, supportive, compassionate) with people?

- Generate teamwork and collaboration among people who have been competing and in conflict for years?

- Create learning organizations when people are so reluctant to take risks and be open about their mistakes?

- Deal with overwhelming workloads while reallocating staff to new initiatives?

- Encourage people to take responsibility for their careers and lives when they feel like victims of uncontrollable circumstances?

- Develop leaders who are powerful without having to diminish the power of others?

- Generate confidence in leadership when the leaders themselves are unsure of what will happen in the future?

This chapter will provide a concrete method for leaders and organizations to solve some of these classic dilemmas. The process is founded on having faith that individuals can solve their own problems (plants grow themselves).

Communication is much misunderstood. The fleet of ships (Chapter 5) does not require twice as much communication as the supertanker but exponentially more. Every captain must understand the mission, vision, strategy and tactics of the entire fleet. Each captain has responsibility, accountability and authority. Each has the power to act.

Creating a Common Vision
What is a "fast" car? To one person it may be a Mercedes-Benz on the Autobahn at 160 miles per hour with such a smooth ride that the coffee in the cup holder doesn't jiggle. To another it might be driving in a Corvette at 50 miles per hour with the top down during the summer. To a third it may be driving an Indy Pace Car on the racetrack.

The only way that I can find out what "fast" means to someone else is to enter into a discussion. It is only through involvement that I create understanding.

Even such a simple concept as "fast" can generate a wide array of understandings. Think of how a vague corporate mission or vision statement could create different understandings. For instance, most mission statements involve serving the customer; however, what if serving a particular customer requires a financial loss? All organizations exist to make a profit. In this situation what should be done? There is no right or wrong answer. Only by discussing the case study will people in the culture come to understand what the mission means.

One of my clients has a goal of achieving 15 percent revenues from entirely new products and services within 12 months. I asked, "How will people accomplish the goal when everyone has to work from line items that lock them into existing activities?"

If managers are expected to create new products and services they will have to engage in activities that they are not currently engaged in. So managers must increase the top line (revenue) or cut costs through efficiency to free up at least 15 percent of their budget to dedicate to researching and developing new products and services. In most organizations, however, any expenditure outside of existing line items must be approved. In this sense the budget locks managers into the current way of doing business. Line items cannot predict future staffing, product and service inputs. Instead of being the master of managers, the budget should be their servant. The better managers are at increasing revenue or cutting costs, the more freedom they should have to act without requiring multiple approvals.

Budgeting, as practiced in most organizations, dictates *how* the organization will work. But what is more important, the method by which the end is achieved or the actual achievement of the result? In dictating the *how*, the budgeting process often denies people the flexibility required to achieve the ends.

Budgeting, in fact, puts the cart before the horse. Before budgeting, everyone in an organization needs to know where the organization is going (vision) and why the organization exists (mission). Once everyone in the organization has a deep understanding of the mission and vision, budgeting will be an easier, speedier process. The budget, then, is a guideline, a rough outline of the best prediction of where the organization will allocate resources to achieve its vision over the next year. The budget is the servant, not the master.

In *Reinventing Government,* Osborne and Gaebler point out that:

> Most organizations are not driven by their missions but by
> their rules and budgets. They have a rule for everything that
> could conceivably go wrong and a line item for every subcate-
> gory of spending in every unit of every department. The glue
> that holds bureaucracies together, in other words, is like
> epoxy: It comes in two separate tubes. One holds rules, the
> other line items. Mix them together and you get cement.[1]

While the mission and vision of an organization are different, the process outlined below to achieve consensus for either within an organization is the same. In the example below, I will refer to vision. The same process could be used to facilitate the creation of an organization's mission.

Many executive teams believe that their employees understand their organization's vision. This is because the executive team has been deeply involved in the process of developing it. However, front-line employees often don't understand their organization's vision. They haven't grasped what its implications are for them, for their department or for their future.

Even people who believe in the vision and are committed to it may have entirely different understandings of its implications! How can that be?

Back to the simple word "fast." What is a fast car? It could be many things. But I only understand what a fast car is to you when I am in dialogue with you. So a CEO can present his or her vision of the future, but employees may not understand it, agree with it or be willing to commit to it. Trying to force a vision on an organization is like trying to push a string. It's far more effective to pull it. It's far better to have employees understand, agree with and be committed to and excited by the vision of their organization than having the executive team continually try to sell it.

How can a CEO pull the vision through the organization? By involving people in the process of developing, refining and clarifying it. Here is a simple principle: no involvement, no commitment. Paradoxically, the more a CEO holds on to control, the more out of control the organization is. The more a CEO lets go of control, the more powerful the organization is.

For most organizations, creating a vision of the future is a one-way, top-down process. The assumption is that the CEO or executive team has better predictive powers; therefore, charting the organization's course is left to them.

There is no doubt that the executive team has special talents. The organization needs to create the best vision possible. Just because this group cannot control the whole process doesn't mean that they should be excluded. In fact, the executive team, in most cases, will have many of the most important and richest insights and contributions to make to the process. Letting go of controlling the process, however, doesn't mean abdicating responsibility for the overall operations of the organization. The executive team will guide the process throughout the organization.

Co-Creating Mission & Vision: Parallel Processing

Normally, in a strategic planning session involving the top 20 executives in an organization, one person is speaking and 19 are listening. It is like having a 20-cylinder engine but using only one cylinder at a time. How can more creativity and power be released through the planning process? How can an organization generate more commitment to change in its employees?

The following process works well in creating a common mission or a common vision for a group. We will use the example of vision here. For an executive team of 20, I break up the group into 10 pairs. Each pair discusses its vision of the future in five years until it reaches consensus. The hallmark of a good vision is one that is exciting and compelling, a future that people will gladly work toward.

As each pair concludes its discussion, it brings its written vision to the front of the room where I am working with a typist. The typist keys the visions into a computer that is projecting them onto a large screen so that everyone in the room can read them. Once the last group is finished, each pair presents its vision to the group. This allows a synergistic, cross-fertilization of ideas. No matter how brilliant each pair is, no one will have perceived all the areas where the organization can seize opportunities to develop new markets in the future. The presentations get everyone thinking creatively.

The groups are not allowed to comment positively or negatively on the other visions. They only listen. This creates an atmosphere of respect where individuals feel able to share ideas that may be "off the wall."

I then break up the pairs and form new groups. Before beginning the next round, each person receives a hard copy listing all 10 visions from Round One. This serves as the input for the new discussion.

If we are taking a full day to develop the vision, the group would be formed into new pairs. If we are developing a vision in only half a day, I would compress the process, forming seven groups of three people or five groups of four people for Round Two.

Again, once each group has reached consensus, its vision is posted using the overhead projector. When all groups are finished they present their vision to the entire group. A fascinating dynamic occurs: the visions move closer together.

The process is then repeated for Round Three with four groups of five people, ensuring that the groups comprise people who haven't yet worked together. Round Four might be three groups of seven people and Round Five, two groups of ten people.

What staggers me each time I facilitate this process with an executive team is that the vision is almost exactly the same for the final two groups of people. The wording may be slightly different and one group may have four main points and the other three, but the two visions will be roughly the same. Executives are blown away!

The final discussion is as a large group working out the final wording of the vision.

Two-Step Vision Development

When there are strong disagreements, these need to be aired, discussed and debated. If it boils down to two protagonists, I ask each to fully air his or her views and why he or she feels the future will follow that path. Once both views have been fully aired we go back into the groups and resume parallel processing. In this way the focus is taken off the individuals and is brought back to the ideas. The groups wrestle with the question as to which view of the future is more likely to unfold. The groups not caught in an either/or approach often identify third alternatives that take into account aspects of both views.

Where there is no vision, the people will perish.
Proverbs 29:18

In the traditional way of developing a vision with a large group—where one person speaks at a time—the force of a personality, power of a position or tenacity of an individual can sway the group. But in this process an individual initially can only influence one out of ten groups. The power, personality or position of one individual doesn't have as great an influence on the whole group. The compelling nature of the ideas rules. At the end of Round One an individual can influence only one of the nine visions. The individual is then forced back into discussion with two, three or four other individuals and his or her opinions are continually challenged.

If you do not know where you are going, then any road will take you there.
The Koran

Even more important is that the entire group has been discussing the vision in parallel. In a normal meeting of 20 people only one person is talking at a time and 19 are listening. So at the end of a four-hour meeting there has been four hours of talking. In the parallel process there has been over 20 hours of discussion, the equivalent of a three-day meeting! But even more important, there has been a cross-fertilization of ideas. People have been excited, galvanized by the process.

Round #	# of groups	People per group	Time	Total # People	Av. Time Talking (minutes)	Total Time per round (minutes)
1	10	2	30	20	15	300
2	10	2	30	20	15	300
3	7	3	30	20	10	200
4	5	4	30	20	7.5	150
5	4	5	30	20	6	120
6	3	7	30	20	4.3	86
7	2	10	30	20	3	60
				Total time talking (mins)		1216

This first stage — reaching consensus on the vision of the future — is the most exciting part of the process. The second step is to identify the barriers that will prevent the organization, in its current state, from achieving the vision. Again, we go through the same process until we have an agreed hierarchy of restraining forces. For instance, the organization may not have the information technology infrastructure to achieve the vision. Employees may require more training. The organization may have to develop new core competencies.

The amount of time spent on each round will vary depending on how quickly the groups reach consensus or how divisive the issues are.

Once the process has created consensus on the major problems facing the organization, the group then goes through the same process a third time to develop action plans to overcome the top three limiting factors. Again, each round varies in time depending on how long the team wants to dedicate to creating a common vision of the future. It can range from a one- to three-day process.

At the end of the strategic planning session, the group of 20 people has a widely shared, commonly understood vision of the future — one that everyone agrees with and is committed to. Additionally, the group has agreed upon a hierarchy of limiting factors that will prevent the realization of this vision. Finally, the group has developed a series of action plans to overcome these obstacles. The executive team is motivated, excited and ready to take on the world.

However, the rank and file of the organization have not had the same galvanizing experience. So the next step is to take this process to the front-line staff. Executive committee members are now responsible for facilitating the same process in their respective departments, perhaps with the assistance of the human resources department. In this way ideas from front-line people bubble up and influence the overall vision of the organization.

If you don't know what you stand for, the marketplace is an expensive place to find out.[2]

Adam Smith, economist

A colleague of mine, Robyn Allan, asks, "What was Thomas Edison's greatest discovery?" Answers that immediately spring to mind are the lightbulb and phonograph. She answers, "The discipline and process of discovery."[3] In other words, the methodology of uncovering new knowledge.

Edison patented 1,093 inventions in his life, including the incandescent lightbulb, the typewriter and phonograph. He credited hard work for his success, as he had to experiment with 6,000 different materials for the filament in his lightbulb before finding one that worked. He used to say that, "Genius is one percent inspiration and 99 percent perspiration."

Similarly, Allan asks, "What was Henry Ford's greatest invention?" Her answer is, "Not the Model T, but the process of breaking manufacturing down into its component parts and creating the assembly line. Ford said that if his car didn't sell he would simply find something else that people wanted and manufacture it."

Edison was disciplined in his approach to creativity. He was self-reflective and self-correcting. He kept journals about his insights that run into the thousands of pages. Similarly, Ford was conscious of how he saw production, realizing that his contribution was not the product (the car) but the process of manufacturing. Today security comes from being self-reflective and self-correcting. The process outlined above is a disciplined approach that brings out the best ideas that people have.

How can an organization create a five-year plan? How can people have any sense of what to do in the organization? Why is this process so important?

The process of reinventing the organization on the basis of a rich, widely shared vision of the future is not an easy, linear process. It is messy, circuitous, disorganized and chaotic. In hindsight a discovery makes perfect sense but in foresight it is impossible to see. Otherwise, someone would have already seen it!

Gary Hamel has a dry wit. We were both speakers at a conference in 1995. He launched into a line of questioning that I would paraphrase as, "Who is closest to the future, the 65-year-old who doesn't know how to turn on a computer or the 18-year-old who surfs the World Wide Web every day? Who does all the strategic planning? Who is most disenfranchised from the planning process? Is it any wonder organizations get incremental change?"

First, I do not want to be ageist. I don't believe the saying "You can't teach an old dog new tricks." Having gray hair or no hair doesn't prohibit learning. I look at Andy Grove, CEO and chairman of Intel, who was born in 1937, and Gordon Moore, the chairman emeritus, who was born in 1929. These two gray-haired, balding individuals have been leading the microchip industry and changing the world. Gray hair coupled with attitude, discipline and practice is a potent force. In fact, the most dangerous dogs are old dogs who learn new tricks because they can take you by surprise! Gray hair is hardly a barrier to learning, and youth does not always spell cutting-edge brilliance. But it makes sense that a company's culture benefits from a blend of ages, cultural backgrounds and expertise. Remember Hamel's story about genetic diversity at the boardroom level.

While it is common to stand in awe of the 18-year-old computer whiz, don't confuse technical competence with business wisdom. The 18-year-old who knows how to surf the Web wouldn't be asked to design the organization's strategic plan. That would be like going to someone who knows how to run the photocopier and asking, "What will the future bring?" And then betting the company's future on the answer. Companies need to marry the new technical skills of the 18-year-old with the deep business wisdom of the 65-year-old. It's not either/or, it's and. If an organization's CEO is not on the cutting edge of learning the new technologies firsthand, what systems and structures exist within the organization to ensure that those developing the new technical competencies are briefing the senior team that does all the strategic planning?

Strategic planning in the past assumed that a group of very bright individuals could figure out the market and then write a plan for others to implement. The underlying assumptions were that you just need bright people at the top and if you study the market long enough you will create the perfect plan.

However, these assumptions are fatally flawed. Not even the brightest people can predict the future. Remember the quotations from the experts (Chapter 4), or the fact that Bill Gates was blind-sided by Netscape.

The second assumption has a danger of leading to analysis paralysis. Is it likely that a child's first step will be perfect? Why do adults assume that we will get things right the first time, when scraping our knees is part of the learning process?

The same is true of strategic planning. If an executive team studies the market until they identify the perfect product or service and the perfect strategy, and then calculates how to perfectly reorient their organization to produce the product or provide the service, they will wake up one morning to find that a competitor has stolen the market before they have begun implementation. This is analysis paralysis. In

> Don't be afraid of opposition. Remember that a kite rises against the wind, not with it.
>
> Hamilton Mabie, newspaper editorialist

today's rapidly changing marketplace, by the time you have figured out the perfect product, service and implementation plan and then executed it, market requirements have changed. At the heart of the analytic model is a desire for control. But remember the paradox: the more in control an executive team is, the more out of control the organization. Where leaders exercise control is by working on the context of the organization, creating the systems and structures in which employees work. People are then free to be creative within that framework. Leaders cannot control creativity. Controlling creativity is an oxymoron.[4]

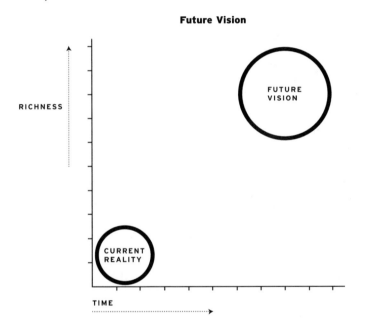

Future Vision

A heuristic approach is to take the best guess at what will work, do it, learn from the mistakes, then refine the implementation. It's Think-Do-Fix rather than a Think-Think-Think-but-Do-Nothing approach. Inherently there is a bias for action and a recognition that the only way we learn and understand as human beings is by doing. It's the difference between head knowledge (knowing what needs to be done) and hand knowledge (practical experience). In the long run a heuristic approach will succeed.

In real life it is very difficult for adults to accept that we achieve a high score in a game and then our performance falls. No one can post a new high score in a game every day. Advances are followed by the return to old levels of performance. But over time performance improves.

Progress Toward Future Vision

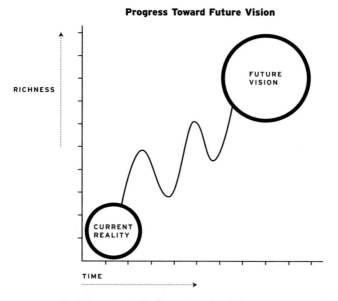

Golf is all about discipline. After a bad shot, a pro golfer can't afford to get angry and frustrated and beat him- or herself up over it. After a great shot a pro golfer cannot afford to get cocky and complacent. After every shot the pro must have the discipline and concentration to make the next shot exceptional. Consistency and discipline. The same is true of an individual learning to play a new game or a corporation playing in the marketplace. Consistency and discipline.

The nature of leadership today (Chapter 4), is that leaders are gardeners, creating in their organizations the optimal environment for growth. A leader's most important contribution to the success of an organization is ensuring that the organization has in place processes that guarantee innovation and creativity by ensuring that the learning is shared throughout the organization.

The process outlined above guarantees that the organization is able to evolve and respond quickly in the rapidly changing business environment.

The Head, the Hand, the Heart

Change for an individual comes about by involving the head, the hand and the heart. Everywhere I go, people talk about the need to change. Clearly, people know that they have to change (head knowledge). However, many fear change (heart). They dislike the feelings of fear, frustration and inadequacy that they experience when learning. Their fear may be so strong that it paralyzes them, preventing them from taking action (hand).

Many business people believe that if employees within their organization just had more knowledge (head) they would be able to change the practices within their organization (hand). They believe they can think their way into new action. But I cannot read my way into physical fitness no matter how much I would like to. I don't mean to disparage head knowledge — changes in thinking can lead to new behavior.

New action leads to new learning, feeling and thinking. It is an organic process. A child will not become an Olympic hurdler on the first day of learning to walk. So think and start small. Learn from mistakes. As competence increases, the risks that an individual is willing to take increase. Similarly, a team working to develop new products and services in an emerging market develops experience and practical insight as the market emerges and becomes more clearly defined. In this way individuals and teams act their way into right thinking. Insight flows out of experience. The more the team goes through the learning paradox, the greater their emotional courage becomes to face uncertainty, fear and ambiguity. The greater the experience (hand) of developing new markets, the greater the courage and faith (heart) and the more willing (head) the individuals, teams and organizations are to embrace new markets even when the new ventures appear risky. It's not either/or, we need all three: the head, hand and heart.

> **We are more likely to act our way into feeling than feel our way into acting.**
> William James, psychologist

Communication: Push/Pull

Ravi Vijh[5] is a consultant who advises North American organizations wanting to enter international agreements. He was helping a North American company negotiate an agreement with a Middle Eastern company. The English contract was translated into Arabic and the Arab executives were aghast by what it proposed. Ravi told them, "Don't worry, translations create misunderstandings." He hired another translator to translate the Arabic back into English. Then the North American executives were shocked, saying, "We didn't mean that." So they went through a process of clarifying what they had intended to convey to their prospective Middle Eastern partners.

This went back and forth, with new translators frequently brought into the process until the misunderstandings were eliminated and both parties understood the contract and all of its details and implications. The story is powerful because we often assume that we understand each other when we speak the same language. If we applied the same diligence when working out mutual understandings in a win-win relationship, we would have fewer problems at the back end.

It is a sign of a healthy corporate culture when any employee feels comfortable approaching his or her team leader with problems.

Creating Future Security

Companies must continually add value to their core products or services to create future security. No customer writes to an airline president to say, "Thank you for the flight from New York to Paris. We landed safely and I am deeply grateful." We've come to expect the service. So airlines must differentiate themselves on items further and further from their core business of flying and landing planes.

A company must begin at the core of its business and add value. If the core business is faulty, adding value won't matter. If planes crash frequently, it really doesn't matter how good the airline cuisine is.

The idea is there, locked inside. All you have to do is remove the excess stone.
Michelangelo, sculptor

The Value Vortex

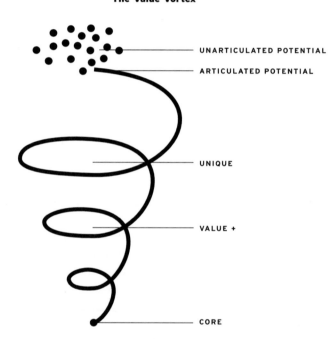

UNARTICULATED POTENTIAL

ARTICULATED POTENTIAL

UNIQUE

VALUE +

CORE

Customers today expect more than customers did a century ago, ten years ago or even last year. Any successful product or service goes through a predictable life cycle. When first introduced, the product or service is unique and offers competitive advantage to its creator. Margins are high. There is no competition. As others begin to mimic the product or service, it becomes a value-added service. Margins begin to compress as competition increases. Eventually, customers come to expect the product or service. If you don't offer this product or service you will lose customers. Competition is intense, margins are tight. At this stage, the product or service tends to become a price-driven commodity. Operational efficiency — working on the denominator — becomes key.

What was unique four years ago has become value-added today, and it will join the core service offerings tomorrow. The banks that had automated tellers in 1980 were on the leading edge. But today, I would not use a bank that did not have widespread distribution of ABMs and that was not connected to the Interac or CIRRUS network.

Value Vortex

Companies create a value vortex by continually adding radical new value to their core products or services. A value vortex is like a whirlpool that sucks new value to the center. The process is swift and fundamentally redefines the market. Companies that adopt a value vortex philosophy continually throw their competitors off balance, expand rapidly and enjoy higher margins than their competitors.

By definition every problem you solve will create another problem (Chapter 2). In the PC industry, every bottleneck that is solved exposes another bottleneck. In such a rapidly changing industry, leading-edge companies are continually creating innovative solutions to the bottlenecks that PC users encounter.

For instance, in the early 1990s one of the slowest aspects of personal computers was the way in which graphics were displayed on the monitor. While the average central processing unit (CPU) ran at 33 MHz and was a 32-bit chip, the motherboard bus that carried the graphics information to the monitor ran at 8 MHz and was only 8 bit. It was like having a Ferrari engine in a farm tractor. The brains of the computer could think quickly but the body couldn't keep up. Consumers could buy computers with fast CPUs but had to wait while their monitor refreshed the screen.

As a result, a number of companies created graphic accelerators (special PC cards) to speed up system graphics. These companies expanded and became very successful. But Intel began making motherboards for its chips to ensure that bottlenecks such as the slow graphics bus were eliminated. The companies doing a booming business on graphics accelerators had to find new products and services as their value was sucked into the core products that Intel provides today.

In other words, the value that PC consumers used to get by buying separate add-ons for their computer, was brought right into the core product, the CPU and motherboard. The net effect has been that Intel has doubled the average amount of money it makes on every PC sold, from under $100 in 1985 to almost $200 in 1997.

Intel's Value Vortex

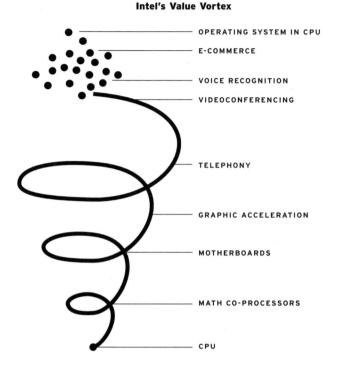

OPERATING SYSTEM IN CPU

E-COMMERCE

VOICE RECOGNITION

VIDEOCONFERENCING

TELEPHONY

GRAPHIC ACCELERATION

MOTHERBOARDS

MATH CO-PROCESSORS

CPU

In 1997, Intel introduced chips with MMX technology, a new set of instructions that allows the chips to perform certain graphics functions faster. MMX technology will enable videoconferencing at the desktop level across the Internet. While the Internet is still too slow to allow full-motion video (30 frames a second) this new technology paves the way for videoconferencing to become an integral part of business. This makes the PC more valuable. And that means that as videoconferencing over the Internet becomes widespread, a whole new category of consumers will begin to purchase PCs. It also gives compelling reasons for individuals and organizations with older computers to buy newer ones.

Companies that practice the value vortex are always rapidly bringing high value into the core of their products or services, thereby creating an effective monopoly and continually redefining the nature of the market.

What will airlines that rely on high-margin business fliers to remain profitable do when executives reduce their traveling because they can videoconference from their desktop? (For executives, the real cost of traveling is time away from their families.) This is an example of how the practice of value vortex radically redefines competition and the market. When videoconferencing becomes widely practiced, Intel innovation may threaten the profitability of airlines. With serious reductions in high-margin business travelers, tremendous consolidation may occur in the airline industry.

Microsoft aggressively pursues the value vortex. Microsoft's new versions of *Windows* create opportunities for other software companies to develop niche markets. For instance, Norton (owned by Symantec) sells utilities for *Windows*. *Defrag*, a disk-defragmenting utility, is one of the most popular features. It was the reason many users bought *Norton Utilities*. *Windows 3.11*, when it was released in 1993, included the utility within the operating system.

A tree grows by adding to its outer layer. Information is added to your hard disk in the same way. When you edit an existing document, the new text can't be physically stored next to the original text on the hard disk. Over time the data on the hard disk become fragmented. For instance, your hard disk may have to access ten different spots to open a single document. Defragmenting your hard disk eliminates all the fragments, reconfiguring the data on your hard disk so that all the data for a single document reside at the same physical location on your hard disk

With the release of *Window 3.11,* Microsoft added peer-to-peer networking capabilities into its operating system. Until then, Novell had dominated the market for networking software. Novell's specialized software runs computer networks. Called *NetWare*, it was the software that large companies purchased to run complex networks. Microsoft included rudimentary networking software in *Windows 3.11*, allowing PCs to communicate with each other.

Windows 3.11 was inferior to Novell's software. However, by practicing the value vortex philosophy, Microsoft selects only the most important features from competitive products to bring into its core products. Pareto's Law applies for software: 80 percent of the excitement that mass-market consumers have for software comes from 20 percent of the features. Microsoft product managers work to identify the features that will compel the largest number of customers to upgrade to a new software release or to switch to Microsoft products.

Microsoft keeps adding functionality (or building value) into its programs. New value can be identified by many sources. In addition to focusing on successful competitors' products, Microsoft creates value proactively through a number of strategies. In usability labs, development teams study users as they work on PCs trying to complete certain tasks without assistance. By studying the problems that users have, developers work to make the software more intuitive so that users can more easily figure out how to use features on their own without calling Microsoft's help desk.

The help desk has input into new releases that are being planned by listing the features that generate the most help calls. Given that each call to the help desk costs Microsoft $12, there is a strong incentive for improving features that users have the most difficulty with. Finally, the development team creates new features on their own to add value to the software.

Once the list of new features is identified and ranked in terms of hierarchy of importance, the Microsoft development team begins writing code. In the case of competitive products Microsoft may license code from a competitor. This was the case with Symantec, where Microsoft licensed the defragmentation utility.

By only focusing on the most popular competitive features and continually incorporating them into software releases, Microsoft gains market share. At the core of the philosophy is a commitment to progress rather than perfection. Microsoft identifies the most important features that most software buyers want and incorporates most of the functionality of those features — leaving its competitors to compete over niches.

Outer Reaches of the Value Vortex

The greatest security, the highest margin, the most excitement and the greatest customer delight lie in the far reaches of the value vortex. This represents products and services that do not exist yet and they fall into two categories: those that customers can articulate and those they can't. Some customers will be able to tell you what it is they want, but that no company in the marketplace is meeting their need. This offers great opportunity and the focus groups and market research can help refine the product because prospective customers can talk about what it is they want. The furthest away is unarticulated, potential products. Here, customers cannot even tell you what it is they want. I argue that tremendous opportunity exists at this level. For instance, our need for the personal computer existed before Steven Jobs invented it. Also, the laws of physics that would enable the invention of semiconductors existed before engineers uncovered them. Customers just didn't know that they needed personal computers. Think of the president of Digital Equipment's comment, "There is no need for anyone to have a PC in their home." This shows that executives or consumers, even when a new invention is presented to them, may not see its value until they begin to use it and incorporate it into their lives.

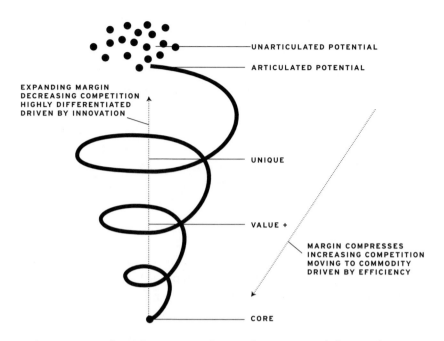

As you struggle with constant change, keep in mind the good news: Organizations that continually create unique products and services that delight customers continually create high-margin business and future security. As products and services move from the outer rings to the core, competition increases and margins compress. At the outer fringes companies enjoy no competitors and have high margins. The core, with its many competitors, demands operational efficiency. Organizations that continually reinvent their products and services live in the outer ring.

True Measure of Success

As Gary Hamel notes in a *Fortune* cover story on strategy,

> In a survey of 550 U.S. CEOs, 38 percent said that industry newcomers—non-traditional competitors—had taken the best advantage of change over the past 10 years. When asked how the newcomers had succeeded, 62 percent said they had profoundly changed the rules of the game. Only 31 percent thought the newcomers had won through better execution.[6]

Hamel proposes a fascinating way of measuring success, not sales growth or profitability, but the creation of new wealth (the numerator).

Share of new wealth creation must be measured with respect to the total amount of new wealth that has been generated in an industry over time... A rough indication can be derived by comparing a company's current share of the total market capitalization of its relevant competitive domain with its share a decade ago.[7]

For instance, between April 1995 and April 1996, the capitalization of Internet-related companies rose from zero to almost $10 billion.[8] By comparison, IBM's total share of the computer industry, including office equipment, has fallen from 45.9 percent in 1988 to 14.2 percent in 1997.[9]

How can companies create new value? What will drive the process? The mission and vision of the organization.

Mission as a Way of Being

Johnson & Johnson (J&J) was founded in 1886 as a medical supply company. Robert Wood Johnson, the son of the founder and chairman from 1938 to 1963, was responsible for shaping the company's philosophy and culture. He believed that large, ponderous organizations were ineffective and that small, autonomous units were inherently superior. In 1943, Johnson formalized his beliefs on corporate and social responsibility in the company credo. In 1979, then-CEO James Burke perceived some degree of tokenism regarding the Credo. He described his actions:

People like my predecessor believed the Credo with a passion, but the operating unit managers were not universally committed to it. There seemed to be a growing attitude that it was there but that nobody had to do anything about it. So I called a meeting of some 20 key executives and challenged them. I said, "Here's the Credo. If we're not going to live by it, let's tear it off the wall. If you want to change it, tell us how to change it. We either ought to commit to it or get rid of it.

The meeting was a turn-on because we were challenging people's own personal values. By the end of the session, the managers had gained a great deal of understanding about and enthusiasm for the belief in the Credo. Subsequently, Dave Clare and I have met with small groups of J&J managers all over the world to challenge the Credo.

Now, I don't really think that you can impose conviction or beliefs on someone else.[10]

The strongest evidence of the Credo's power was in the company's response to the Tylenol crisis. In 1982, seven people died after taking Tylenol capsules that had been tampered with and laced with cyanide. Even though the poisoning was limited to the Chicago area, J&J took immediate action and withdrew all Tylenol capsules from the U.S. market at an estimated cost of $100 million. The company developed tamper-evident lids, reintroduced Tylenol and consumer confidence was not only restored but grew to new heights.

In 1996, Johnson & Johnson, with $21.6 billion in sales, is the world's largest manufacturer of health care products serving the consumer, pharmaceutical and professional markets. J&J has about 90,000 employees and more than 170 operating companies selling products in over 175 countries.

J&J organizes each business around a given market and a given set of customers. So how does such a diverse organization of over 170 operating companies work in unison? What organizes all of the activities? The Credo (see next page).

In her book *Leadership and the New Science: Learning About Organization from an Orderly Universe*, Margaret Wheatley asks the reader to think about an atom and all its parts: the proton, neutrons, electrons. And she asks, which part is in charge? The answer is none. So where does leadership come from? The laws of physics. What organizes the behavior of 170 different companies within J&J? The Credo and the vision of each separate operating company.

Beginning the Change Process

I am often asked, "If a company has not changed for many years, how should executives lead their organizations through change?" Begin by involving people in developing the mission and vision of the organization. There is far more understanding (head knowledge) of the need to change in any organization than most people realize. People need to have a strong understanding of where they are going, why they must go there and how they will get there.

Pareto's analysis applies to the willingness of people to change an organization that has not been involved in change. In a stable organization 20 percent of employees will rapidly embrace change, the bulk of employees will adapt a wait-and-see attitude and 20 percent will oppose change. Begin with individuals who are excited and committed to change.

Credo

We believe our first responsibility is to the doctors, nurses and patients, to mothers and all others who use our products and services.
In meeting their needs everything we do must be of high quality. We must constantly strive to reduce our costs in order to maintain reasonable prices. Customers' orders must be serviced promptly and accurately. Our suppliers and distributors must have an opportunity to make a fair profit.

We are responsible to our employees, the men and women who work with us throughout the world. Everyone must be considered as an individual.
We must respect their dignity and recognize their merit.
They must have a sense of security in their jobs. Compensation must be fair and adequate, and working conditions clean, orderly and safe. We must be mindful of ways to help our employees fulfill their family responsibilities. Employees must feel free to make suggestions and complaints. There must be equal opportunity for employment, development and advancement for those qualified. We must provide competent management, and their actions must be just and ethical.

We are responsible to the communities in which we live and work and to the world community as well. We must be good citizens – support good works and charities and bear our fair share of taxes. We must encourage civic improvements and better health and education. We must maintain in good order the property we are privileged to use, protecting the environment and natural resources.

Our final responsibility is to our stockholders. Business must make sound profit. We must experiment with new ideas. Research must be carried on, innovative programs developed and mistakes paid for. New equipment must be purchased, new facilities provided and new products launched. Reserves must be created to provide for adverse times. When we operate according to these principles, the stockholders should realize a fair return.

Johnson & Johnson Family of Companies

Work with this group of committed people to create early, quick, small victories. Continue to build upon them. As momentum grows, employees who took the wait-and-see attitude will see the success and get involved. Once the bulk of this middle group has embraced the change initiatives, the final group will have a choice: join the new culture or leave. People have an inherent capacity for growth and learning, but after years of no change, don't expect employees to change overnight. Change takes time, patience and perseverance.

Receptiveness to change in stable cultures

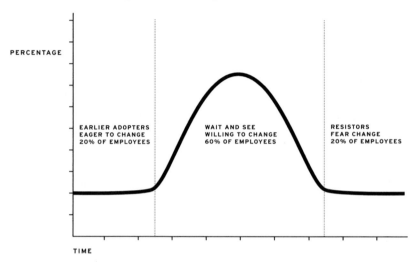

PERCENTAGE

EARLIER ADOPTERS
EAGER TO CHANGE
20% OF EMPLOYEES

WAIT AND SEE
WILLING TO CHANGE
60% OF EMPLOYEES

RESISTORS
FEAR CHANGE
20% OF EMPLOYEES

TIME

To summarize:

- Top-down strategic planning is dead. Strategic planning now requires the involvement and input of everyone in the organization. People at every level must begin to think strategically to create new products, services and markets.

- The more tightly a CEO or team leader holds on to control of developing the vision/mission, the more out of control the organization/department. The more that people can challenge, clarify and refine the vision, the greater their commitment to and understanding of it.

- There will be reverses in performance. Individuals (and most organizations) will not post high scores every day.

- Planning should not be academic but be action based.

Workshop Questions and Activities:

- How could you significantly increase value for your customers?

- How could you use new technologies or processes to simplify or streamline the delivery of your products to your customers? Are any other organizations better qualified to do this? Will they take your customers? Should you make them your partner? Or should you acquire them?

• What existing products or services, if enhanced, could create effective monopolies?

• Using the process outlined in this chapter, prepare a mission statement for your department, division or organization. What is the corporate vision? What will the company look like in five years if it is to be successful?

Reflection:
• Is there any difference between my understanding of the mission/vision of my department/organization and that of others?

• What is the key learning/insight for me in this chapter?

Action:
• What one action shall I take tomorrow to move learning into action? And over time repeat, to move action into habit?

Shifting to the New Realities

Each of the following chapters explores new ways of perceiving an aspect of the business environment. Adopting these new paradigms will fundamentally change the way leaders perceive the market, threats and potential opportunities. The chapters are designed to provoke discussion within organizations, divisions and departments. At the end of each are a series of questions designed to stimulate discussion within your team after everyone has read the chapter. The shifts are:

- The rise of the new economy (Chapter 7).

- The importance of people and development (Chapter 8).

- Focus on customer retention and delight (Chapter 9).

- Information technology (Chapter 10).

- The Internet as the key to future commerce (Chapter 11).

- The environmental imperative (Chapter 12).

Everyone in an organization must ask how these shifts challenge existing policies, systems, structures, products and services, and what opportunities they create. By continually scanning the horizon and questioning assumptions, leaders can help build a new security for all stakeholders in the organization.

E-mail your feedback to jimh@strategicadvantage.com. Suggest new case studies, information or improvements to the text. If your suggestions result in changes to a subsequent edition of the book, I will send you a complimentary audio tape.

the new economy

History is a series of rolling waves of change, wrote Alvin Toffler in *The Third Wave*.[1] The first wave occurred when the agricultural revolution transformed hunter-gatherer tribes into agrarian societies. In 8000 B.C. nomadic tribes began to settle. Societies grew as farming sustained larger populations. Arts and culture flourished as survival no longer consumed every waking minute. The city-state evolved. In short, everything about life changed.

The second wave swept through Europe at the end of the 17th century, when the industrial revolution unleashed a dramatic new era of mechanical production. While human labor alone fueled the first wave, gas, oil and coal drove the second. The state began to assume many of the traditional functions of the family: health care, education and social security.

The third wave began in 1955 when for the first time in history white-collar workers outnumbered blue-collar workers. We entered the information era of the knowledge-based economy where employees are valued for their brains, not their brawn.

This brings the learning paradox into sharp focus. Much of today's management theory is still based on the industrial, or second wave, systems and structures. Progressive companies have adopted third-wave management theory, where value is first created in the mental realm and then in the physical realm. This has forced business leaders to *unlearn* principles that were successful in the past in order to *learn* new strategies for the new era. Starting from zero is sometimes an advantage. Imagine having to unlearn a bad golf swing.

During the industrial revolution workers were known as "hands" because that was what people contributed to production. Workers had to be physically present on the production line for their shift. Henry Ford broke production down into simple steps and created the assembly line. Like Charlie Chaplin in *Modern Times*, workers on Ford's production line performed simple, repetitive, boring tasks. Bosses and time-motion experts did all the important thinking. Everyone else merely "wielded" the screwdrivers.

But in the third wave, knowledge is required. When Toffler wrote *The Third Wave* in 1980, he predicted widespread and dramatic change. Today the evidence to support his view is all around us. Economist Nuala Beck has researched the economic growth of knowledge-based companies. As she says, the old, material-intensive economy is in decline while a new, knowledge-based economy is expanding. Some staggering facts highlight the power of the new economy:[2]

- The personal computer didn't exist in 1979. By 1997, the PC hardware market was worth $185 billion, adding software and services brings it to over $500 billion.

- More North Americans make computers than cars.

- The average replacement cycle for cars lengthened tremendously between 1980 and 1997, and will probably continue to grow as automakers try to compete on better warranties and higher-quality products. By comparison, computer replacement cycles have shortened because innovation is so fast and furious.

- Young, aggressive, computer companies such as Sun Microsystems are driving the market. Sun was founded in 1982 and by 1996 its sales reached almost $7 billion. Sun pioneered and has become the worldwide leader in "distributed computing" — the linking of powerful workstations in a network where some computing is done on the server and some on the workstation. Sun's slogan is, "The network is the computer."

- Software sales have been growing 25 percent annually for more than a decade. Microsoft's market value exceeds that of General Motors! While American automakers have been closing plants and laying off employees, Microsoft, which was founded in 1975, adds 35 "knowledge workers" a week to its staff of 20,500.

- On July 16, 1997, Microsoft slipped ahead of Coca-Cola to become the second-largest company in the United States. Microsoft's value rose to US$176.5 billion, ahead of Coke ($174.9 billion). General Electric is still number one ($242 billion).[3]

- Computers account for 20 percent of all U.S. non-agricultural foreign trade ($26 billion). Add another $22 billion — or 17 percent of all exports — for software export earnings.

We have now entered the "fourth wave." Using Toffler's terminology, the third wave is a knowledge-based economy. But knowledge is no longer enough. Knowledge has become a commodity. Why hire a North American graduate for $30,000 a year when an equivalently educated person in China costs $1,200? And knowledge has a half-life — if you have a PhD, you know a lot about old stuff.

We have entered the fourth wave, which is a learning-based economy. In this economy the ability to learn (as an individual, team and organization) is what counts. The fourth wave is driven by organizations that focus on "meta" processes — the conscious processes of learning, thinking, innovation, working as a team and as an organization. To succeed in the fourth wave, organizations must institute processes that guarantee self-reflection and self-correction. Individuals, teams and organizations must think about how they think, learn about how they learn, become more innovative about how they innovate, as a team reflect on how they work as a team and as an organization reflect on the systems and structures that promote learning in the organization.

The fourth-wave economy is based on generating new knowledge, products, services and markets. The fourth wave also involves applying existing knowledge in new ways, thereby creating new value for customers. The systems and structures within organizations that promote learning at the meta level are what create success in this new era.

Innovation is this new era's most powerful force. The following story drives home the point.[4] An American company bought a British high-tech firm with a stunning track record for innovation. Six months after the takeover, the U.S. company decided to estimate the future earnings of the new acquisition and meet with its employees, suppliers and customers. So an executive traveled to the United Kingdom.

One way to gauge a company's future success is to count its number of new patent applications, and using the company's past track record for turning patents into market winners, predict future revenue. The executive reviewed the patent applications and returned to the United States. with both good news and bad news. The good news was that 22 new patents had been filed in the previous six months. The bad news was that one scientist's name appeared on more than half of them, and he had left the company six weeks after the takeover! While he appeared nowhere on the balance sheet, this scientist was the company's greatest asset.

All our assets have legs.

Louis Burgos, president, Royal LePage Commercial

This shift from the second wave to the third wave, and from the third wave to the fourth, turns upside down many of our assumptions about business and how to measure success:

In the old economy, the value of material assets depreciates, while in the new economy, as employees learn and develop new skills, their value to the corporation appreciates.

Such old-economy assets as buildings can be rebuilt in weeks if they burn down, but the scientist who leaves can't often be replaced as easily. It may take years of highly specialized training and/or experience for someone to reach the required level of competence in a unique field. Thus, people have time-developmental value. Employees, if they are continually learning, increase in value over time. If employees are not continually learning, the value of their static knowledge decreases over time. What I learn today about computer programming languages could have little or no value in five years.

In the old economy, protecting assets was a matter of buying insurance. In the new economy, it's a matter of treating your assets — your employees — well.

In the old economy, it was easy to protect assets with, for example, fire insurance. But what do we use in the new economy — employee retention insurance? In the old economy, installing water sprinkler systems protected assets. In the new economy, progressive and fair human resource policies do the job. In the old economy, if you treated your producing assets badly, they couldn't walk out and set up shop to compete against you. But, in the new economy that certainly can happen. In the case of the U.S.–U.K. high-tech firm, further research revealed that Dr. Scientist had set up his own company and had already filed three new patent applications. His track record indicated that the patents would make money, but not for the new U.S. owners.

In the old economy, bankers made loans against such tangible assets as real estate and machinery that could be sold off in case of repayment default. But in the new economy, what's the banker's security in a new software company? Only the soundness of the company's business practices, including its ability to attract and retain the brightest people and its ability to create systems that draw out the full talents and creativity of its people.

In 1950, 73 percent of U.S. employees worked in manufacturing. In 1996 it was less than 15 percent.
US Department of Commerce

Imagine that we were directors on the board of Microsoft in 1975 and were making a presentation to a board of bankers for a loan. Bill Gates begins by describing his vision of the future: the *MS-DOS* operating system will revolutionize computing and will make a new era of personal computers possible such that by 1995, the system will be used on 200 million PCs worldwide.

> **Bankers:** "That's very exciting, Mr. Gates, but what are your assets?"
>
> **Gates:** "I just told you. I have this revolutionary idea and incredibly talented programmers working on the project."
>
> **Bankers:** "Yes, Mr. Gates, we heard that part, but what are your assets?"
>
> **Gates:** "As I said, this compelling vision of the future, the incredible talent of the programmers, our ability to work together as a team and the relentless drive we have to dominate the market."
>
> **Bankers:** "Sorry, Mr. Gates, we've decided to lend our money to Olympia & York."

How do you measure drive, innovation, tenacity, knowledge and creativity? Or the ability to identify and exploit new opportunities that no one else can see yet? Have you ever seen a creativity meter?

> In the old economy, there are limits to the profitability of resources. But what are the limits to innovation in a mental economy?

Physical assets are limited, the law of diminishing returns governs. In mining iron ore, the deeper the mine goes, the more expensive mining becomes. The richest veins of ore are mined first, leaving less profitable ones for later. At some point, the shafts become so deep and the ore of such a low grade that the mine is no longer profitable.

But in a mental economy, there are no limits to creativity and ingenuity. Alexander Graham Bell didn't exhaust the supply of innovation when he invented the telephone. Nor did Einstein become less creative or intelligent after he had discovered $E=mc^2$. Knowledge is a constantly expanding resource. Each innovation opens the door to new possibilities. The more creative I am, the more creative I can be. Rather than the law of diminishing returns, the new economy functions according to the law of increasing returns. Creativity breeds creativity, ingenuity fosters ingenuity, innovation drives further innovation.

The shift from the second to third to fourth wave economy challenges the theory of management on almost every front. The shifts are summarized:

Old Economy	New Economy
material	mental
primarily physical value	primarily mental value
buildings, machinery	ideas, people
tangible	intangible
declining resources	expanding resources
protect by sprinklers	fair human resources policies
assets depreciate	assets appreciate
assets have dollar value	assets have time-developmental value
assets don't compete	assets can compete
assets on balance sheet	assets not on statements
assets easy to value	assets hard to value
zero-sum gain	unlimited potential
diminishing returns	increasing returns

Innovation Drives High Margins

There are four ways to increase profitability. One is to increase production efficiency—for example, by installing robotics within a manufacturing environment; by implementing just-in-time (JIT) inventory systems to eliminate the warehouse and inventory carrying cost, or by implementing quality initiatives.

The second way is to increase the efficiency of distribution. When Michael Dell founded Dell Computer Corporation in his university dormitory room in 1984, the company's greatest weakness was that it had no distribution partners and no retailing presence. Dell's competitors, IBM and Compaq, dominated the distribution and retail channels. At each level of distribution—manufacturers, distributors, wholesalers and retailers—there was a mark-up. Dell sold directly to customers by advertising in magazines and newspapers, thereby eliminating overheads, distribution layers and mark-ups. As a result, Dell was able to sell higher-value products at a lower cost than his competitors.

Each additional step in a value chain adds significant cost. If a PC maker produces PCs in one location, maintains regional warehouses, deals with distributors who in turn sell to value-added resellers (VARs) who in turn deal with end customers, each layer in the distribution chain adds significant cost. If each level maintains 30 days of inventory, there are 120 days of inventory in the chain at any one time. Costs are duplicated at every stage of the value chain—inventory, warehousing, financing, shipping, administration and accounting. But the largest cost is the cost of carrying 120 days of inventory in an industry where component part prices are always falling.

When a manufacturer produces the latest, greatest, hottest new computer, should it advertise immediately? If consumers stop buying the old systems, the distribution chain is stuck with 120 days of slow-moving inventory. Discounting is usually the solution. For manufacturers who are committed to providing customers with leading-edge technology, a multiple-step value chain works against them.

Price protection is common policy in the industry. It is the manufacturer's way of shielding distributors against price drops. If a distributor maintains 30 days of inventory and the manufacturer drops prices by 20 percent, the manufacturer pays the distributor the 20 percent difference on its existing inventory. In this way the value chain creates a disincentive for manufacturers to be always lowering their prices.

Repairs and returns add significant cost within the value chain, as returned or defective products are handled at every stage. This creates delays in returning products to the ultimate customers, thereby decreasing customer satisfaction.

Finally, each distribution level puts distance between the manufacturer and the customer. By dealing directly with the customers, Dell got immediate feedback and was able to solve customers' problems quickly. Better service generated strong customer loyalty.

Traditional Value Chain

MANUFACTURING   REGIONAL WAREHOUSES   DISTRIBUTOR   RESELLERS   CUSTOMER

Dell's in-bound and out-bound telemarketing sales force learned firsthand the problems and desires of customers. These sales reps became the advocates of the customer within the company. The distribution structure forced Dell to be sensitive to the needs of customers, thereby developing customer intimacy and delight.

In the new economy, key assets are mental, not material — innovation and teamwork are the driving forces.

As Dell's success grew, what was once IBM's and Compaq's greatest strength became their greatest weakness. All their distribution and retailing partners vehemently resisted their attempts to develop direct sales programs. This allowed Dell to flourish. Finally, the paradigm shift was recognized and now everyone sells direct, even IBM. Meanwhile Dell, founded in 1984, exploded to a $7.8-billion *Fortune 500* company by January 1997.

Dell Value Chain

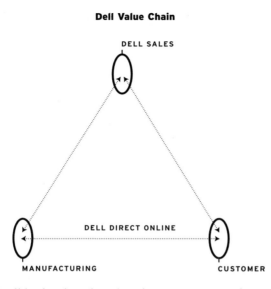

By 1997 Dell had reduced on-hand inventory to 13 days sales – down from 31 days in 1996! Dell has further compressed the value chain by allowing customers to order PCs directly over the Internet, eliminating internal salespeople from the order-taking process. Dell Direct Online gives customers up-to-the-minute real-time pricing, availability and order status, allowing Dell to provide the lowest-priced PCs in the market. These facts explain why Dell's sales grew 47 percent in 1997. As of March 1997, Dell Direct Online was selling $1 million a day of products over the Web. By August 1997, Dell's Web sales had doubled to $2 million a day! On an annual basis that's two-thirds of a billion dollars!

The third way to increase profitability is to develop a personal relationship with customers and treat them as unique individuals. Companies today are moving to develop one-to-one relationships with their customers.[5] Many women can't find standard-size jeans that fit. Now they can go into a Levi Strauss store, have six measurements taken and 10 business days later, a "personal pair" of custom-cut jeans will arrive in the store for $10 more than the regular rack price. For additional courier costs, customers can have them delivered to their door. The move is designed to fight off private-label jeans manufacturers who compete on price and between 1990 and 1995 increased their market share by over 30 percent.[6]

The fourth way to increase profitability is through innovation. Contrast the old philosophy of IBM and Intel. In the history of IBM, engineers occasionally went to the executives and said, "We have found a way to produce a mainframe that is twice as powerful as our existing

121

systems at half the cost." The executives would respond, "That's great, but if we market these new computers, no one will buy our older, slower, more expensive ones. We would kill our existing markets." And so they held back the technology.

This strategy works as long as you're the only game in town. But if you can invent a machine that's twice as powerful as the leading model at half the cost, chances are that someone else can and will. By not making its own products obsolete, IBM allowed other companies to step in and do the job.

Intel's philosophy sharply contrasted IBM's. Intel produces central processing units (CPUs) for microcomputers. Since the introduction of Intel's first chip in 1971, processor power has doubled in power every 18 months. This exponential growth in processor power (measured in millions of instructions per second) revolutionized business by enabling it to fundamentally alter information distribution, decision-making distribution, organizational systems and structures, and the way businesses relate to customers and suppliers.

Intel had two development teams working at all times, leapfrogging each other. As one team developed the CPU chip for the XT computer, a second team was developing the next generation chip, the 286. As soon as the XT was in production, the XT team began designing the 386 chip, even before the 286 chip was prototyped. As soon as the 286 chip was in production, that team began designing the 486. As soon as the 386 was released, its team began designing the 586 (known as the P5 or Pentium). Once the final version of the 486 was released, that team began designing the 686 or P6 (Pentium Pro), and then the P7 (Pentium II). Intel's strategy is to always make its own products obsolete. The result has been an explosion of the market. Radical technology breakthroughs that have allowed Intel to continue to double the power of its microprocessors every 18 months have ensured Intel's security and success.[7]

This philosophy of relentlessly obsoleting its own products has become essential for Intel because the company now has an 18- to 24-month window of opportunity in the market until its competitors copy its latest chips. Two years after the introduction of the first Pentium chip, AMD, Cyrix, IBM and Motorola had chips that perform at comparable speeds.

In 1997, Intel will invest $2.5 billion in research and development. What is R&D but investing in people? Knowledge, innovation and creativity drive R&D and these come from people, not from financial resources or capital equipment. And training and education fuel people.

Intel Invests in its Future[8] (in billions $US)

	1992	1993	1994	1995	1996	1997
Revenue	5.8	8.8	11.5	16.2	20.8	n/a
R&D	0.6	0.8	1.0	1.1	1.8	2.5
Capital Additions	1.2	1.9	2.4	3.6	3.0	4.5

In 1997 Intel will invest $7 billion in research and development and new plant facilities, equal to 34 percent of its 1996 sales! The company's security is in its ability to reinvent itself—its products, its services, its culture.

Commodity markets are price sensitive. Market share is easily gained by lowering prices, but easily lost when a competitor lowers prices. But companies that create effective monopolies through innovation, creativity and ingenuity can charge whatever price the market will bear. This strategy is known as "price skimming." Thus Intel sustains healthy margins by allowing for heavy investment in research and development to ensure effective monopolies in the future.

The only reason that Intel can continually invest so aggressively in R&D is that it has high margins and dominates the chip market. Why? Because it always has a new chip on the market. In 1997, Intel was the only company offering a 300 MHz chip with MMX technology. MMX chips are designed to run graphics-intensive applications faster.

> Only the paranoid survive...
> Andy Grove, chairman, Intel

The key to high margins and high profitability is innovation, which comes only from people. At the base is continual investment in the skills of people through training and education. In the new economy, training and education are to the human asset what R&D is to technological advancement. And the two are inextricably linked.

The Value of People

The old economy is based on zero-sum thinking, which assumes that the pie is only so large. If you have more of it, I have less. But the new economy is built on the concept of unlimited potential. In the old mindset, companies typically opposed profit-sharing because if they gave profits to the employees, there would be less for the shareholders.

The opposite attitude is a growth mentality that recognizes that the pie is not fixed in size. New thinking advocates giving away part of the pie because this way the whole pie grows larger. And while our percentage of the pie may decrease, our overall or absolute earnings will increase. After all, would you rather have 100 percent of $1-million profit or 50 percent of $10-million profit? The percentage is smaller but the absolute value is greater. Recent studies show that whatever measure you use—ROI, sales per square foot or absenteeism—profit-sharing companies outperform their competitors because employees have a sense of ownership and they benefit personally from efficiency.

Liquid Intellectual Capital

If people are the only asset of a high-tech company, how can a learning-based company retain its liquid intellectual capital? Only by rewriting the rules of business and creating an entirely new business culture.

High-tech companies have done just that. In 1985, the total value of shares granted to American employees totaled $59 billion. By 1996 the figure had risen to $600 billion.[9] Microsoft went public in 1986 not to raise cash, but so that employees could increase value and cash in stock options. In 1992, a Wall Street analyst estimated that 2,200 of Microsoft's 11,000 employees held options worth over $1 million. Given that Microsoft's stock has risen dramatically (60 percent a year compounded annually since 1986) and the company has granted generous options (57 million in 1996, or almost 2,500 per employee), workers have been willing to accept low pay, keeping salaries down and earnings high.

In high-tech companies where people are the primary asset, options create the incentive that fosters a learning organization. The wealth is shared with the people who created it. This is key to attracting and retaining the best and brightest executives, engineers and salespeople. The old mentality is that options are only for executives. In 1997, Intel expanded its option plan to include every one of its 50,000 employees. And Intel's treasurer, Arvind Sodhani, believes that, "Eventually, every corporation in the United States will give every employee options."

Over 1995–1996, Intel issued $111 million of options (2 percent of profits), Microsoft issued $570 million (26 percent of profits) and Netscape issued $61 million (291 percent of profits).

Options dilute the total number of shares outstanding. Gordon Moore's 16.5 percent stake when he founded Intel in 1971 has been eroded to 5.5 percent in 1997. But Moore is not complaining. In 1997, his stake was worth more than $6 billion.

Some people might think, "That's fine for high-growth, high-tech companies, but not for mature companies and industries where growth is harder to count on." Even mature industries' growth is really only limited by our perception: in the gas market for home and office heating, a company may think that it can grow only by taking market share from other gas companies. The market in the mind of executives is limited by consumer demand. Challenging the paradigm would require taking a fresh look at what business a gas company is in. Does

> Using best available technology, we can maintain our current lifestyle using only one-quarter of the energy we currently use!
>
> Amory Lovins, energy conservation expert

the company exist to sell gas or meet the heating and air conditioning needs of customers? If the purpose is to meet the needs of customers in the best way possible, then the market is infinitely larger.

A gas company could sell or lease energy-efficient furnaces, or create partnerships with construction companies and offer new homeowners the option of upgrading to the highest-grade insulation. Currently, the best-insulated homes have cut their gas bill by over 75 percent! Instead of paying the construction company thousands of dollars for upgrades, the new homeowners would pay for the insulation via their heating bills over a multi-year period—in essence, leasing the upgrades. The heating bill would equal the average bill if the upgrades had not been installed, but 75 percent of the monthly heating bill would pay for insulation and 25 percent for gas.

Let's assume that the gas company does not enter these markets, and that over time furnace makers begin promoting high-efficiency furnaces that dramatically reduce consumer demand for gas. Meanwhile, construction companies begin aggressively marketing high-efficiency insulation in new homes. Won't the appliance makers and construction companies become the gas company's competition, killing the market for natural gas heating?

Of course, making significant paradigm shifts depends on people, their ingenuity, creativity and lateral thinking. But how do we value human assets? There is still much work to be done in this vital area. And yet the value of knowledge workers cannot be underestimated.[10]

The new economy has introduced many new rules, yet many established companies still measure success by old rules that are no longer relevant. It's like using a 1980 tax guide to fill out a 1998 tax return.

General Motors decides to launch a new car. The company spends millions or billions of dollars developing the prototype. Then customers can walk into any dealership, describe the options they want and preview the car on a computer screen where it's rotated three-dimensionally. The customer then presses a button to confirm the purchase, keys in a credit-card number and the car is instantly replicated at the dealership. The production of the car costs the dealership nothing. A ludicrous business model? That is exactly what software maker Netscape does (Chapter 11). Millions of dollars have gone into the development of the new versions of Netscape's Web browser. Customers can download the software across the Internet! The replication of the product presents no cost to Netscape. The physical limitations—manufacturing and distribution—of yesterday's production model disappear.

In our vastly changed economy, the most successful organizations are rewriting the rules of business. Here are some questions and clues to determine whether a company is up to date:

- Are people throughout the organization empowered to use their knowledge creatively? At Sun Microsystems the philosophy is: In the absence of policy, make a decision. You will make mistakes. Worse than making a wrong decision is making no decision at all. The best organizations draw on the full talents of their people. Management philosophy and structures ensure that leaders continually challenge people but allow freedom.

If 25 percent of my work is not substantially different from last year, I get worried.
Everett Anstey, president, Sun Microsystems

- The best companies recognize that the team approach is the most effective. How a company's culture and strategic plan encourages team effort says a lot about its openness and ability to grow.

- How quickly can the organization change direction when it recognizes that the current strategic direction is wrong? What structures exist to continually challenge the senior leaders? Do the leading technologists, regardless of their age or seniority, brief the executive team on potential future opportunities or threats?

- How effective is the organization at converting R&D spending into marketable products? What percentage of the R&D budget is spent on refining existing products and what percentage is spent on making the company's core products obsolete?

- How much does the organization invest in technology? If the company's computers have been at the company longer than the average employee, then the company's days may be numbered.[11]

Organizations that place high value on the minds that produce knowledge will far surpass those that cling to physical assets. Locked out of the mental economy, old-style producers will be left in the dust of the new economy.

Companies must begin now to set up the infrastructure that will attract individuals capable of producing ideas and prosperity. Training and educational investments must be made in order to tap the full potential of people within the organization. No matter how rich the mental resources within the workforce, if they're left untapped they will produce nothing. The success of any organization depends on the degree to which it successfully releases its human potential for knowledge.

To Summarize:
- While the third wave was knowledge based, the fourth is learning based.

- Individuals and organizations need to develop practices that ensure self-reflection and self-correction at all levels of the organization. The leader's role is to ensure that the systems and structures within the organization promote learning at the personal, managerial, executive and organizational levels, and within the value chain as a whole.

- People are an organization's most valuable resource.

- There are few limits to profitability in the learning-based economy.

Workshop Questions and Activities:

In the late stages of the last wave, many companies competed successfully with one or two core competencies. Federal Express and UPS developed outstanding logistics management abilities through proprietary software that optimized truck routes to pick up a maximum number of packages with a minimum number of trucks. This lowered operations costs by reducing the number of trucks required per market. Both companies eventually packaged and sold this capability as software (Roadshow, for example), having dramatic impact on the direct store delivery industry. This best-practice transfer quickly became a basis for competition in the soft drink industry where bottlers bought this expertise for a few thousand dollars and instantly had world-class delivery capability.

- What are the biggest cost and information hurdles facing your company? How do people in other industries do a better job than you? How could these capabilities be transferred? What would the impact be if another company does this first?

- If these hurdles were removed, what would your company need to focus on?

Particularly for successful companies, it is difficult to find the motivation for radical innovation. However, technology has reduced the entry barriers to many industries, making industry leaders more vulnerable than ever. In the production of packaging for consumer products, for instance, one of the most lucrative steps used to be the production of film separations. Today, however, digital photography is poised to all but wipe out this step, as photographers can capture an image with a digital camera, manipulate it electronically and send it directly to press without ever creating film.

- In most companies, the people create value. In fact, in many start-ups, venture capitalists require "key-player" insurance to protect the company against the loss of key employees through death or injury.

Who are your key players, and how much would you insure them for? Why?

- Where could your teams look for new learning that might change your products, provide new ways of doing business or create new business?

- How can you empower your company's employees to take more responsibility in the absence of policy or authority?

- How can the link between formal training and job performance be made stronger?

- How does your organization promote self-reflection, self-evaluation and self-correction among individuals, teams and the entire organization?

Reflection:
- What business are we really in?

- What is the key learning/insight for me in this chapter?

Action:
- What one action shall I take tomorrow to move learning into action? And over time repeat, to move action into habit?

CHAPTER 8

Valuing People

A hologram is fascinating. Should one break, you could pick up any shard, hold it to the light and the entire, intact hologram will appear. The whole is revealed in the part. The way organizations treat employees — their internal customers — tends to be reflected in how employees treat external customers.

Want to Delight Your Customers? Delight Your Employees!

The same is true of an organization. A company cannot claim to value the customer and talk about customer service while treating employees poorly. It is essential to understand employee needs and how they can be met and exceeded.

"We'd go bankrupt paying them what they want!" is a common management refrain. If money is a sore point in the organization, then either salaries aren't competitive (by region, length of service, level or industry) or the unhappiness springs from such non-monetary sources as lack of empowerment and dated management systems that are out of sync with the lifestyle realities of today's employees.

Creating an Empowering Environment

For companies wanting to draw out the full talents and resources of people, as well as attract and retain the best and brightest employees, authoritarian responses to employee challenges no longer work. Yet many companies cling to old, hierarchical systems. Companies that treat people poorly may last for a while, but eventually they destroy employee motivation, creativity and productivity.

A new model for leading people has evolved. Leaders understand that quality and productivity are directly linked to the job satisfaction of each employee, or each part of the whole organization. There will always be a need for limits, and for employees to be given a clear understanding about what is expected of them, but within this framework there is much room for creativity, decision-making—and mistakes.

Imagine a construction crew roofing your dream home. The guy next to me, Joe, is doing a sloppy job and there will be leaks in your living room during the first rainfall. Will I stick my neck out to correct this guy? And if he doesn't listen to me, would I complain to the supervisor? What if the supervisor is a friend of Joe's? Would I continue to push the issue? What if the situation got ugly and I was labeled a troublemaker on the construction crew? Would I appeal to the company president? What if the president stands behind management and management stands behind the other employee? I might even get fired. Knowing all this in advance, is it likely that I will correct Joe? And if I do, is it likely that I will have the character and determination to pursue it regardless of the consequences?

> **Life is one indivisible whole. One cannot do right in one department of life whilst he is occupied in doing wrong in any other department.**
>
> Mahatma Gandhi, Indian spiritual leader

But now, imagine that you are helping the construction crew build your own dream home. What if you see the guy next to you doing a rushed job? Will you correct him? You bet! Do you care if you have a problem with the supervisor? What if it goes right up to the president? "Too bad! This company isn't getting paid until the job is done right!"

Ownership creates commitment. To create ownership, organizations must put in place processes that allow employees to have creative input into their jobs. Hired hands do what they are told and expect their payment at the end of the day, owners care deeply and go the extra mile. If business sticks to the authoritarian model, will there be commitment to high standards? What will employee satisfaction and morale be like?

Disputes within organizations can be resolved by returning to the mission (why) or vision (where), which are like a blueprint (which everyone contributed to and understands). In this case the supervisor might say, "Yes, Joe is a good guy, but he isn't doing a great job and that goes against our mission to produce high-quality work."

Rather than immediately blaming Joe, a good supervisor asks some questions first. Was Joe properly trained? Do our reward systems promote undesirable behavior? Are we rewarding workers on the basis of how many shingles they lay an hour rather than the quality of the work done? Does Joe understand the mission? Focus on the problem, not the person.

Within the traditional hierarchical model, the supervisor might decide to take Joe discreetly aside and discuss how his efforts affect the entire company. Within a team environment, peers rather than a manager might correct Joe. Within a team environment, the function of leadership is to ensure that systems and structures are aligned with creating the desired behavior. The team, through the process of self-reflection and self-correction at the team level, will correct the problem.

If all efforts to correct the situation fail, the company must take a hard look at its hiring processes to reduce the odds of making such a hiring mistake again. Hewitt Associates interviews prospective candidates an average of five times before making a hiring decision, while Microsoft hires only two to three percent of the candidates it interviews.[1] Hence, a great deal of time and money is invested early in the hiring process, resulting in fewer problems downstream and a higher-caliber workforce.

In the long term, we want to create teams that are self-regulating. The team will ultimately govern performance. Each person should assume responsibility and leadership within the scope of their job descriptions. Access to the blueprints allows each person to do that.

To paraphrase Confucius:

> *Tell me and I will forget.*
> *Show me and I will remember.*
> *Involve me and I will understand.*

The final line of this saying is often interpreted as "Involve me and I will be committed" — an equally powerful insight.

Question Industry "Wisdom"

At one time, the New York Fire Department's rule book stated, "Upon arriving at the scene of a fire, immediately place a ladder against the front of the building." It was the first commandment of fire fighting in New York.

There was a fire. A brigade arrived. Its lieutenant saw that the fire was raging at the back of the building and ordered everyone around to the back without putting a ladder against the front of the building. The crew put out the blaze quickly, minimizing damage and potentially saving lives.

But one of the fire department inspectors was in the area. And what was the inspector's job? He noted the absence of the requisite ladder and began disciplinary action. Then the union got involved and a court case ensued.

In court, the defense lawyer for the lieutenant began by asking, "Why does the department have this rule?" No one knew. He even subpoenaed the chief of the fire department. The chief couldn't answer.

The defense lawyer had done his research. He brought in an 89-year-old historian who hobbled up to the witness stand and testified that nearly a century earlier in New York City there were no full-time, paid firefighters. All the brigades were voluntary, and the insurance companies paid only one brigade, the first one at the scene of a fire. How did the insurance firms determine which brigade was first? Whichever brigade had its ladder against the front of the building!

This raises several interesting points. The first is that policies, procedures or practices are usually a logical response to a problem. But if we teach a practice without the underlying principle (teach the *how to* without the *why to*) and circumstances change, people have difficulty taking decisive action. Leaders need to teach principles (the *why*) so people can adapt as circumstances change.

I ask audiences, "What is the universal mission of a fire department?" Within 30 seconds the group has come up with four key points: to put out fires, to save lives and property, prevent fires and provide education. We all intuitively know the mission of a fire department.

In the case above, what was the inspector communicating to firefighters through the disciplinary actions? That the rules should be followed without exception.

The late Edwards Deming, who is widely credited with founding the quality movement, said 94 percent of problems in organizations are due to bad systems and structures, not bad people. People are well intentioned and want to do well. Misaligned systems and structures create the problems.

What if the lieutenant of the brigade was fired for failing to place the ladder against the front of the building? You are the next lieutenant arriving at the scene of a fire and you notice the fire is around the back of the building. What will you do? You have the ladder placed against the front of the building because you know the consequences of not following the rules. In the extra few minutes that this takes, the fire spreads to a gas main that explodes. Four children die in the fire. How do you feel about the organization?

The systems and structures of organizations create misalignment. In disciplining the lieutenant, the inspector's actions sent a clear message: the organization's purpose is following rules, not saving lives. An organization cannot be both mission driven and rule bound. Leaders must create the atmosphere in which employees can break the rules if they are serving the mission.

Systems must be flexible. Principles for decision-making, rather than etched-in-stone rules, will enable every employee to make reasonable decisions in keeping with the mission to uphold the organization's values. Then the organization can expect to become fast, flexible, focused and friendly, and unleash the inherent power in people that is required to thrive in the rapidly changing business world.

Contrast the New York Fire Department story with the following. The Four Seasons Hotel chain is world renowned for its customer service. How has it achieved this reputation for excellence? By allowing its employees the freedom to make decisions within the realm of their responsibility. Here is an example: while checking out of the Four Seasons Hotel in New York City, you forget your briefcase at the front desk. The bellhop grabs it, flags a cab and chases you to the airport, where he tracks you down and gives you the briefcase before you board your flight.

Now, where in the policy manual does it say, "If a guest leaves briefcase at front desk, flag cab, chase to airport...?" No one can prescribe what to do in every situation. Instead, employees need to treat customers the way they themselves would want to be treated (the golden rule). Even better, follow the platinum rule—treat the customer the way the customer wants to be served. Because of cultural, income and age differences, the customer will define value differently than the employees.

Empowerment has failed in many organizations. Often, people at seminars are very cynical about the principle. A man said to me, "What if a busload of senior citizens arrived at the hotel while the bellhop is away. With no bellhop to unload their luggage, empowerment has resulted in poor customer service!"

When experiencing the first problem with empowerment, some organizations retreat into the old management mode where managers go back to making arbitrary decisions. However, adjusting to new initiatives is never easy, there is always a learning curve. If returning briefcases to forgetful clientele proved to be a recurring problem, let the bellhops find a permanent solution.

"Imagine you were the team of bellhops. How could you get the briefcase back to a client and maintain the same service levels so that a busload of senior citizens would not be kept waiting? Answers I have heard include: "Get the cabby to take the briefcase and chase the limousine to the airport." "Hire more bellhops." "Call the customer's office, find out his next destination and courier it to him there." "Have someone from the kitchen dress in a bellhop uniform and cover for the absent bellhop." "Call the limo company and have them radio the car."

All of these are great ideas, but as humans we tend to take the first available solution. I challenged the audience again, "How could you creatively eliminate the potential problem at no cost to the hotel?"

"Front-desk staff should ask clients if they have all their luggage," was one suggestion. The best answer was, "Make the bellhops responsible for selecting the limousine company that wins the contract for the hotel. Among the contract's conditions is the requirement that all limousines be equipped with two-way radios tuned to a base station at the bellhop desk. If, by chance, a guest leaves something behind, the bellhop can radio the driver immediately, to return to the hotel."

Here, in a ten-minute discussion, an audience with little experience in bellhop procedures came up with an elegant solution that would cost a hotel nothing to implement! Would bellhops, who know their customers and suppliers better, have been able to arrive at the same solution?

As an audience we had an unfair advantage in that we had more than 100 people brainstorming for a solution in an environment where there where no wrong answers. In other words, people felt comfortable suggesting off-the-wall ideas.

The role of leadership is to create a climate in which such a process can take place. Given enough time, the bellhops would have arrived at an equally elegant, inexpensive solution. However, organizations often do not encourage or even welcome employee input. If they do, the process of working through numerous solutions is often flawed.

Some seminar participants have argued that the bellhop problem is simple, but with complex business problems it is unrealistic to put constraints on the process—for example, challenging people to identify an elegant solution at no cost. This may be true in some cases, but if the first proposal to solve every problem is to throw more resources—money, staffing—at it, then corporations are becoming intellectually lazy. Resources are substituted for creativity as the primary means of solving problems and taking advantage of new opportunities. That is not to say that organizations should not invest resources in creating new opportunities, new products, new services or adding new value to existing products or services.

Trust: Essential for Empowerment

Technology is advancing faster than management philosophy. We can give front-line people all the information they need to make real-time decisions, but if we hold on to an old management paradigm, our efforts will fail. In essence, organizations need to create trust.

The former chairman of Matsushita Electric in Japan, Konosuke Matsushita, hit at the core of this faulty western management paradigm when he said:

We are going to win and the industrial West is going to lose. There's nothing much to it, because the reasons for your failure are within yourselves.

With your bosses doing the thinking while the workers wield the screwdrivers, you're convinced deep down that this is the right way to run a business — getting the ideas out of the heads of the bosses and into the hands of labor.

For us, the core of management is the art of mobilizing and pulling together the intellectual resources of all employees in the service of the firm. We have measured the scope of the technological and economic challenges. We know that the intelligence of a handful of technocrats, however brilliant, is no longer enough. . . .

Only by drawing on the combined brain power of all its employees can a firm face up to the turbulence and constraints of today's environment.

This is why our large companies give their employees three to four times more training than yours. This is why they foster within the firm such intensive exchanges and communications. This is why they constantly seek everybody's suggestions and why they demand from the educational system an increasing number of graduates as well as bright and well-educated generalists — because these people are the lifeblood of industry.

New economic and social realities are forcing organizations to adopt more open and rewarding relationships with employees. Companies that remain stuck in an old, command-and-control, militaristic management paradigm will fall further and further behind in their ability to compete in the dynamic, rapidly changing business world. Organizations that hold to the notion that you can't trust people with anything more than a simple task (the thinking inherent in the production line) are doomed to fail.

Involving Staff

When researching *The 100 Best Companies to Work for in Canada*, a government agency impressed me — Canada Mortgage and Housing Corporation (CMHC). One of the goals of senior management was to be ranked in the book and the team communicated this goal to everyone in the organization. So when any decision had to be made, people at CMHC asked, "If we expect to be one of the 100 best companies to work for, what should we do in this situation?" The process of making decisions in light of this mission created a compassionate workplace.

When CMHC was ordered by the government to cut its budget by

25 percent in 1985, the executives went to the employees and said, "Look, we don't like this any more than you do, but our hands are tied. We have to cut the budget by 25 percent. You tell us how to do it."

The employees formed committees and came up with a series of recommendations:

- Institute an immediate freeze on external hiring.

- Offer all employees a voluntary leave of absence for up to two years, for any reason, with benefits and guaranteed job security. [Through the leaves of absence the organization temporarily shed staff. The intervening two years allowed normal attrition to reduce staff before those on voluntary leave returned.]

- Offer truly voluntary early retirement with a package that is more generous than required by law.

- If the first three strategies haven't reduced staff enough, offer voluntary severance with a package that is more generous than required by law.

- If after all these efforts, CMHC had still not reduced staffing levels by 25 percent, those whose positions were eliminated would be put on a priority list. The freeze on external hiring would continue until all these people were brought back into the corporation. If no one on the list had the skills necessary for an available position, CMHC would provide training for the most suitable person on the list.

How can an organization cut staff by 25 percent (in this case, CMHC went from 4,000 to 3,000 employees) and have morale increase? Only by empowering the staff and involving them in the decisions. In times of change, ignorance breeds fear. Typically, the atmosphere of an organization undergoing downsizing is one of fear, uncertainty, confusion and stress. No one knows what is happening, rumors run rampant and everyone feels helpless. Feelings of victimization breed anger and resentment. But at CMHC employees were not only informed but empowered. They weren't helpless, they were driving the process and were in control of their destinies.

Don't just aim to make your company one of the best companies. Expect that it will become one of the best and make all decisions based on what the best would do!

Dennis Waitley, author of *The Psychology of Winning*, tells of an experiment that highlights the importance of expectations. Three high school teachers were called in to the principal's office and told they had been specially selected to participate in a secret experiment because they were the best teachers in the school. The classes they were going to be assigned in the fall would be made up of the brightest pupils. At the end of the year, the progress of their students would be compared with that of average students in the school. But the teachers were not allowed to tell anyone else—the students, parents or other teachers.

These teachers were excited. They spent the year fostering and nurturing their students. In everything they did, their expectations shone through, "You are the best. You are the brightest. You will excel." Sure enough, at the end of the year, the progress these students had made was phenomenal. It was better than that of the students in the rest of the school, the area and the state. The teachers, who were proud, said, "Well, it's a fantastic achievement, but then our students are the best in the school."

The teachers were staggered when they found out that their students had only been average, randomly selected from the student body.

But after reflecting for a minute the three teachers perked up, "Well, that's understandable. We're the best teachers!"

"No," came the reply, "your names were randomly selected from a hat containing the names of all teachers in the school."

The teachers believed their students were the best, and so they became the best. Belief, or expectation, is a powerful force. Creating high expectations—believing in people and their inherent capacity to do well—is a powerful motivator. If you really believe you are the best, you are forced to live up to that image.

When the executive team made it their explicit goal to make CMHC one of the best companies to work for in Canada, that expectation permeated the organization.

At Federal Express, a manager is a productivity enhancer or facilitator, not the "boss." A manager's job is to provide employees with the training, resources and staff support to help them do their jobs better, not tell them what to do. Managers are champions of new ideas, change and improvement.

FedEx is perhaps the best example of the inverted pyramid. If an employee is unhappy with a manager's decision, he or she can challenge it. The manager's manager is called in. If the problem is not resolved to the employee's satisfaction, the vice president of human resources becomes involved. The next step for a FedEx subsidiary outside of the United States is that the most senior executive for the country gets involved, and finally everyone is flown down to Memphis, where a tribunal is established. The employee selects the majority of people on the tribunal. Tremendous expense is incurred to ensure fairness. The enormity of the expense ensures that managers do their best to ensure that conflicts don't escalate and that solutions are readily found. The system forces communication from the bottom up. Employees cannot be silenced by authoritarianism. Ideas cannot be stifled. Unfairness must be corrected.

The FedEx philosophy overturns the traditional view of management. In the hierarchical, top-down model, if an employee is consistently late, the manager calls him or her into the office and says, "If you're late again, you're fired."

At FedEx, the manager invites the employee to come and talk about the issue and asks if there are any problems. It may be that the employee has two toddlers who are difficult to bundle up and get to day care in the morning. Because the onus is on the manager to work out a mutually agreeable solution, he or she might suggest that the employee work another shift.

In a typical, hierarchical company, if an employee in a similar situation was disciplined or fired, his or her co-workers would undoubtedly interpret it as unjust, which would only create tension between employees and management.

Back to Deming's point that systems and structures determine performance. FedEx has created communication structures that encourage managers to get at the root cause of problems. Managers cannot act in an authoritarian way and make arbitrary decisions that could threaten livelihoods. As a result, fear can't flourish. Morale is consistently high.

The New Training Paradigm

Every company provides training of some sort. Even within an organization without a formal training budget, "informal" or "unstructured" training occurs. People often start a job with little or no experience and eventually become competent at their work. They learn by trial and error, by asking questions of colleagues and bosses and through self-study. Most North American employees get their training this way. Japanese, German and French investment in on-site training and education is significantly higher. The cost of the learn-as-you-go approach is enormous, yet it is invisible and unmeasured.

One thing worse than training employees and losing them, is not training them and keeping them.

Dr. Ed Metcalf, professional speaker

Studies show that employees who develop their skills through unstructured training are half as productive, or less, during the developmental period than those with formal training. Yet a staggering three-quarters of Canadian companies spend absolutely nothing on formal training! Even those with a training budget may be quick to reduce or eliminate it in times of financial stress. This is because training expenses are considered "soft" and are difficult to quantify. Companies that spend little or nothing on training may think they're saving money, but in the long run they lose a fortune in lower productivity.

138

Here's a math problem about two new average sales representatives in a clothing store:

> Sales rep "A" is put on the sales floor on Day One and takes 48 weeks to become proficient at selling $4,000 of clothes per week.
>
> As an experiment sales rep "B" is taken off the sales floor and given an intensive, four-week, $6,000 sales course, after which she begins immediately selling $4,000 of clothes per week.

Which rep will have the highest net sales for the company? Here's how the solution is calculated:

> Sales rep A's average sales are $2,000 per week. (Starts off at zero and ends up at $4,000 per week; therefore, A's total sales are 48 weeks x $2,000/week = $96,000.)
>
> Sales rep B starts off behind because she sells no clothes for four weeks, which means she has only 44 weeks for selling clothes. But the moment she gets out on the sales floor she begins selling at a rate of $4,000 per week. So 44 weeks x $4,000/week is $176,000. But the four-week course cost $6,000. So B netted the company $170,000.
>
> Given that $170,000 is greater than $96,000, this highlights how an HR professional can prove that formal training is more profitable for the retailer.

We can see this example in the graph below:

Cost benefit of training

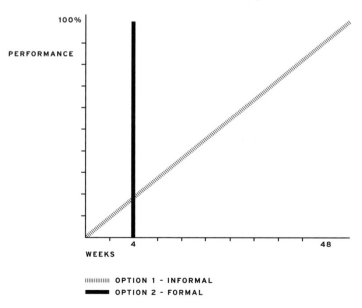

OPTION 1 - INFORMAL
OPTION 2 - FORMAL

Would we take a learn-as-you-go approach with commercial airplane pilots? Imagine boarding a plane and hearing the following announcement: "Welcome aboard Flight 907 to Miami. We'll be cruising at an altitude of 30,000 feet. Joe Henderson, one of our pilots-in-training, will be your captain today. Please fasten your seatbelt. It may be a rough ride as it's Joe's first flight. We thank you for flying A Wing & A Prayer Airlines."

While the above example may appear exaggerated, it makes the point that in a highly competitive business environment, investing in employee training and education is investing in the future.

What is the lifetime value of a loyal customer? For a luxury auto dealership that delights its customers, a customer's lifetime worth can exceed $300,000! If the delighted customer convinces his or her friends to buy from the dealership, the value of that initial customer can exceed $1 million. If salespeople working at the luxury-car dealership know that anyone walking in is potentially worth $1 million, do you think that knowledge affects their perception and treatment of potential customers? If the dealership did not invest in training and educating its salespeople, it could potentially allow new sales or service people to alienate million-dollar customers! Isn't that like letting untrained pilots fly an airplane?

The onus should be on human resources professionals to assess the cost of failing to invest in formal training. For example, poorly made products or poor service can be thought of as economic losses because the customers are less likely to return. By quantifying this loss, training professionals can demonstrate the value of training.

> When you buy a piece of equipment you set aside a percentage for maintenance. Shouldn't you do the same for people?
> William Wiggenhorn, president, Motorola U

The True Costs of Not Training
An organization that fails to invest in formal training will experience:

- Fewer skilled employees
- Lower-quality work
- Poor customer service
- Substandard customer satisfaction
- Higher customer turnover
- Increased marketing costs to attract new customers
- Slow corporate growth and lower corporate profitability
- Lower job satisfaction and a less motivated workforce
- Higher employee turnover and absenteeism

- Increased workload on employees in high turnover departments, leading to an increase in burnout and even higher employee turnover
- Higher recruitment costs
- Reduced ability to attract high-caliber employees (Lower-caliber applicants require more training, which, if not provided, results in a vicious cycle.)
- High "informal" training costs
- Inability to change swiftly in a dynamic business environment (When a crisis occurs, downsizing is usually seen as the answer.)
- Slow corporate turnaround for projects, proposals and bids
- Slow responsiveness to new competitors
- An inflexible organization entrenched in the way things have always been done (Employees who are not continually learning produce fewer fresh ideas and are less innovative, resulting in the organization having to compete in lower-margin "commodity" markets.)
- Employee battles over turf, politics and office size. Politics, not competency, is valued
- Decreased ability to use the latest high-productivity, high-yield tools.

In short, an organization that fails to adequately invest in training will not be focused, fast, flexible or friendly—the four characteristics that Rosabeth Moss Kanter, former editor of *Harvard Business Review*, says are essential for organizational survival. The mission will not be effectively implemented, resources will often be misallocated and internal processes will be antiquated, time-consuming and unable to adequately meet customer needs. Such an organization's chances of competing in a rapidly changing economy are poor.

Executive Development
Who needs more training and education on a 747 crew—the pilot or the flight attendant? One requires over 10,000 hours of flying education and experience to qualify, while the other requires two weeks of training.

The higher individuals are within an organization, the greater their commitment must be to lifelong learning because the consequences of error are far greater. Executives must continually be thinking "paradigmally" and strategically, reading widely, spending time with their organization's technical people, managers and project leaders who are working on the cutting edge. Executives must be leaders in learning.

Support is Expensive Training

A study of Fortune 1,000 organizations by Nolan, Norton & Co. revealed the tremendous hidden costs associated with personal computers.[2] The price of a computer is like the tip of an iceberg—it represents only a small portion of the overall cost. The average PC costs $18,000, of which:

Cost of a PC

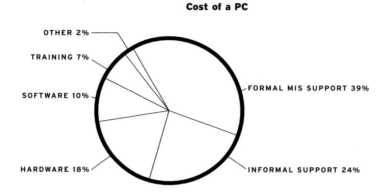

OTHER 2%
TRAINING 7%
SOFTWARE 10%
FORMAL MIS SUPPORT 39%
HARDWARE 18%
INFORMAL SUPPORT 24%

Most of the costs associated with a PC are typically unmeasured. They are:

- 7 percent training
- 10 percent software
- 18 percent hardware
- 24 percent informal support from colleagues
- 39 percent formal support from IS professionals

These last two categories are "hidden" and rarely measured, but together they total 63 percent of the cost of a personal computer—a staggering $11,340!

The corporate information systems (IS) department provides users with formal support. "Informal support" occurs when, for example, John can't paste a spreadsheet table into his word-processed document so he interrupts Sally, who takes 30 minutes from her work to teach him. Both categories represent hidden costs that go completely unmeasured and unmanaged, representing the bulk of the total cost of ownership (TCO) of a computer.

The Nolan, Norton study shows that IS support and informal training subsidize underfunded training expenditure. This is a huge waste of resources. Highly specialized, highly paid IS professionals may end up teaching end users how to turn on their computers. The IS professional will likely lack the patience required for training and get frustrated with "dumb users" asking "stupid questions." Users sense this and after an initial experience may hesitate to ask for help. They struggle along, never fully utilizing the software. Nor is an adequate solution to have a well-meaning colleague who lacks competence provide assistance. If the company increased its training commitment, end users would learn to use the systems to much better advantage as well as ensure that employee skills are continually upgraded.

If organizations doubled or tripled their formal training budgets, the hidden costs of "informal training" could be halved, resulting in a huge net saving.

Managers making computer purchases often conduct basic cost comparisons of hardware and software without considering the largest costs: ease of use and training. It's like comparing the tips of icebergs: the visible costs hardly matter!

The Gartner Group's 1996 TCO model confirms the Nolan, Norton findings. Gartner studies show that computers' capital costs average 21 percent, technical support 21 percent and administration 12 percent, while managing the end-user accounts for 46 percent! In this final category, 8.3 percent is formal learning, 7.0 percent data management, 6.5 percent application development, 5.5 percent informal learning, 3.2 percent supplies and 2.0 percent peer support (with a 14 percent fudge factor).[3]

Comparative Training Expenditures

A 1996 Conference Board survey of Canadian firms offers interesting insights.[4] A total of 219 organizations, mainly in the private sector and ranging in size from under 500 employees to over 10,000, reported spending an average of C$842 on training and development per employee per year.

A 1995 American Society of Training and Development (ASTD) study of its members involved in a benchmarking forum revealed average expenditures of $1,352 per employee per year, representing over two percent of payroll expenses.[5]

Surveys on training can be somewhat misleading as companies that fail to make training a priority rarely respond.

Three-quarters of Canadian firms spend nothing on training and education, and overall per capita training in Canada is at half the U.S. levels. German and French firms spend 2.5 times as much as American companies on training and education, while Japanese companies spend four times as much! Training and education is to people what research and development is to technological advancements.

Learning By Doing

Different people learn in different ways. Some people need written material, manuals and handouts. For others, manuals never suffice. They learn by listening. People also want training that relates to their specific job situation and skills. The needs must be assessed and the training approach customized according to individual preferences.

In universities, the co-op model has shown incredible results. Microsoft hires more software engineers from Canada's University of Waterloo co-op programs than from any other university in the world. In a co-op program, students study for four months, then work for four months at a company in their field of study, then return to studying for another four months. Degrees take students a year longer than at other universities, but graduates are more qualified because what they have learned is integrated with workplace practice. It also means that professors can't teach mainframe computing theories from a 15-year-old curriculum because students know from their experience that demand for mainframe programmers is declining.[6] The whole department is market driven.

In the same way, we need to develop a new model of organizational training, one that is interactive and demand driven. The old model was to take a two-day computer course. The new model is to have 15 minutes of customized on-demand training tied specifically to the need. When I need to print labels from a database to do a mailing, I first go to the on-line help menu or printed manual and look up "print—labels," but it's not there, so I try "labels—print," but it's not there. In the end I find it was under "mail merge." Of course, why didn't I look there to begin with? Stupid me.

At this point I don't need a three-day course on how to use the program. All I need is 15 minutes of customized, contextualized training. Likely I will call the software company's help lines or, as discussed above, take one of my colleagues from their work to show me. In this way help lines are really providing informal training. Given that the average help call costs Microsoft \$12,[7] making software easier to use in the first place is one of Microsoft's major goals.

Most computers sold after 1995 include a CD-ROM drive. I predict that interactive training on demand will be one of the fastest-growing segments in the training market. When I want to produce a slide presentation for the first time, I don't need to take a full-day course. I just need 15 or 20 minutes of instruction and then, time to try it myself! CD-ROMs are perfect for this kind of piece-by-piece, on-demand training. A rapidly growing alternative will be Web-based training.

While training focuses on such specific skills as being able to merge computer files, education deals with conceptual development. Education must be tied to business goals, yet not so tightly that it doesn't allow room to "play." Courses should allow for interplay between theory and practice. The old model for education was to take a three-day course and then return to work. Studies show that unless new learning is applied within 48 hours, most of it will be forgotten.

One thing is clear: organizations significantly underestimate the amount of time, effort and expenditure involved in bringing about change. What's needed is a fresh education model that allows students to apply newly acquired knowledge immediately and for an extended period. Otherwise, the course will not prove worthwhile. One model might be to take a one-day course followed by three weeks of applied experience in the workplace, a half-day refresher for questions and problems, another two months of experience and another full-day refresher, and so on.

Perhaps there is only one valid instance in which training is not necessary and that is when a company creates a rapidly changing learning organization in a rapidly evolving industry. Learning in a "bleeding edge" environment isn't formal, it's informal and experiential. The only courses of value in this environment are ones that focus on the process of learning, the process of team facilitation, the process of creativity itself. In other words, courses on how to learn, how to be more creative and productive in teams.

> The unexamined life is not worth living.
>
> Socrates, Greek philosopher

Companies such as Microsoft and Netscape are always reinventing themselves. These organizations are on the bleeding edge and formal training may not exist or help them. Instead, they practice continuous team-based learning. In *Microsoft Secrets*, Michael Cusumano and Richard Selby take a look inside Microsoft:

> Rather than investing heavily in training programs, formal rules and procedures, or even detailed product documentation, Microsoft tries to hire people who can learn on their own on the job. It relies on experienced people to educate and guide new people: Team leaders, experts in certain areas, and formally appointed mentors take on the burden of teaching in addition to doing their own work.[8]

Microsoft and Netscape hire only the best and brightest programmers. Problem-solving ability, proactivity, a continual quest for the excitement of challenge and change are the key characteristics that executives search for in candidates. These companies hire only the most creative, intelligent people. The working environments always give employees more responsibility than they would get anywhere else, continually challenging them to produce results. The result is company cultures that thrive on change. On the bleeding edge, Netscape and Microsoft have "excitement" capital to attract the intellectual capital they need to maintain their leadership positions.

Organizations on the bleeding edge must put in place practices that ensure self-reflection and self-correction at the individual, team, managerial, organizational and even the inter-organizational level. Individuals, teams and organizations that are venturing into uncharted waters need to be continually asking themselves, "Are we headed in the right direction? What are the perils? What are the opportunities?" And in response to these questions, they must be vigilant in correcting their course.

What would comprise formal learning courses for managers and leaders of bleeding-edge companies? Managers' courses would focus on organizational systems and structures that facilitate learning, change and creativity. For leaders, courses would focus on how to increase creativity within their organization as well as between organizations as they work to optimize relationships within the whole value chain.

Prove the Value of Training

CEOs are typically bottom-line oriented. Shareholders judge the CEO's success or failure in terms of profit, return on investment (ROI), dividends per share and market share. Facts, figures, proof and profit are the language of a CEO. Human resources (HR) and training professionals, by contrast, tend to be more concerned with people and teams in the organization.

To gain credibility with CEOs, HR and training and development professionals are increasingly tying training and education programs to corporate objectives in meaningful ways that can be measured. Almost 16 percent of all training and development activities in the Conference Board of Canada's 1996 study are subjected to ROI evaluation, while the American Society of Training Development's 1995 study shows that 40 percent of U.S. training and education initiatives are measured in terms of their bottom-line impact.

In 1979, Donald Kirkpatrick proposed four levels to evaluate the effectiveness of training. Level I diagnostics measure participants' reaction to a course, usually in the form of a survey, often called a "smile sheet." Level II measures learning. Participants complete surveys before and after the course to measure changes in self-reported attitudes and knowledge. Level III focuses on changes in behavior. This involves surveying the co-workers and supervisors of participants before and at least three months after the course to see if their behavior has changed. Finally, Level IV diagnostics seek to tie the training to business results and assess the financial impact on the bottom line. Each level is progressively more difficult and expensive. Working at Level IV is what will give HR and training departments increased respect in organizations.

The HR department, like any other department, exists to serve the overall corporate mission. HR programs must be designed to meet corporate objectives, including increasing new product innovation, team performance, creativity, sales, quality and/or customer satisfaction and decreasing costs. Creating an ROI is increasingly the aim and justification of any HR investment.

Training professionals must learn to quantify the unquantifiable. They must speak the language of the CEO. As HR professionals gain credibility with CEOs, they may begin to teach CEOs the language of HR.

The Cost of Disrespect

How do you quantify the cost of disrespect? Take the case of an HR professional in a manufacturing company who knew there was a lot of tension on the production line, where workers felt they received no respect. This company manufactured new product lines every year, from prototype through to mass production. The engineers who did the design work had an arrogant manner toward the production-line workers. Further, the design engineers described their designs using sophisticated, complex, academic terms that the production workers couldn't always understand. Clearly, there was a problem within the company. Pride and arrogance came ahead of the overall corporate mission.

The HR professional calculated the cost of such tension. The total wages of all the engineers and line workers involved in prototyping were $18,500 per day, and on average it took seven days to go from prototype to actual production, a total cost in wages of $130,000 per prototype. In addition, a lot of scrap was produced during prototyping as line workers tried repeatedly to create what the engineers wanted. This totaled $10,000 worth of wasted metal per prototype. Finally, there was the lost profit of having the line out of production for seven days while the machines were being retooled to accommodate the new runs. The average profit on the line for seven days of normal runs was $80,000. Adding up these three costs showed that each prototyping of seven days cost the company $220,000. The company went through prototyping seven times a year, for a total cost of about $1.5 million.

The HR professional then estimated that a custom-designed training program would heighten the engineers' awareness of the problem and its cost, increase the line staff's knowledge of engineering terms and do some team-building, halving prototyping time and saving $770,000 a year. The program would cost $200,000 to design (a one-time charge) and then $200,000 to operate every year.

If you were the CEO and saw this analysis, would you invest in the training initiative? The HR professional demonstrated the value of training in bottom-line terms. In addition, she could have argued that the company would also benefit from shorter cycle times (time it takes from concept through design, prototyping and manufacturing), thereby enhancing the company's ability to win contracts based on speed. When presented in these terms, funding for training is seen as an investment, not as a cost.

Continuous Challenge and Change

In her book *The Plateauing Trap*, Judith Bardwick examines the learning curve. She says that in the first three months of a new job, employees are almost totally green. They really don't know what they're doing and have to ask a lot of questions. The next 18 months are characterized by rapid learning, in which they are also acquiring new skills. After two years, they reach a plateau where they become "expert."

Research shows that challenge and growth are the primary motivators (see Herzberg's study, discussed later in this chapter). How can we keep people continuously challenged in their work?

> To gain or regain our employees' loyalty we must grow their independence! This is the win-win corporate paradox. It is difficult for leaders to embrace, but embrace it we must.
>
> John Kempster, former president, Hallmark Cards

Typical Learning Curve

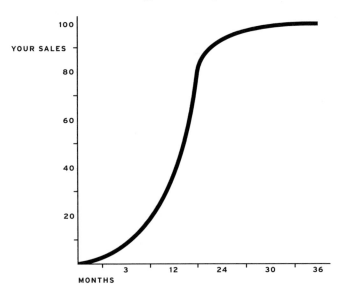

148

Pillsbury hires a lot of career-driven, hot-shot MBA graduates. These individuals are hungry, aggressive and driven. They thrive on challenge. Secretly, MBAs know in their heart of hearts that "YES, some day I will be president." Given that Pillsbury hires 70 MBAs every year, the response to this is NOT. So Pillsbury has a problem. It's called "plateauing." There is little chance of promotion for these MBAs because their boss may be as young as they are and likely will not retire for 20 years. How can a company meet the needs of ambitious employees without offering upward mobility? Through lateral moves. The corporate ladder has given way to the corporate spiral. Employees move sideways three times before being eligible to move up.

We acknowledge the paradox that people must be treated differently in order to be treated fairly.
LEGO Statement

Employees who have a high need for challenge and diversity are moved laterally every two years. This may seem counterproductive. Why move them right after they become fully competent or "expert"? Because the goal is to keep them excited by their work.

In the past, department heads at Pillsbury have complained about having to move good people to a different department. But the president always contended that it's more important to keep good people challenged and working for another department than to lose them to a competitor.

There is a new social contract: Job security has given way to employability security.
Rosabeth Moss Kanter, author

Lateral transfers have numerous benefits for the company, including increased internal communication and a new synergy in the workplace. Productivity increases because the product development department understands marketing, marketing understands production and so on. It also means that executives who have come through the ranks of many departments do not have tunnel vision.

For employees, there is the benefit of future employability. After eight years, they have four skill sets instead of one. Even more important, employees have learned how to learn. They know that no matter what new job is thrown at them, through study, trial, error and perseverance they will be able to succeed. They have faith in their ability to learn, no matter how difficult the situation. This is the ultimate form of intrinsic security. It is essential for peace of mind in today's turbulent world, where the traditional concept of one job for life has gone. As previously mentioned, statistics show that in their working life, most employees will have ten jobs over the course of three careers.

Rotating people and letting them work in different assignments is an excellent way to keep a person's work interesting. In addition, it serves to enrich and develop the employee's skills. It's a pity that it isn't practiced more widely.
Andy Grove, CEO, Intel Corporation

According to psychologist Abraham Maslow, the greatest human need is to achieve self-actualization, a state in which we blossom, realizing our full potential.[9] With the "plateauing" crisis, smart companies have realized that they must find new ways to keep their employees challenged or risk losing them.

I once met a 28-year-old manager at Microsoft, who was responsible for the worldwide marketing launch of a product. Putting a 28-year-old in such a demanding position is empowering, to say the least. This sends the message, "As a company, we believe in you. We know you are capable of meeting this challenge. We have faith in your talents and your ability to continue growing." Talk about motivation! If you had a Geiger counter to measure on-the-job satisfaction, his would be off the scale! He probably worked 80-hour weeks, partly because at 28 he could, but more importantly, because he wanted to.

"Isn't he a candidate for burnout?" I am often asked. "No, because he loves his work. He doesn't perceive it as work. It is more like the video game than writing with the other hand. He sees it as pure fun, challenge and play. His avocation has become his vocation."

Burnout, by contrast, occurs when an individual perceives that the costs of work exceed the rewards. In other words, work really is work. An employee might say, "I have to drag myself to work every day. Office politics take more of my energy than the work itself. There is little incentive to do a better job."

Don't misunderstand me, I don't want to celebrate workaholic 80-hour-a-week schedules. Balance is essential. Companies must be happy with employees who work 40 hours per week or less. Companies are finding innovative ways of evaluating the contribution people make. Corporations should be concerned by the statistic that 73 percent of North American employees feel their work is boring.[10] If their work allowed for passion, excitement and involvement, what would their commitment, contribution and productivity be? If employees were truly doing what they loved to do, would they consider it work? The productivity of impassioned employees is phenomenal.

This philosophy of continuous challenge and continuous learning, which relates to our deeper desires, is growing with the demise of the traditional notion of job security. In the Pillsbury example, employees are secure in the knowledge that they have many marketable skills because they worked in a different department every two or three years.

But this new approach requires a heavy investment in training. We can't just throw employees into the deep end of a pool and expect them to know how to swim.

The smaller the company, the tougher it may be to move people laterally. In a large company of thousands, it doesn't matter whether the accounting department has 150 or 151 people. But in a company of 25 people, there is a big difference between one and two accountants. Functional divisions, however, are blurred as people pitch in to do whatever is needed. Thus, many small businesses offer even more opportunities for broader work experience than in "silo" organizations, where functions are clearly delineated and separated.

I listened to Harvey Mackay, author of *Swim with the Sharks*, talk at a conference about learning to speak Russian. Apparently, it takes 400 hours on average for an English-speaking person to learn Russian.[11]

After Harvey's talk I began to think about what it would really be like to learn Russian in a 40-hour-a-week immersion course. In the first week, nothing would make any sense. Try, try, try and nothing makes any sense. It's all Russian to me. One word sounds exactly like the next. Every time I take a drink of coffee, the instructor says the same thing. I guess she means "cup." After 40 hours in the first week I have learned only "cup," and a few other words! Big deal! In the second week, every time I take a drink the instructor says a different word. I get the impression she means the verb to drink. I learn how to conjugate drink (I drink, you drink, we drink). I learn some other words such as "beer," "another," "please," "washroom." So while I have learned some important things, I would hardly say that I can speak Russian. The experience is still characterized by frustration, like writing my name with the other hand.

The first two weeks would be characterized by pain. I would feel like a failure for 80 consecutive hours. And the pain, fear and frustration wouldn't stop at two weeks. It would continue for months. And then

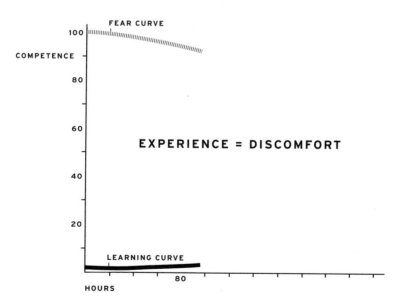

Feelings Early in the Learning Curve

I only gain a little understanding here, have a little Aha! over there, but I can't understand the language. I'm in the dark. But at some point around 400 hours everything clicks into place. There is a profound Aha! And now everything makes sense. It's like a join-the-dots picture where not all the dots are joined yet, but I can see the whole picture. I even understand words that I have never heard because I can figure out what they mean from the context of the sentence. I can now say with confidence that I speak Russian. All the grammar, all the rules of construction, all the principles of the language and how to speak it make sense. I experience the YES! that kids get when they master a video game. We can plot the experience:

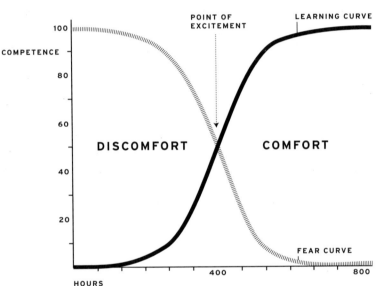

Learning and Fear Curves

As I approach that magical point of 400 hours my frustration, fear and anxiety have been decreasing weekly while I have been learning scattered bits of Russian. But at some point, and it is different for every person, I get the Aha! experience. I have a sense of mastery and control.

As adults we tend not to tolerate the frustration and anxiety of learning new skills. We don't have the patience required to persevere without gratification.

A child taking a first tentative step wobbles and falls over. If it takes 900 falls before the child learns balance, were the 900 scraped knees failures or necessary steps in learning the delicate art of balance?

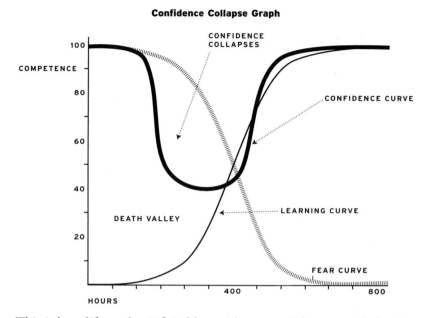

Confidence Collapse Graph

This is how life works. Life is like a video game. There are rule books, such as the wisdom literature of the world's religions, but like kids with the video games, few people read the instructions first. We go through life and we make mistakes. We are doomed to make the same mistakes over and over again until we learn the underlying principles. If we learn the principles we graduate to the next level and assume more responsibility in life.

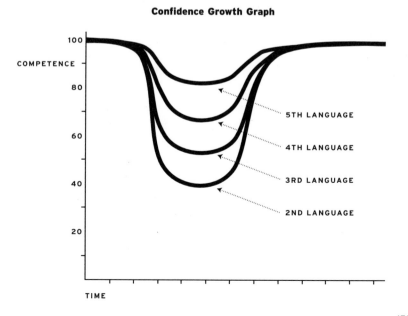

Confidence Growth Graph

We make new mistakes because we face a higher order of challenges. Are the mistakes failures? No! Were the child's scraped knees a failure? Only by giving up the game do we stop learning.

Thus courage and tenacity are characteristics of leadership. Children will naturally continue struggling to learn to walk because the drive is innate. But adults do not naturally struggle to learn new skills. As adults we must be proactive. Only continuous effort brings success. Adults need to develop the "no fear" attitude that children show in learning to walk.

Mackay noted that most of his fellow students quit Russian class after two weeks because they didn't get it. Really, however, they had just not got it "yet." Most people learning a difficult language like Russian quit. And they can honestly say, "I tried my best. I gave it my all for two weeks of intensive study, and I still can't speak or understand Russian." We significantly underestimate the amount of time and effort required to change. That is why 75 percent of quality initiatives in North America fail and two-thirds of reengineering undertakings fail to deliver their promised results.

Think back to the story about Martin Rutte learning to dive in Chapter 2. Four stages are involved with learning how to dive. The first is when you don't know anything and your coach must tell you what you did wrong or right. The second stage is when you think you have done something wrong, check with the coach and jointly figure out how to solve it. In the third stage you know when you have done something wrong. You don't have to check with the coach and you also know how to correct it. The final stage is when you know in advance what conditions lead to a mistake and prevent it before it occurs.

At the end of one presentation, a successful executive came up to me and said, "I have just taken a French course and you are missing the confidence curve." "The confidence curve?" I asked. "What is it? Help me understand."

"It is what happens to your confidence in this process," he replied. "When I started the course, I was very confident. After a couple of weeks of not getting it, my confidence plummeted. I wanted to quit. But I hung in there. As soon as I had the Aha!, my confidence shot up again." Salespeople call this plummet "Death Valley." If new reps can survive Death Valley in their first few months they usually will be good in sales.

How far would learners' confidence fall while learning subsequent languages? In learning a third language — Spanish, French or Italian — confidence would remain high longer, and when it did fall, it wouldn't fall as far as it did in learning the second language. Learning a fourth language would be easier because of similarities with the languages

It's not so much that we're afraid of change or so in love with the old ways, but it's that place in between that we fear. It's like being in between trapezes. It's Linus when his blanket is in the dryer. There's nothing to hold on to.

Marilyn Ferguson, author

already spoken. Any dip in the confidence curve would be later and shallower. By the fifth language, learners would have complete confidence in their abilities. No matter what the language or how difficult, learners know they will succeed. They are now truly secure. They have faith in their abilities to learn. This faith can translate into a general faith in the ability to face challenging new situations and learn the necessary skills to succeed.

What Truly Motivates People?

I often ask audiences, "Who feels that their organization is utilizing the full talents of all employees?" People only raise their hands after they look around and see their boss in the audience.

How can organizations tap people's full potential? American pollster Dan Yankelovich defines "discretionary effort" as the difference between the maximum contribution an individual can make to his or her organization and the minimum contribution necessary to avoid being punished or fired. The incremental effort that employees could make, the care and concern they could demonstrate for customers and their colleagues, the creativity that they could contribute, is the discretionary effort. How can organizations elicit employees' full effort?

Demotivators and Motivators

The goal for organizations should be to unleash the full potential of employees, to provide the training and knowledge, as well as physical, financial and human resources necessary for them to reach their full potential.

We often think that money motivates employees most. Frederick Herzberg, in what is considered a classic study, examined the nature of motivation in his 1968 *Harvard Business Review* article "One More Time: How Do You Motivate Employees?" His conclusions are both simple and powerful.

Herzberg argues that only challenging work and responsibility really motivate people. Money turns out to be seventh on the list of motivators.

The "dissatisfiers" are interesting as well. For instance, salary can be a bigger dissatisfier than a motivator. Underpaying employees will create more lasting unhappiness than overpaying will create lasting happiness. If a salary isn't competitive by industry, region or level within the organization, it will create dissatisfaction. But being within the highest pay range by industry, region and level will not create the satisfaction one would expect, as other factors are more important. Thus, salaries should at least equal the industry average, taking into account regional cost-of-living differences. But once the perception of fairness is addressed, other issues such as achievement, growth and advancement matter more.

For training, Herzberg's research has important messages. If achievement, growth and learning motivate people most, organizations should be continually giving employees new challenges and allowing them to direct their careers and invest in education and development. The results are a more excited and committed workforce with lower turnover, higher job satisfaction, higher productivity and higher-quality work.

Valuing people requires many businesses and organizations to look at their human resource, training and education policies in a new light. The new realities demand new approaches that will be inherently challenging for HR professionals. Few industries or professions can avoid facing up to the learning paradox.

To Summarize:

- Informal training costs are hidden and enormous compared to formal ones.

- Investing in training and education to meet employees' growth needs is essential for survival in the new economy.

- Employee motivation and subsequent innovation produces higher profits.

- Salary is not at the top of the list of human motivators.

- Courage and tenacity overcome the fear of change.

Workshop Questions and Activities:

- Informal, on-the-job training will always play a role in organizations. How can you do it better?

- There are many ways to create ownership within an organization beyond actually giving stock in a company. Many companies use such standard measurements as output per shift across plants, for instance, as a way of spotlighting performance and encouraging the transfer of best practices. In the best cases, pride develops among employees for the performance of their units. How can you create greater ownership for results in each area in your organization?

- What is the fundamental "industry wisdom" where you work? If you want to understand it clearly, listen to the new person. New people have not been indoctrinated in your industry's paradigms and will usually ask questions that fundamentally challenge these paradigms. How could you facilitate the implementation of the best suggestions?

- Does your organization trust its people? As a test, think about the reporting and management rules. Would you use these rules to run your family? Why or why not? Do these rules allow for innovation, or stifle it? What would you do to open the lines of communication?

- List the ways your company can enhance the working lives of employees. Rank them according to which ones will enhance satisfaction the most, which can be implemented the fastest, at the least cost, with the least amount of disruption.

- Which of these do you think will be the most important to attract and retain new people with the new skills required for your company to successfully evolve? Are these different from the ways you would enhance the work environment for existing staff? How? Why?

- List the possible benefits of increasing employee satisfaction to your customers.

- List the outdated company rules that ought to be eliminated and give your reasons. What effect would the following rule have: for each new policy introduced, the organization will eliminate two old policies.

- How much does your organization spend on training per person per year? How does this compare with national and international industry averages?

- What resources exist in your organization, community, industry or professional associations to foster continuous learning? What structures within your organization would promote continuous learning?
- Using the example on pages 137–138, create a cost/benefit analysis of how training and development in your organization would save money or increase revenue.
- Calculate cost of employee turnover in your own department and/or company.
- Develop an education plan with objectives for your organization. Provide at least one example where this would be effective. Why?
- How much of your time is spent learning? Is it enough? How would you make more time for learning?
- How much time do you spend thinking about opportunities as opposed to problem solving?
- How many meetings are open—where new ideas are welcomed and encouraged?
- On a personal note, does your job provide you with the opportunities to do things that enhance your employability? Remember, formal training is important, but what is more highly valued is actual experience performing tasks and functions that are in great demand. Does your current role allow you to do this?
- How could this happen?
- Describe your dream job. How can you create it?

Reflection:
- What is the key learning/insight for me in this chapter?

Action:
- What one action shall I take tomorrow to move learning into action? And over time repeat, to move action into habit?

CHAPTER 9

Keeping Customers:
Exceeding Expectations

We've all heard about exceeding customer expectations and delighting the customer, but to really understand the importance of customer service we need to work through some basic questions: What is customer service? Why is it so important? How do we measure customer satisfaction? What proof is there that poor service has a negative impact on financial performance?

U.S. researcher Jack Parr set out to discover how customers felt about a large, well-known American company's goods and services. He surveyed 6,000 customers. These customers represented a wide cross-section of industries and organizations.[1] His findings are typical of ratings for most companies.

Customer Satisfaction

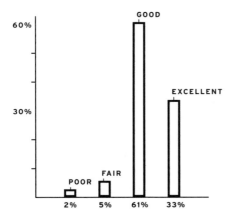

The first graph shows that only 2 percent of the customers surveyed said goods and services were poor; 5 percent rated them fair; 60 percent said they were good and 33 percent reported they were excellent. Executives in most organizations would look at these results and say, "Great! A full 93 percent of our customers say our goods and services are good or excellent. Aren't we doing an amazing job? Why should we change any of our policies or practices? It's time for big executive bonuses around here!"

However, such a conclusion would have been premature. Customer responses to the next question, "How willing are you to purchase from the company again?" were staggering.

Willing to Purchase Again?

Of those who say they experienced poor goods and services, none wanted to be repeat customers. Of those who rated the goods and services fair, a mere seven percent were willing to purchase from the company again. Of those who rated the goods and services as good, that is, acceptable but not impressive, only 62 percent were willing to purchase again! But of those who had an excellent experience, a full 95 percent were willing to be repeat customers. This research clearly demonstrates that the key to high-repeat business is delighting the customer. This is a typical finding in customer research. No wonder there's so much talk about the need to exceed customer expectations.

Such findings also reveal how disastrous it would be to consider the average customer satisfaction rating acceptable for any organization. Good is not good enough! Satisfaction is not enough. Delight is what we're after.

In the graph below, the first bar represents the percentage of customers who responded by rating the goods and services as poor, fair,

> There is only one boss - the customer. And he can fire everybody in the company from the chairman on down, simply by spending his money somewhere else.
>
> Sam Walton, founder, Wal-Mart

good or excellent. The second is the number of retained customers in each category.

Predicted Future Customers

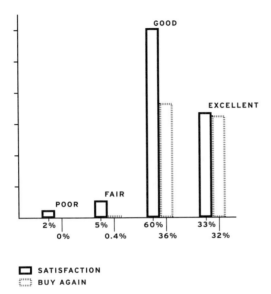

SATISFACTION
BUY AGAIN

No organization can keep all of its customers forever. The graph above shows that if an organization consistently offers excellent goods and services to its customers, it generally keeps them. However, companies that settle for average ratings will continuously lose significant numbers of customers. In fact, according to Parr's study, a company with an average customer satisfaction rating would keep only 68.8 percent of its customers after one business cycle. In the construction industry, a "cycle" may be many years, while in the grocery business, people shop every week. On the other hand, even if customer satisfaction is only "good," you may not lose customers if you have a convenient location and no competitors. In short, good is not good enough.

But in a fierce market where competitors are always improving, an average company must attract over 33 percent of its business from new customers every cycle just to maintain its revenue base!

The key to real growth in any business is customer retention. And the key to customer retention is continual improvement in products and services. This increases customer satisfaction and moves the bulk of customers from the good into the excellent category.

Studies show that it costs five times as much to attract a new customer as it does to retain an existing one. Organizations should put

Studies show
that on average
only one in five
dissatisfied
customers will
complain
directly, even if
you provide a
1-800 telephone
number.
Customer
research studies

five times more effort into keeping their existing customers satisfied than into prospecting for new business.

But very few do. How often do you hear from salespeople? Every day I hear from people trying to sell something. I receive faxes, letters and brochures. How often do I get the same attention from the people I already do business with? Usually, the only time I hear from my suppliers is when I receive an invoice in the mail.

Total Future Customers

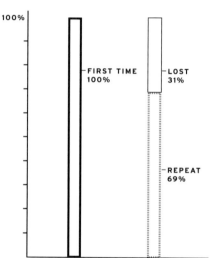

What Determines Excellence in Customer Satisfaction?

Perception is reality in the eye of the beholder. Executives need to perceive customer service as the customer does.

Learn to listen, so you can listen to learn.
Anonymous

What is excellent service? Contrast these two examples:

After buying a computer and carting it home, I found that it didn't work. I called the store and was told to bring it back in. So I brought all the boxes up from the basement, repackaged everything and drove back to the store. Of course, the nearest parking spot was two and a half blocks from the store, so I lugged the boxes back into the store one at a time. The sales rep greeted me with the news:

"It has to go to the wholesaler, who will send it to the repair depot. We'll have it back for you in two to four weeks. We'll call you when it's in."

This was done with an "I'm-really-going-out-of-my-way-for-you-and-you-should-thank-me-for-this-great-service-I'm-giving-you" attitude.

"Well, what do I do for a computer in the meantime?"

"I'm sorry, sir, it's the manufacturer's fault. We aren't responsible," the salesperson said.

"But I bought it from you," I pleaded.

"Well, sir, I'm afraid it's the manufacturer's warranty. I'll see if I can get them to speed up the process."

When customers do complain, company representatives explain why things are the way they are in such a way that customers end up feeling guilty or stupid. Most people feel that it is pointless to complain. Why bother? This explains why only one in five dissatisfied customers actually do complain. Complaints offer a golden opportunity to discover new products or services that the company can offer to customers.

Now compare my experience with that of a friend who purchased a notebook computer from Dell Computer Corporation. The day after he bought it, he noticed that one of the plastic clasps that allows the screen to flip up was broken. The notebook worked fine, it was just cosmetic damage. He called Dell. The next morning a Dell representative was at his office with a brand-new notebook.

From these two examples it's easy to identify which company designed its service policies with the interests of the customer in mind and which company will get repeat business.

Why Not Ask?

There is an old Sufi story about perception. A child is playing in the garden and remarks, "What a beautiful, pink flower this is." A honey bee flying about the flower responds, "The flower is not pink. I know it by its red and white stripes." A cat, who can only see the underside of the flower, chimes in, "It is neither—it is gray." Perception depends on perspective. We need to experience both satisfaction and dissatisfaction as the customer experiences them.

At a seminar, the executive director of a hospital related her experience in planning a hospice for elderly patients. Her executive team had worked to anticipate the needs of their customers: high-quality nursing care, lounges with lots of light on every floor and a sound system allowing residents to listen to music in their rooms.

Before commissioning the architects, the executive team interviewed future residents on what they considered design priorities. The answers were surprising. The overriding concern was privacy. This was a palliative care hospital, mainly for elderly women. Many knew they would die in this institution. They wanted to be able to meet privately with their families and clergy in their rooms. They knew that with health care cutbacks, their rooms would not be private, but they still wanted to have a sense of privacy.

The women interviewed made it clear that they did not want to have to traipse down a hall to use a public phone for their private conversations. They wanted private phones in their own rooms.

They also didn't want lounges that resembled doctors' waiting rooms, with last year's magazines. They wanted a variety of lounge facilities designed for interaction and meaningful activities: a music room, a beauty salon, a bridge room.

With this feedback the executives were able to modify their plans and place client needs first.

While the executives had every intention of providing excellent customer service, they were missing what future customers considered most important. Customer satisfaction is highly subjective. Researching what customers want is not only necessary, it yields fascinating results!

Organizations should survey prospective and exiting customers, asking them to rate 40 or 50 points of service, including price, service, quality, product features, delivery, billing and promptness of response: 1) Rank each service in terms of its importance to your overall satisfaction. 2) How well or how poorly is the organization meeting each need?

Importance versus Performance

Point A is something the organization is doing exceptionally well but that customers do not consider a priority. For example, if the hospice had built a sound system into every room, it would have spent thousands of dollars needlessly. Point B is something like a telephone in every room. It's exceptionally important to customers but the organization's original plans didn't call for it.

Using this information, plot the results on the two dimensions (importance and performance). First we will plot importance: everything above the horizontal mid-point line is important to the customer, everything below the line is unimportant.

Everything to the right of the vertical mid-point line means the organization is doing well in the customer's opinion and everything to the left indicates the company is doing poorly (see next page).

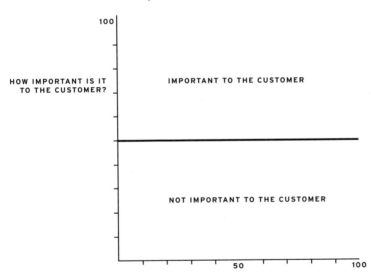

Importance to the Customer

100

HOW IMPORTANT IS IT TO THE CUSTOMER?

IMPORTANT TO THE CUSTOMER

NOT IMPORTANT TO THE CUSTOMER

50   100

We now get four quadrants. The top-left quadrant (QI) contains items that are very important to the customer but on which the organization is doing poorly. The top-right quadrant (QII) contains items that are very important to the customer and on which the organization is doing very well. The bottom-left quadrant (QIII) contains items that are not important to the customer and on which the organization is doing poorly. The bottom-right quadrant (QIV) contains items that are not important to the customer, but on which the organization is doing very well.

Rating of Company Performance

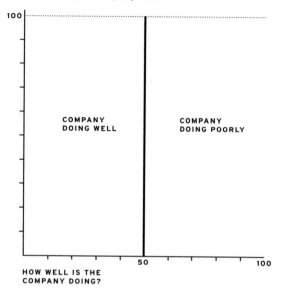

Importance versus Satisfaction

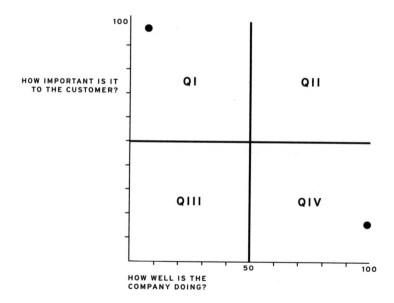

Quadrant IV activities are clearly a waste of money. The organization is doing a great job, but customers don't care. The activities don't add value from customers' perspective. Quadrant III really doesn't matter. The organization is doing a bad job, but the customers don't care. Quadrant I is the quadrant of crisis. It contains items that really matter to the customer but on which the organization is doing poorly. The organization needs to stop investing in the activities in Quadrant IV, invest all the savings of time, energy and money into points of customer service in Quadrant I, thereby pushing the ratings on those dimensions of customer service into Quadrant II. Simply put, the organization should do best what customers value most.

Rationalizing Improvements

Sun Microsystems has taken this two-dimensional model (importance versus performance) and further refined it. Sun takes customer feedback and prioritizes the areas of dissatisfaction by asking employees, "How much of an improvement can we make on this issue? Knowing our internal processes, do you feel we can make a 5 percent improvement or a 100 percent improvement? How much will it cost us? How much time and effort will be required to bring about the improvement?" These three new dimensions, added to the initial two, give a more complex analysis. Sun can then calculate what improvements to its products and service will increase customer satisfaction most, for the least expense, in the shortest time frame. In other words, Sun works to get maximum results for its investment.

An organization that takes an undifferentiated approach to serving its customers — by treating all clients exactly the same — will treat its best customers like its worst ones and its worst like its best.

Customer feedback can also take into account competitors' strengths and weaknesses. Customers can be asked, "How does our service in a particular area compare with our competitors'?" "If we matched their level of service, what effect would that have on your loyalty?" Organizations need to continually focus on how they can add the most value for the lowest cost with the least amount of effort, and in a way that will benefit the largest number of customers.

When the Chips Are Down

When he was president of Loblaw International Merchants, Dave Nichol hired a high-powered, well-educated team of consultants to study the cookie market. They came to a startling conclusion: People who eat chocolate chip cookies like chocolate chips!

(I know the results are staggering! I was blown away myself when I read the report. But then, that's why consultants get the big bucks.)

They also found that the more chocolate chips you put in a cookie, the more customers like it!

So Nichol and his team went to the bakery that had been making the cookies and said, "We would like you to double, possibly triple, the number of chocolate chips in *No Name* chocolate chip cookies, and we'll reposition the new product as *President's Choice Decadent Chocolate Chip Cookies.*"

"But Dave," said the baker, "you don't understand our baking process. We bake the cookies by sending them through ovens on a conveyor belt. The chocolate actually melts during the process. If we use that many chocolate chips, there's not enough batter to keep the cookie together. There will just be a pile of cooked batter in between pools of melted chocolate when the belts emerge from the oven." In essence, the bakers were saying, "We can't change our process."

Nichol said, "Thanks, it's been great doing business with you all these years." Five bakers later, he found one who didn't know it was "impossible" to bake such cookies. The result was *President's Choice Decadent Chocolate Chip Cookies*, the top-selling cookie in Canada. But, it's only available at 20 percent of retail outlets. How do you have a number-one brand when it's only available at such a limited number of retailers? By delighting the customers and exceeding their expectations.

Exponentially Increasing Margin

The impact of treating the best customers well is awesome. In a *Harvard Business Review* article, Alan Grant and Leonard Schlesinger note:

> Given the fixed cost structure of a grocery store, the contribution margin from each additional dollar spent by a customer can earn 10 times the store's net profit margin. Thus, the company found that even small improvements in any one of the many customer behaviors led to very significant profitability gains. Expanding the customer base by two percent with primary shoppers, for example, would increase the store's profitability by more than 45 percent. Converting just 200 secondary customers into primary customers would increase profitability by more than 20 percent. Selling one more produce item to every customer would increase profitability by more than 40 percent. Persuading every customer to substitute two store-brand items for two national-brand items each time they visited the store would increase profitability by 55 percent.

In other words, expanding the base of primary shoppers — the store's best customers — by a mere two percent increases the store's profits by 45 percent! [2]

How do grocery stores define convenience for customers? They have special checkouts for people with 10 items or less. They treat the worst customers the best! The people who buy little or nothing get out of the store fastest. This concept probably came from supermarket executives wanting to compete against convenience stores. The average family spends $400 to $500 a month ($6,000 a year) on groceries.[3] What are supermarkets doing for their best customers? They have to wait in huge line-ups. Why not have a frequent-shopper gold card that allows the best customers to check out in special, preferential lines? First, the store would have to know who its best customers are in order to be able to treat them preferentially.

A study by the National Retail Federation in January 1996 found that nearly half the consumers surveyed feel that shopping is a hassle and try to avoid it![4] A staggering 75 percent of men and 58 percent of women said they sometimes walk out of a store because the wait is too long! If I were a retailing executive, I'd be worried. The market is ripe for companies offering alternative shopping experiences to grow rapidly.

The Dreaded Shopping Experience
Round up the children. Bundle them into snowsuits. Strap them into car seats. Search endlessly for a parking space. Try to find a quarter for a shopping cart. Fight for space at the deli counter. Take the kids to the washroom. Stand in long checkout lines. Carry out 19 bags, two of which are ripping. Dent the car with the shopping cart. These are just a few of the images that come to mind when we contemplate grocery shopping. The fact is, consumers dislike grocery shopping. According to *American Demographics*, grocery shopping is the second-least popular activity of 22 daily tasks. In fact, it only rates ahead of going to the dentist as the activity people most hate to do.

"People spend the equivalent of two-and-a-half [work] weeks each year in the grocery store, and that's not counting driving time," says Andrew Parkinson, co-founder of Peapod, a computer grocery shopping and delivery service. "This breaks down to a 66-minute major food shopping trip each week, with more than one 16-minute, fill-in trip."

Peapod, the largest interactive on-line grocery shopping and delivery service in the U.S., serves over 50,000 customers in Chicago, San

Francisco, San Jose, Columbus, Boston, Houston, Austin, Dallas and Atlanta. With a computer and modem, customers log on to Peapod's Web page at www.peapod.com or dial up directly to shop. Customers can download the software over the Web, call a 1-800 number or pick it up at select stores. Peapod offers over 20,000 items for sale on-line.

On-line versus In-line Shopping

Customers can shop from the office or home or anywhere they have a computer and modem. With Peapod, shopping can be a 15-minute experience with a glass of wine while listening to your favorite music after the kids have gone to bed, or during your lunch hour at work. It's the beauty of on-line instead of "in line" shopping and it plays to Peapod's motto: Smart Shopping for Busy People.

Peapod halves average shopping time. Time is one of the things that baby boomers (born between 1946 and 1966) are most pressed about. With aging parents and young children to look after, time is one thing that baby boomers who are sandwiched in midlife have very little of. As a group, boomers are computer literate, so Peapod appeals to them.

Customers can comparison shop (Coke versus Pepsi versus generic pop), easily find sale items (marked with a red tag) and check their running total of purchases at any time. Customers automatically get any in-store sales that apply to their order and can use manufacturer and electronic coupons. They can view the product picture, price, nutritional information and whether it is kosher. The computer allows the shopper to shop from their last order or to create frequently ordered items lists (i.e., weekly list, summer BBQ, dinner party, baby), reminding them of items that they might otherwise forget. By reminding customers of items they might otherwise forget, Peapod increases incremental sales, adding to profitability. Peapod offers on-line recipes that are educational and promote new item sales.

Enter the snacks aisle and you'll find cookies. What kind? How about chocolate chip? Click on that and get a variety of brands. They're listed alphabetically, but click again and they're listed by price and price-per-ounce. Concerned about calories? That information is there, too. Select the one you want and it goes into your virtual shopping cart.

Many new consumers may be reluctant to let someone else choose their fresh fish or strawberries, but the personal shoppers choose only the freshest and best-looking items. "Members have an option to make comments on the computer screen, instructing shoppers, for example, to buy only green bananas or to substitute sirloin if T-bone steak isn't available," says Parkinson. If the produce, meat or deli item is not up to Peapod's standards, the shopper does not fulfill the request and explains why. Groceries are delivered in temperature-controlled coolers. Peapod guarantees each order they deliver, and members can reject any items that aren't satisfactory.

Peapod's monthly membership fee varies by market and in 1997 ranged from $4.95 to $6.95. It includes three hours of dial-up shopping and free e-mail. After three hours, customers pay $2.95 an hour. Customers who get their e-mail elsewhere are unlikely to incur additional charges. Peapod charges a per-order fee, that again varies by market, ranging from $1.95 to $6.95, plus five percent or less of the total order as a delivery fee. Orders are delivered to the doorstep in three hours. Specifying a half-hour time frame—such as between 3:00 and 3:30 p.m.—costs an extra five dollars. If a profit can be made on delivering a $10 pizza to your door within 30 minutes, why can't a profit be made on a weekly $120 grocery order for a total of $6,000 a year?

> We get the behavior we tolerate.[5]
>
> Maurice Mascarenas, consultant

Peapod's clients are predominantly women (77 percent), a remarkable number given that only one-third of on-line users are women. Over 60 percent are professionals in dual-income families and 56 percent have children under 18.

Increase Margin by Preventing Defection of Best Customers

Companies can increase customer retention and prevent customer defection by allowing the customer to build equity with their products or services over time. Microsoft *Word's* auto-correct feature is a case in point. I frequently type "beleive" instead of the proper spelling "believe." When I run the spellchecker, I can define a misspelled word to be corrected automatically. Every time I mistype the word in the future, the software will automatically correct it. The more words that I define to be automatically corrected, the less spelling I have to correct in future. The feature also allows me to create short-hand phrases. For instance, I can define "wrt" as "with respect to" or "MS" as "Microsoft" or "org" as "organization." Over the course of a year I will likely work on my word processor 1,000 hours. I am unlikely to switch to another word processor because I have built hours of equity in the product.

Similarly, airlines encourage customers to enroll in their frequent flier program to build equity. When a customer flies a certain minimum number of miles, they achieve a frequent flier status, giving them special benefits, speedy check-in at the first-class counter, use of special airport lounges with free drinks and upgrades from economy to first class.

How much does it cost the airlines to treat frequent fliers preferentially? What is the cost of allowing them to use the first-class check-in line? Or the airport lounges? Or to upgrade to first class when seats are available? These are all low cost to the airline, but have tremendous perceived value to the customer. Frequent fliers get addicted to the preferential service and are often unwilling to switch airlines for fear of losing it! For this reason, some travelers will even take a non-direct flight with "their" airline, rather than take a direct flight with a competitor.

Allowing customers to build equity with your product or service means that the more they use it, the harder it will be for a competitor to woo them away.

Federal Express: A Case Study in Customer Service

Federal Express requires every executive to work on the front line serving customers for two weeks each year. Executives gain firsthand experience and quickly discover any systemic problems that prevent front-line staff from providing exceptional customer service. This maintains a tight information loop between executives and the front line. Executives hear customer complaints and frustrations directly. This simple policy helps to orient the whole organization to the customer. Executive time is at a premium. An executive spending two weeks on the front line sends a clear message throughout the organization: customer service is essential. This policy is leadership by example.

Mathematical Measurement of Performance

At Federal Express, the culture and the processes are all built on a huge investment in information technology (IT). The company measures almost everything that affects its business, and ultimately, the bottom line: service quality, customer satisfaction, employee satisfaction, employee performance and management performance. FedEx's extensive use of IT enables these performance measures and helps to create an environment of continuous improvement. Underlying the measurement, logistics systems and IT investment is the FedEx People-Service-Profit philosophy that dictates how the systems will be developed and implemented. This heavy IT investment has been one of the key reasons for FedEx's staggering growth. The company was founded in 1973 and as of 1996 employed 124,000 people, moving 2.5 million packages a day to and from destinations in more than 211 countries. With 563 aircraft, Federal Express has the world's largest cargo fleet.

"Hard" Management

When I think of Federal Express' management, the word that consistently comes to mind is "hard" because it always knows what is going on. The company is able to confront problems and issues because it has gathered the necessary information. Logistics is the key to running a successful courier company. On a typical day, 2.5 million packages travel through the system, so the possibilities for errors are staggering. Federal Express' goal is for 100 percent accuracy, quality and customer satisfaction on all transactions. Nothing short of the 100 percent goal is acceptable.

Most people wonder why any company would be so relentless in its pursuit of 100 percent accuracy, quality and customer satisfaction. What is wrong with 98 percent? When FedEx ships a package, many different employees handle it as it moves from its pick-up point to its destination. If 10 employees handled a package during its trip and each one performs his or her job to 98 percent accuracy before passing it off to the next person, what is the net effect?

$$98\% \times 98\% \times 98\% \times 98\% \times 98\% \times 98\% \times 98\% \times 98\% \times 98\% \times 98\% = \mathbf{82\%}$$

The cumulative effect is only 82 percent accuracy! This is unacceptable in terms of quality and resulting customer satisfaction. If 20 employees handle the package and each performs his or her job to 98 percent accuracy, the cumulative effect is a product with only 67 percent accuracy!

$$98\% \times 98\% \times 98\% \times 98\% \times 98\% \times 98\% \times 98\% \times 98\% \times 98\% \times 98\% \times$$

$$98\% \times 98\% \times 98\% \times 98\% \times 98\% \times 98\% \times 98\% \times 98\% \times 98\% \times 98\% = \mathbf{67\%}$$

Only 100 percent is acceptable.

Of the 2.5 million packages handled daily, more than 99 percent reach their destination on time, undamaged and with the right paperwork. The remaining one percent represents 25,000 potentially unhappy customers. Not all customers with a late package are unhappy but, if all 25,000 are unhappy, the company will likely hear from fewer than 7,500. How do you design a logistics system that supports 100 percent accuracy? How can a company move closer to the virtually unattainable goal of 100 percent accuracy?

Federal Express instituted the Service Quality Indicator (SQI) in 1988 with a goal of reducing the service and quality failure by 90 percent by 1993. The company identified points of service and quality failure from the customer's viewpoint and then weighed each item according to the level of dissatisfaction it caused customers.

When a FedEx courier picks up a package, he or she scans the bar code on the waybill with a "supertracker." When the courier returns to the van and puts the supertracker in its holster, the information is downloaded from the hand-held unit and transmitted, by radio, to a FedEx station. From the station, the information is relayed to the central computer system, which tracks packages from pick-up to delivery.

A package is scanned an average of seven times between pick-up and its final destination. So when it is delivered and given its final scan, the company knows what time it was delivered and whether it met its committed delivery time. If the package was scheduled for 10:30 a.m. delivery, but the courier dropped it off at 10:32, that would register a failure of one point in the SQI index as a Right Day/Late Delivery. If the customer requested an invoice adjustment, that would add another failure point. A single package could add many points to the SQI: if it was initially a missed pick-up (10 points), if the package was not delivered on time so the customer called to ask for a trace (1 point), if the call was disconnected (1 point), or if the package was delivered on the wrong day (5 points) and with water damage (10 points). This one package could have potentially added 27 failure points to the SQI.

When Federal Express introduced the SQI in 1988, daily failures accounted for 150,000 points. The company announced its goal of reducing the SQI by 90 percent in five years. During the first year, actual service failures decreased 11 percent despite the fact that package volumes grew by 20 percent.

FedEx Service Failure Ratings

Item	SQI
right day late	1
wrong day late	5
late pick-up stops	3
traces	3
complaints reopened	3
damaged packages	10
lost packages	10
invoice adjustments required	1
missing proof of deliveries	1

The graph below highlights the relationship between the SQI and package volumes. While the number of packages almost tripled between 1987 and 1995, the SQI failures fell:

Service Quality Index

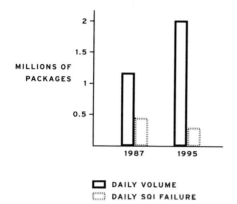

DAILY VOLUME
DAILY SQI FAILURE

Proactive Measurement of Customer Satisfaction

Given that fewer than 20 percent of unhappy customers will ever call to let you know where, when or how your products or services are failing to meet their expectations, a toll-free phone number is not enough. Organizations must be proactive in getting customer feedback. Every quarter, FedEx randomly selects a new group of 2,100 customers to survey daily. During a 10-minute interview, customer satisfaction is gauged on 50 points of service on a scale of zero to 100 percent satisfaction. FedEx also conducts targeted customer satisfaction studies around such specific procedures as Saturday delivery and invoice adjustment. The company also solicits feedback via comment cards at all FedEx service centers. FedEx annually surveys its 34,000 largest customers, whom the company equips with *PowerShip* shipping and billing computer systems. These users account for half the company's total package volume.

Balancing Qualitative and Quantitative Customer Feedback

Customer surveys provide good quantitative data, allowing the organization to benchmark itself against competitors and the best businesses in other industries. Quantitative information is "left brain" (mathematical, linear, logical); it doesn't give any feedback on feelings or emotions. While a statistically significant survey such as FedEx's survey of 2,100 randomly chosen customers provides good feedback, it doesn't answer the question, "Why are customers satisfied or dissatisfied?" That is where qualitative information comes in, generally through the use of focus groups.

Focus groups provide executives with insight about how their customers relate to the company's products and services. Focus groups also allow researchers to explore customer ideas. They are "right brain" (emotional, intuitive, holistic). The research for *The 100 Best Companies to Work For in Canada* was to a large extent based on focus groups conducted with the employees of companies under consideration.

Companies focused on customer and employee satisfaction need to balance quantitative and qualitative research. Both are important. For instance, the Survey Feedback Action (SFA) program at Federal Express asks all employees to rate their managers and work environment. The quantitative data will show whether employees are unhappy in a particular department. Once the problem is identified, how can it be solved? Qualitative information gives the clues. A non-threatening discussion with employees led by trained facilitators will uncover the reasons for the discontent. Both quantitative and qualitative research methods are necessary to create understanding: quantitative research gives you the hard facts and numbers, qualitative gets at the reasons behind customer or employee attitudes and preferences.

The researchers need to pit points of customer satisfaction against one another to create a hierarchy of needs. If the organization had only one additional dollar to spend per customer, what investment would yield the greatest delight?

Some interesting research was done by a jet manufacturer a number of years ago. Executives who bought corporate jets were asked a series of questions, "Would you like mahogany paneling in the interior?" *Yes.* "Would you like wider seats?" *Yes.* "Would you like built-in cellular phones?" *Yes.* "Would you like a shower in the plane?" *Yes.*

Then, when the executives were asked, "Would you be willing to pay an extra $250,000 for these added features?" their tune changed. *No way*, they said. When asked what features really mattered, their answer was, "Skip all the amenities and just make the planes as fast as possible and with the longest range." Executives who buy these jets spend a lot of time traveling. What they want is to spend less time in the air. Therefore, range is important because refueling requires landing and creates the potential for long delays. So all engineering efforts were invested in increasing the range and speed. Not surprisingly, these jets have sold extremely well.

There Is More Than One Customer
Surveys show that people born before 1950 have been slow to use ATMs. These people may not be comfortable using computers. They often fear the technology because it wasn't user friendly. By contrast, people born after 1950 are rushed for time and prefer ATMs. But rather than blame older people for not using new technology, developers have to always work to make their products and services easier to use.

There is a great example of this in my neighborhood. One of the local banks has a branch located right under a seniors' residence. Seniors like human contact. In fact, they like line-ups because they can chat with other people in the line. It's a social outing. The branch only recently installed an ATM. But half a block away in a 24-hour drug store, the same bank has had an ATM for years. Baby boomers like late-night shopping. They are so pressed for time with their careers and looking after the kids that they shop based on convenience, location and speed of getting in and out of the store. If they can get cash where they buy toothpaste, they feel pleased. So within the same block the bank's marketing strategy addresses the needs of two completely different customer markets.

Organizations have more than one customer in another way. I remember a fascinating presentation by the president of a chocolate-bar manufacturer. His company's products were sold in convenience stores. So there were two customers with different needs — the chocolate-bar buyer and the convenience-store owner.

If you conduct street interviews, you'll find that no one eats chocolate bars. "No. Not me. I run five miles a day. I only eat alfalfa sprouts and granola. Chocolate bars never cross these lips. Nope. Never." If marketers could only find the one person in North America who is eating all the chocolate bars, it would be a major coup! It's interesting to note that customers will sometimes not tell us what they really feel or do because it's not fashionable, polite or politically correct.

The end customer wants a great-tasting product at a good price. The store owner is concerned about delivery times, delivery frequency, storage, spoilage in summer heat, attractive packaging, credit terms, display racks and whether the product is in high demand.

The food company studied the convenience-store owner's needs, force-ranking 40 separate needs. This analysis is essential because corporate resources are scarce and becoming scarcer, and executives want to make the most effective use of them. If the food company has $400,000 to spend, what would make the greatest impact? Doing more product testing with a view to changing the taste of the product? Redesigning the packaging to make it more attractive to the end customer? From the convenience-store owner's perspective, what would have the greatest impact? Better credit terms, free display racks or $400,000 of television advertising? After extensive research, the company found that redesigning the shipping carton for the candy bars so that it doubled as a marketing display when cut open, made the greatest difference to increasing sales. As a result, the company pushed two of its chocolate bars into the highly competitive top-20 bar category.

This significantly increased market share, as only the top 20 bars are carried in every store in the country.

Find out who your customers are, identify their needs and then tailor your services to them.

Dell Computers: A Case Study

Excellence in customer service must be defined from the customer's point of view. The truth is that many organizations have designed policies and practices from the company's point of view, policies that make it easy for the accounting department, the inventory department or the sales reps. But in a successful business, the focus must be the customer's point of view; other interests should be subordinate to that.

Dell Computers has been rated number one in terms of customer satisfaction in numerous independent computer surveys. Why have Dell's sales grown exponentially?

Dealing directly with customers allowed Dell to not only sell a higher-value product at a lower price than its competitors because of lower overheads, but it also allowed Dell to enter into a direct relationship with its customers, gaining a better understanding of their point of view and needs.

Founded in 1984, it took Dell just 13 years to become a $7.8-billion Fortune 500 company.

The secret of Dell's exponential growth is simple: listen to and understand your customers, then satisfy their needs, always exceeding their expectations. If customers can't find service or value as good as yours, they will keep coming back. The key to Dell's growth has been retention of customers.

Dell Sales

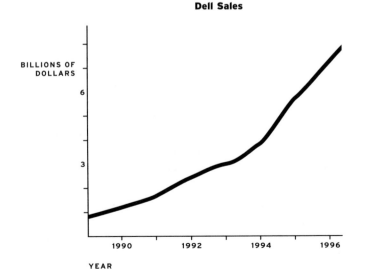

Techno-typing

Dell "techno-types" its customers into seven broad categories. It's a basic approach of segmenting the market.

Dell's research in 1993[6] found that 55 percent of North Americans were technophobic to some degree—32 percent of all adults were intimidated by computers and worried about damaging a PC if they used it without assistance. Most adults found the new technology difficult to understand (51 percent) and the rapid rate of change in technology confusing (58 percent).

Techno-typing recognizes that a "one size fits all" strategy doesn't work because large segments of the population have radically different primary needs. Each segment will create a different hierarchy of needs. Dell designs products to meet the force-ranked needs of each segment and then targets markets to each segment.

First is the Techno-Wizard. These are the computer "techies" who live on the "bleeding edge." They want the latest and greatest—machines that scream, the fastest hard disks, the fastest video graphics, the most RAM. These are the early users of technology. They are not price sensitive. They do, however, want good value and demand very little support.

Then there is the Techno-Teamer. This second type is typically an information systems professional, responsible for a LAN (local area network) or WAN (wide area network). They want high-quality, net-work-ready systems. What such types fear most is network failure because every hour the system is down, the company may lose tens of thousands of dollars. Reliability, service and system recovery speed are the Techno-Teamer's main concerns. Even better than recovering from failure is anticipating it in the first place. This group wants diagnostic tools to anticipate when the network is likely to fail.

Prevention strategies require a focus on reliability of the hardware and duplication (i.e., two power supplies, two sets of hard disks, two sets of CPUs), so that if one set goes down, the system itself doesn't go down. This is obvious. For non-critical computers that don't have duplicate parts, this group wants diagnostic software that monitors the LAN and pre-emptively warns of impending failure, so that spare parts can be ordered and switched in before failure occurs.

Then there is the Techno-Traveler. This third type spends a lot of time on airplanes, so the primary concern is notebook battery life. Dell has developed a series of notebooks to satisfy this group.

The Techno-Plug-and-Play group wants the computer to work the moment it is taken out of the box. No loading software, no configuring the modem or solving conflicts, just unpack the computer, plug it in and away we go. This group also wants service. When something goes wrong, this group wants someone on the other end of a 1-800 number to walk them through an easy solution.

The other market segments identified by Dell were Techno-Critical (primary concern is the network being down), Techno-Boomer (doesn't want to make a wrong buying decision) and Techno-Phobe (avoids technology whenever possible).

Dell's customer service includes setting up the network so the LAN administrator doesn't spend the day unpacking boxes, setting up systems and configuring the addresses of each computer. For an extra fee, Dell will send a technician out for a full day to set up the entire system and orient the new computer user(s).

Service is one of the key areas that differentiates Dell from many competitors. Dell offers lifetime, unlimited, toll-free 24-hour, seven-days-a-week, 365-days-a-year telephone support with a guaranteed five-minute response time. There's also a 30-day money-back guarantee on all systems and a full year of next-business-day, on-site service for some systems.

Within the broad range of each segment, Dell is able to further customize orders according to individual needs. Techno-typing helps to zero in on a customer's expectations and also gives marketers the insights they need to develop mass advertising/marketing programs aimed at customers and potential customers in each segment.

In numerous independent surveys of the computer industry, Dell has been named best at providing service (including twice winning the J.D. Power award for customer service). In 1994, the company had a rude awakening when Hewlett Packard was awarded the top honor, which goes to show that even the best companies dare not become complacent. Being the best and remaining the best requires relentless work to improve the company's product and service offerings.

The rise of Dell computers is an excellent example of the rise of the private label. IBM created the PC market. Compaq came along and offered a better product at a lower price and created the clone market by using the same off-the-shelf components as IBM but branding the PC under Compaq's name. Dell is another example of a private-label manufacturer that rose to such prominence it became a brand. When the components of the underlying computer are identical, consumers look for better value. When all else is the same, price matters most. That is why innovation is so essential. Unless a company can differentiate itself and offer higher-value goods and services in key areas that customers value most, the company will have to compete on price. Techno-typing, or market segmenting, highlights how different customers have different hierarchies of needs. Some place service first, others reliability, ease of use or price. Dell has successfully positioned its products to meet broad techno-type categories and then has customized its products within each segment.

Creating an "Unimaginable" Future

Customer satisfaction information systems are essential, but relying solely on customers to tell you what they want is not always effective. Here is an example: German companies were once the pre-eminent camera makers. German cameras were simply the best. Imagine conducting focus groups with owners of German cameras in 1980 and asking participants, "What can we improve? What don't you like about your camera?" The owners would say: "We love everything. There's nothing you can improve. You make the best cameras in the world."

But the customers couldn't predict the invention of auto-wind cameras that allowed photographers to shoot a whole roll of film in a minute simply by holding down the shutter release, or auto-focus cameras that allowed people with no experience to shoot professional-looking pictures. Japanese firms thought of these added features and the resulting market-share loss for the German companies is history.

Nissan Motor Cars of Japan has attacked the problem of sleepy drivers with an electronic system that warns of drowsiness. A video camera mounted on the car's instrument panel takes photographs of the driver's face and a processor analyzes the length and frequency of eye blinks, which correlate to alertness. Too many long blinks and the processor knows the driver is falling asleep, triggering an electronic beep, while a disembodied female voice implores, "Please take a rest." If the driver ignores the warning, continues driving and falls asleep, the car shoots a blast of lemon-scented methanol at the driver's nose and screams at him to pull over. Nissan hopes to have the product in car models by the year 2000.[7]

How many customers do you think are demanding such a feature? Companies can't rely only on customer research to understand customer needs because customers don't always know what they want or what is possible.

Customer needs exist before their discovery, just as the principles for flight existed in nature before we uncovered them. The possibility of the transistor existed before scientists "invented" it. All our needs exist. It's up to smart individuals and companies to uncover them.

Most people have a hard time articulating what they want. In fact, customer opinions can be deceiving, sometimes suggesting the opposite of what they really want. In a focus group on credit cards, participants are asked which they would prefer to have: a card with a low interest rate or one with all sorts of benefits (insurance, frequent flier air miles or 30-day purchase/return guarantees) and a high interest rate. Participants will often answer that they would rather have the feature-less card with the low interest rate. But at the end of the focus group, offer them a card as a reward for participating in the group, and most will choose the card with special features. So what consumers say can be inconsistent with what they actually do. Again, researchers don't always get accurate or truthful answers from consumers, who will often give politically correct answers when what they truly feel is embarrass-ing to admit. Successful organizations create systems and structures that help uncover customers' unarticulated or hidden needs.

So how can organizations uncover customers' unarticulated needs? Often, customers can't articulate what they want, but can articulate what upsets them. For instance, if I was in a focus group for a car com-pany, the researcher would likely ask me what I do and don't like about existing cars, but this information will only help a car company refine existing features. How can a company come up with completely new features, products or services?

The researcher might ask me what upsetting experiences I have had while driving, making it clear that the answers don't have to be tied to the company's cars but just with driving in general. In response, I relate an actual incident on a six-lane highway (three lanes each way). A truck in the far outer lane and a car on the far inner lane both moved into the center lane at the same time, colliding. Both drivers had prob-ably checked their rearview mirrors, but neither had obviously looked opposite them.

Upon colliding, the car swerved back to the inner lane and then hit the guardrail. It bounced back into the center lane where it hit the truck again and did a complete 360 and spun out of control back into the guardrail. The truck had swerved initially and then, when hit by the car again, went careening into the ditch. All this happened only 100 yards in front of me at 60 miles per hour. I watched in horror as the whole scene played out in slow motion. If I had been 50 yards ahead of where I was when it happened, I would have been involved. Ever since, I have had a terrible fear of changing lanes, particularly into the center lane of a three-lane highway.

What I am really saying to the researcher is that I would like the car company to develop an infrared or sonar-based sensor on the side of my car that can warn me when I am about to hit another car in my blind spot. Consumers may not be able to articulate what they want (positive), but they can often articulate what upsets them (negative).

Therefore, organizations must first work to uncover what upsets customers and then create solutions to these problems in the form of new features, products or services.

Visa's Neural Network

A neural network is a computer program that identifies patterns. The neural network can't explain why a particular pattern occurs, it only identifies that the pattern exists. Visa has used neural nets to cut fraudulent credit-card transactions by up to 90 percent in some jurisdictions.

A neural network is a program that "learns" by recognizing patterns. If a jewelry shop in Iowa requests authorization for a $5,000 purchase on my card, the computer looks at my pattern of spending and asks, "Has Jim ever been in Iowa?" *No.* "Has he ever purchased jewelry?" *No.* "Has he ever bought anything worth $5,000 using his card?" *No.* The neural net identifies that this requested transaction is outside of my usual purchasing pattern, predicts that it is a fraudulent transaction and requests that the store clerk get photo identification. If it's a thief, he runs out of the store at this point. If I am buying an engagement ring for my fiancée in Iowa, I provide the required identification.

After one seminar a participant told me that his gas card had been stolen, but that he really didn't worry about it too much. After all, how much gas can a thief steal? At the end of the day he reported it stolen and discovered that the thief had run up a $2,000 balance, going from gas station to gas station buying cartons of cigarettes! Here is a perfect case for a neural network to identify a pattern. Has this customer ever bought cigarettes? No. Well, then why is he buying 100 cartons today? It's probably fraud.

Neural nets can be used to identify overall patterns of behavior in groups of people. In analyzing stolen credit cards, neural nets came to recognize the pattern that thieves often place a long-distance phone call before going on a spending spree. Throughout the first day that the card is stolen, thieves continue making long-distance calls on the credit card before going back into stores to make more fraudulent purchases. There's a definite pattern: call, purchase, call, purchase. Today, when the neural network sees this pattern, it predicts that the transactions are fraudulent, even if the card has not yet been reported stolen.

It takes human ingenuity to find meaning in the pattern; in other words, to understand why the pattern occurs. How do thieves think? A thief wants to ensure that the credit card hasn't been reported stolen, so a long-distance call is placed to a randomly selected number. If a call is declined, the thief knows the card has been reported stolen and throws it out. The criminal hasn't risked being identified by a store clerk. If the call goes through, his spending spree begins. The thief makes more phone calls throughout the day, checking the integrity of the card.

Here's another application: car buyers in a certain age group, income bracket and geographical area buy a new car every four years, on average. After individuals in this target group buy a new home and take out a $150,000 mortgage, their behavior will change. Over time, a neural net would show that they will buy a new car every eight years as they shift priorities to pay off their mortgage. With this knowledge, a bank could save thousands of dollars in marketing costs by changing its direct marketing programs for cars loans from a four-year to an eight-year cycle for new homeowners.

Many organizations believe that in a recession, consumers are only price sensitive. In fact, they are value sensitive. The best goods and services with the highest value/price ratio almost always win. Certainly, price is one factor that determines customer satisfaction, especially in tough economic times, but price is not always the most important factor.

Your doctor has told you that you will die unless you have triple bypass heart surgery within a month. You find a student just out of medical school desperate for the experience, willing to perform the surgery for 50 bucks. Will you go for it?

Your only other choice in the market is a highly competent surgeon with years of experience who charges $10,000. Which of the two surgeons will you choose? How price sensitive are you?

What is your hierarchy of needs? 1) The competence of a surgeon with an excellent record of patient recovery. 2) Price. In fact, price is not really a consideration. You are completely price insensitive. You are willing to pay one surgeon 200 times more than the other, a 20,000 percent jump!

This reveals a simple principle: find your customers' pain, solve it and they become price insensitive. Similarly, find their delight and satisfy it (remember the chocolate chip cookie story).

A seminar participant once yelled, "But if the purchasing department was selecting the surgeon, they would have chosen the $50 one!" Systems create misalignment within organizations. If the purchasing manager is rewarded based on the lowest up-front cost, don't be surprised that the cheapest surgeon is hired. Organizations need to optimize the whole, not just one department. Ultimately, it is systems (in this case the compensation system) and structures that govern performance.

You do further research and find a second, equally competent surgeon. The surgeon can operate in three months for $2,000 or you can keep your appointment this month for $10,000. Remember, you will die if you don't have the surgery this month. How price sensitive are you?

The hierarchy of concerns has changed. It is now 1) scheduling of the operation; 2) competence of the surgeon; 3) price. It is interesting to note how the hierarchy of needs is fluid. As more information becomes available in the market to customers, their hierarchy of needs changes. Therefore, organizations need to constantly work to understand how the market is changing and how customers' needs are shifting.

The hierarchy of needs among customers is constantly changing as they age and the world around them changes. A new breed of consumer is emerging, one who is wiser and better informed than ever before. In order to thrive in our rapidly changing world, organizations must work even harder to identify the underlying needs and motivations of their target markets.

Baby boomers are under intense pressure. In addition to both partners working, they are often balancing the demands of both young children and aging parents. Quality and service often mean more to them than the best price. To this group, quality has become more important than quantity. When boomers were in their university years they were interested in quantity—buying beer by the case. But now the concern has shifted to quality. Aging boomers are likely to drink only one beer, but a premium brand, likely an import or micro-brewery specialty beer. So the mass-market breweries are facing new competition. Therefore, the challenge for many companies is to shift from a quantity to a quality perspective.

Customers make decisions based on a complex set of factors that they may be unable to articulate. Good market research uncovers hidden attitudes and needs, giving companies opportunities to delight their customers in totally new ways. The goal is to get inside customers' minds, to see and experience goods and services as customers do.

When asked, "What would excite you as a credit-card owner?" during a 1985 focus group, participants would not have answered, "Give me a frequent flier point for every dollar spent on the card."

American Airlines approached American Express in 1985 with a proposal to co-brand a credit card. Amex rejected the offer. American turned to City Bank. City Bank executives were so excited about the concept that to ensure they were first to market, they launched the card without holding focus groups to test customer response. Aimed at upscale personal and business travelers, the City Bank American AAdvantage card was introduced in 1986.

Response to the card was overwhelming. Consumers began charging items to the card that they would otherwise have paid for by cash, check or charged to another card. As a result, City Bank's AAdvantage card gained significant market share. It was the first major-scale co-branded card and was a phenomenal success, exceeding all expectations.

With the obvious success of the concept, every other airline eventually followed suit. But in 1997, City Bank's AAdvantage card still enjoys 34 percent of the market. The second-place card—Amex's Delta card trails far behind at 16 percent.[8]

American Express eventually recognized the error of its decision and co-branded one of its cards with Delta. The Delta card has been gaining market share, rising from number three in 1995 to number two in 1997. So it is important to recognize and correct mistakes. But this case study highlights the importance of being first to market and creating the standard by which all competitors will be judged. Despite Amex's entry into the market, AAdvantage's market share is still more than double Amex's.

Airline cardholders are significantly more affluent, with average home incomes of $71,000 a year as opposed to $47,000 for average classic-card households.[9] In 1997, airline cardholders charge $18,000 a year[10] to their cards while the average classic cardholder charged just over $2,000 a year and average gold cardholders spend just under $4,000 a year.[11] Almost six percent of U.S. cardholders carry at least one airline credit card—for a total of 10 million cards.[12]

These are the only cards in the market that warrant a significant annual fee and are the standard by which all other cards are measured.

Between 1992 and 1997, the annual growth rate in credit card usage in Canada has ranged between 20.6 and 43.5 percent![13] Frequent flier cards have driven most of this growth. Executives are charging expenditures to their personal cards that they never charged in the past and then are being reimbursed by their companies.

Today, $5 billion worth of expenditures are billed to the CIBC (Canadian Imperial Bank of Commerce) Aerogold card every year. For every dollar you spend using the credit card, you receive one frequent flier point with Air Canada's frequent flier Aeroplan. Aerogold cardholders spend $20,000 a year on their cards. CIBC's strategy has literally skimmed the cream off the high end of the Canadian credit-card market. The card has also been a major win for Air Canada.

You miss 100 percent of the shots you never take.
Wayne Gretzky, hockey player

"Lateral thinking," a phrase coined by Edward de Bono, one of the world's leading thinkers on innovation and creativity, is a process to help individuals, teams and organizations be more creative. Our eyesight is perfect in hindsight. But very rarely can we see into the future with accuracy. In that sense we are all blind with respect to the future.

Our brains have right and left hemispheres. The left is linear, logical and hosts our language ability. The right brain is intuitive, holistic and emotional. Western management has come to rely predominantly on left-brain processes (facts, figures, proof). However, how could an individual "prove" the telephone would be a revolutionary invention before its introduction? How could anyone "prove" that credit cards tied to frequent flier points would radically increase credit-card usage before their invention? The ability to think laterally will increasingly determine which companies thrive. We have been educated and rewarded for left-brain thinking. Right-brain thinking is divergent, exploring solutions and possibilities.

Similarly, cross-marketing will become increasingly important. Who developed American Express's front-of-the-line service? The slogan "Membership has its privileges" finds practical expression in this service. American Express cardholders get first choice for the premieres of top musicals in cities across North America, and the program has been a major hit! It's a win-win situation for Amex and the theaters.

Now, what would really motivate the under-30 crowd to get credit cards? Front-of-the-line service for rock concerts?

Creating a Future not Even Customers Can Predict
How can companies create a future when customers have trouble telling us what they want? In *Competing for the Future*, Gary Hamel and C.K. Prahalad compare applied creativity to baseball:

> The number of runs that a batter actually scores is a product of hit rate (batting average) multiplied by the number of times at bat. A player who bats 1.000,[14] but who only goes to the plate half a dozen times a season will be much less valuable to the team than a player who bats a modest .250 but gets to the plate 300 or 400 times in a year. Similarly, a company may be able to boast about its high batting average in new product introductions, but if that average is the result of a cautious, go-slow approach to creating new markets, the company may well capture less of the future than scrappier rivals with inferior batting averages but more times at bat.[15]

It is interesting to note from baseball history that Babe Ruth had the most number of home runs in his time, but he also had the most strike-outs. Creating new value for the customer requires many times at bat trying to anticipate what customers want—with many small tests—never betting the whole business on just one strategy.

Francis Vincent, former commissioner of major league baseball, said:

> Baseball teaches us, or has taught most of us, how to deal with failure. We learn at a very young age that failure is the norm in baseball and precisely because we have failed, we hold in high regard those who fail less often—those who hit safely in one out of three chances and become star players. I also find it fascinating that baseball, alone in sport, considers errors to be part of the game, part of its rigorous truth.[16]

Delighting Customers

What is the "wow" factor in your product? Use direct marketing and test, test, test. Try different offers, the same offer with different price points, and mail the same offer to different mailing lists. American Express will send 100,000 pieces of direct mail to a target audience, offering 1,000 frequent flier points for agreeing to get a second card for a spouse. Then it measures the response rate. The marketers will follow with a second mailing to another 100,000 cardholders with the same demographic background and offer 1,500 points, and measure the response again. Then they perform a cost-benefit analysis and see which is the better route.

Given that companies can buy one frequent flier point for less than a cent, 1,500 points cost less than $15. If a $15 premium generates the sale of a $60 secondary card, it's an effective incentive. Who would have thought of it 10 years ago? Look at how much business is now being generated through using points as incentive premiums!

Everyone Needs Customer Focus

In today's market, consumers are better informed and have greater freedom of choice. In the airline industry, I can buy tickets from a travel agent, directly from the airline, by phone or the Internet.

Jan Carlzon, former president of SAS airlines, a consortium of the national airlines of Denmark, Norway and Sweden, states in *Moments of Truth*:

Last year, each of our 10 million customers came into contact with approximately five SAS employees and this contact lasted an average of 15 seconds at a time. Thus SAS is "created" 50 million times a year, 15 seconds at a time. These 50 million "moments of truth" ultimately determine whether SAS will succeed or fail as a company. They are the moments when we must prove to our customers that SAS is their best alternative.

If we are truly dedicated to orienting our company toward each customer's individual needs, then we cannot rely on rule books and instructions from distant corporate offices. We have to place responsibility for ideas, decisions, and actions with the people who are SAS during those 15 seconds, ticket agents, flight attendants, baggage handlers and all the other front-line employees. If they have to go up the organizational chain of command for a decision on an individual problem, those 15 golden seconds will elapse without a response and we will have lost an opportunity to earn a loyal customer.[17]

How will employees act in that moment of truth? There is no time to check with a manager or get authorizations from three people. Employees must fully understand the value of customer service and then decide how to best meet the individual customer's needs.

Who Is the Most Important Person in Your Organization?

The president of a large oil and gas company asks, "Who is the most important person in this organization?" He always answers his own question saying, "The person who answers the phone!"

Providing good customer service is the corporate mission and it starts with answering the phone on the first ring.

But it's not good enough just to set goals; the entire organization must be oriented to support them. Who was on the front cover of the company newsletter after the telephone goal was instituted? The employee who answered the phone 85 percent of the time on the first ring (compared with 65 percent for the company overall).

The mission of customer responsiveness was also defined as getting back to customers within 5 minutes of a phone query and within 24 hours of written queries. Once that became the corporate goal, it forced the elimination of unnecessary bureaucracy. If an agent in the credit-card adjustment department was to call the customer back within five minutes, the company had to eliminate multiple approvals from supervisors and managers. Employees openly questioned policies and practices. Were certain meetings necessary? Were certain procedures necessary? Which approvals were unnecessary? Where should decisions be made? Authority had to be given to the front line to make decisions in order to satisfy the goal of answering customers' queries within five minutes.

The goal permeated the company. Internal departments, such as finance, service their internal clients by answering the phone on the first ring, responding to calls in less than five minutes and replying in writing in less than 24 hours so that the front-line people can fulfill their goals.

The people on the front line feel tremendously motivated when their true value to the organization is appreciated.

Treating employees as internal customers cannot guarantee high-quality customer service, but not doing so ensures that customer service will be performed without enthusiasm. If companies expect employees to "Greet each customer with a smile," they should first give employees something to smile about. At the very least, companies should ensure that internal systems are not increasing the difficulties of employees entrusted with the responsibility of delivering service.

Customer Service of the Future: Mass Customization

As Alvin Toffler points out in *The Third Wave*, production of goods in the Middle Ages was by artisans. When you wanted a shirt, you went to the tailor who measured you and produced your shirt. When industrialization came along, we entered the era of mass production, creating the need for standard sizes. Goods were mass produced.

Today we are poised to enter the era of mass customization. You can already go to some shoe stores where the sales associate passes a light wand over your foot that measures the contour of your sole. The scanner will pass the information to a computer in the back of the shop and three minutes later it spits out a custom-made orthotic insole. The sales rep then takes a mass-produced shoe in your size and the style you like, and slips in the insole. It is the most comfortable shoe you have ever worn. Technology enables us to return to the days of custom crafting. It is enabling the emergence of mass customization. One-to-one customer relationships are hot among leading companies. Levi Strauss' "personal pair" of custom-cut jeans (Chapter 7) is another example.

From Mass Customization to Customer Ownership

In the fourth wave, knowledge is a commodity. Self-reflection and self-correction are required to take us to a higher plane. To get a 10,000-foot view of the situation I would ask, "How do we add significant new value for customers? How do we create top-of-mind position with customers? How do we create customer insistence?" Many credit-card companies provide a toll-free number for you to call to cancel your card if you lose your wallet. If you call before a thief uses the card, you are not responsible for the charges. But most people have quite a few credit cards in their wallet, perhaps a corporate American Express as well as a personal Visa and MasterCard in addition to gas cards, department store cards, debit cards and ATM access cards.

One day in the middle of the mall you start panicking because you realize that your wallet is missing. You don't remember which cards you had, let alone all the toll-free numbers you need to cancel them.

How can a credit-card company such as Visa gain mind share such that when a customer thinks "credit card," the first company that comes to mind is Visa? How could Visa create such new value for its customers that whenever they had a problem with any credit card they would call Visa? And begin to treat Visa as though it were the first point of contact for any credit-card information? How does a company build customer insistence — create a value that is so great that consumers insist on channeling their dealing through only one credit-card company? To achieve this, the thinking has to be at the meta level.

If Visa is striving for top-of-mind positioning, executives must think beyond their own credit card to all credit cards. What new value can be created for customers so that when they think of credit cards they immediately turn to Visa? Visa could record the numbers and expiry dates of all the credit cards their customers possess and provide a toll-free number, something like 1-800-I LOST-IT.

If customers lose their wallet, they call to report the loss or theft and automatically Visa would cancel all their credit cards. The customer service agent could then ask if they would like all their cards automatically renewed, or whether some of the competing cards could be canceled and the limit increased on their Visa. By serving customers in their time of need, Visa would become the single source to turn to for help with credit cards. At times of crisis this would also offer an opportunity to convert more of customers' business to Visa. The service would also give Visa insight into consumers' total credit pattern.

Once the service had gained a dominance in the market such that everyone called this service to cancel all their cards, Visa could begin charging other credit-card companies for the service it provides to them. At that point Visa would have to drop trying to switch credit away from the other cards to Visa.

Leaders must continually venture out of their comfort zone—the familiarity of doing things the old way—and work with teams in their organizations to develop new products and services. This will ensure higher-than-average margins in the long run, but will require many attempts and tolerance for a great number of failures in the short run. This tolerance for ambiguity, acceptance of failure and comfort with not knowing all the answers are at the core of the learning paradox.

To Summarize:

- It costs five times as much to develop a new customer as to keep one.

- Organizations need to perceive customer service as the customer does.

- Everyone in an organization must work from a customer focus viewpoint.

- Imagining a future of possibilities for the customer is the key to growth.

- Employees should be treated as internal customers.

Workshop Questions and Activities:

- How long ago were the current measures of performance in your organization set? Do they represent a balance of customer satisfaction variables (customer/market performance) and economic performance (internal/cost performance) variables? Do they relate your performance to the competition's performance?

- Who are your most important customers, and why? How many individual names of important customers can you name? Do the people making key decisions about the products and services that your organization offers have sufficient experience in using your products or services?

- Pretend that you are the customer of your organization or department. Describe improvements in the goods and services you provide. Use the quadrant graph on page 166 to rate your company's activities versus customer satisfaction.

- Rank all the goods and services you provide according to which ones will enhance satisfaction the most, which can be implemented fastest, at the least cost, with the least disruption. Create a quick implementation plan.

- What new product or service would keep you coming back to your company?

- Suggest on-line services that your company can provide to save customer time while increasing profit.

- At FedEx every executive spends two weeks each year working on the front line. This sensitizes them to how to change the systems and structures to increase customer delight. Using this principle, how could you foster continuous improvement in your organization? What front-line roles would you suggest your executive team try?

- If you were designing a neural network for your company, what information would you feed it?

- How often do your customers buy product? How do they spend their money? Create the demographic, psychographic and geographic profiles of your best customers.

- How could you make it easier for customers to do business with you?

- Design a cross-marketing program for your company. Explore ideas for strategic partnerships. What organization might your company form an alliance with to create more customer appeal? What would these partners bring to the partnership? How would they gain from the partnership?

- Design a new voice-mail system that is easy to use and lets customers get what they need immediately.

- How can you customize your product or service for customers?

Reflection:
- What is the key learning/insight for me in this chapter?

Action:
- What one action shall I take tomorrow to move learning into action? And over time repeat, to move action into habit?

CHAPTER 10

EDI or DIE: The New IT Paradigm

Radical advances in information technology (IT) are fundamentally changing the way companies do business. The scope and depth of the changes wrought by IT are profoundly revolutionary. Organizations that fail to make the transition to the new IT paradigm will cease to exist.

Technology: The Organization's Nervous System

Information technology has become the central nervous system of businesses. In the human body, the central nervous system feeds information to the brain in real time, allowing the body to react almost immediately to a dynamic, changing climate. If I stick my finger in a glass of ice water, I know immediately that the water is cold. My central nervous system connects everything in my body to everything else. It allows my right hand to coordinate with my left. It allows me to react appropriately.

Many companies do not work in "real time" because separate departments have separate systems that can't communicate with one another (Chapter 4). Up to 70 percent of computer-originated information exchanged between businesses is still re-entered into another computer! Electronic Data Interchange (EDI) allows information to flow seamlessly through and between organizations. Worldwide, $15 billion a year could be saved by using EDI, eliminating time-consuming data re-entry and consequently reducing the cost of errors.[1]

Wal-Mart: A Retailing Case Study

Of the top 100 U.S. retail discounters in business in 1976, only 24 remain in existence today! What happened to them? Wal-Mart! In 1983, Wal-Mart's 641 stores had sales of $4.8 billion. By 1993, Wal-Mart had grown to 2,000 stores with $55 billion in sales, becoming the largest retailer in the world. By 1997, Wal-Mart had grown to nearly 3,000 stores with collective sales of over $105 billion. And Wal-Mart still has lots of room for growth, as the company has captured only seven percent of the $1.4-trillion U.S. retailing market.[2]

In 1994, Wal-Mart entered the Canadian market, purchasing 120 Woolco stores. By 1997, the company had become the largest discount retailer in Canada. Some industry researchers estimate that by 2003, just nine years after the acquisition, Wal-Mart will have sales of C$7.5 billion, making it the largest retailer in Canada. Wal-Mart's entry spells a real shake-up for Canadian retailing.

Studies show that when Wal-Mart comes to town, sales for certain retail sectors decline significantly. Losses in hardware, jewelry, variety, shoes and discount sectors can run as high as 30 percent. How can retailers compete against the Wal-Mart onslaught? To find out, we must explore Wal-Mart's philosophy, systems and structures.

Wal-Mart works to eliminate overhead to be able to offer to customers the lowest possible prices. Wal-Mart maintains the lowest prices on 600 items that are top-of-mind items with consumers. Wal-Mart's strategic use of information technology allows it to achieve these objectives.

"Traiting"

In business today data warehousing and data mining are buzz words. But these hot topics have little relevance unless I can understand how databases allow companies to more accurately predict what customers want.

Information technology allows Wal-Mart to "trait" its stores. Before opening a new Wal-Mart, executives study the local geographic, demographic, psychographic, financial and cultural profiles of the surrounding area. Using a relational database, the "traits" of the prospective store are compared with those of all 3,000 stores to find which are most similar. The program then predicts which 70,000 items — known as stock-keeping units (SKUs) — will be the best-sellers in the new location. The choice is made from hundreds of thousands of potential SKUs.

For instance, if the target town is near a freshwater lake, the store will stock freshwater fishing gear. If it's near the ocean, it will stock saltwater fishing gear. If it's more than a given distance from any fishing area, no fishing gear may be stocked. But if a certain percentage of area residents in the catchment area own cottages where there is fishing, the store will stock fishing gear.

"Traiting" allows Wal-Mart to open a brand-new store and immediately begin selling up to $300 of merchandise per square foot, which is more than double the industry average. More importantly, "traiting" allows Wal-Mart to maximize profit per square foot from the beginning.

Wal-Mart's information network fosters continuous learning. Traiting shows how information technology has become Wal-Mart's mind, memory and central nervous system, analyzing the impact and interrelationship of a complex web of factors. The company encourages local managers to play with their product mix after the initial "traiting." They constantly fine-tune the product mix, aiming to increase profit per square foot, which is more important than sales per square foot. Managers are always asking, "What merchandise will sell well in my location and yield the highest profit margins?" When a manager discovers a hot new sales trend, this information is rapidly transmitted through the computer network, and managers of every other Wal-Mart store with similar "traits" begin experimenting with the product mix in their locations.

A Wal-Mart manager noticed a large spike in consumption of two quite different products, Pampers diapers and Budweiser beer, at 6:00 p.m. The manager began asking, "Why?" He thought about scenarios: hubby is working at the office and gets a call from his wife who is at home with the new baby. She says, "Honey, would you pick up some diapers on your way home?" "Of course, darling," he replies. On his way home, he stops at Wal-Mart to buy Pampers and thinks, "While I'm here, what would I like? BUD!" But he has to walk 17 aisles over and two rows down to get the beer.

The manager asks, "Why are we making it so difficult for him?" So he puts a huge facing of Budweiser on one side of an aisle and Pampers on the opposite side of the aisle, right at the front of the store. The result is an increase in sales of both.

This shows an interesting relationship between data, information, knowledge and wisdom. We need to "mine" data for information. We are all drowning in data. There have never been more data in the history of the earth. But data give no strategic information. From data we can extract information—Budweiser sales increase at 6:00 p.m. and Pampers sales increase at 6:00 p.m. But there are 70,000 other items in an average Wal-Mart whose sales may increase or decrease at any

Our technology helps us buy the right merchandise at the right time, and have it in the right place at the right price.

1997 Wal-Mart annual report

given time of day. The information technology sifts through millions of possible correlations in sales to highlight for the manager that these two items increase in sales at 6:00 p.m., predominantly on the same check-out bills. If this information creates a deeper understanding of customers and their behavior, then new knowledge is created.

Knowledge is useless unless it is put into practice. Therefore, Wal-Mart managers must be empowered to make such local decisions as positioning the Bud opposite the Pampers. Action creates wisdom. Wisdom stems from the application of knowledge.

The expression "knowledge is power" is incorrect. Knowledge is potential power. Application of knowledge creates power. This is an example of the learning paradox at its best: organizations need to create new knowledge and then find applications to take advantage of the new understanding.

"Real Time"

Information technology allows Wal-Mart to work in "real time." Just 90 minutes after each store has closed, head office knows the day's sales figures. Analysis can be done by store, by merchandise item, by region or by any other parameter. The cost-effectiveness of regional advertising can be analyzed in relation to a specific product's performance and compared with other areas where there was no advertising. Based on this information, a decision can be made whether the promotion should be continued or altered.

> The people who work in corporations are not the problem; it is the systems and structures in which they work that create the problems.
>
> Edwards Deming

Organizations that compete in real time have a tremendous advantage over those that don't. To realize how powerful an advantage, imagine my body only gave me biofeedback once a quarter!

Wal-Mart's largest suppliers manage their own inventories. This is known as vendor-managed inventory (VMI). Ninety minutes after every store closes, Levi Strauss knows exactly how many pairs of its jeans were sold that day. And not just how many, but what sizes and styles — straight leg, wide leg, boot fit, stone-washed or pre-bleached — and in what regions.

What happens when Wal-Mart competes with another retailer in the same market? Both have 20,000 pairs of jeans in stock. Both begin an aggressive sale of jeans at $19.95 a pair. Both stores sell 5,000 pairs the first day of the sale.

Because Wal-Mart's major suppliers know every night what was sold in what region by size and style, they can go into production that night and the next morning. Since Levi Strauss is on-line with Wal-Mart, it knows how much stock different promotions will require and is prepared for the jeans onslaught, having had past experience with buying patterns and responses to promotions. Levi Strauss guarantees shelf replacement within 72 hours. An order for 5,000 jeans is shipped out within two days to the regional Wal-Mart warehouse. Wal-Mart guarantees daily delivery to its individual stores. The 5,000 jeans arrive on Day Four of the sale.

We work at the other store. Once a week, all the department heads give their orders to the head buyer. The buyer collates these and places the orders with head office. At head office, the orders from 120 regional stores arrive by fax. Then the lengthy process of collating and merging these orders begins. By the end of the second week, orders are placed with the manufacturers. The jeans manufacturer begins production and, by the end of the third week, ships our company-wide order to our main warehouse. This order is then sorted and broken up to fill the individual store orders and shipped off to us by the end of the fourth week (along with everything else our store ordered). By the time we get the jeans on the shelf in the clothing department, it's five weeks later. If there are any other steps in this process—for example, using a distributor instead of dealing directly with the manufacturer—the process takes even longer.

So both stores, selling jeans at the same price in the same market, are moving 5,000 pairs of jeans a day. Both stores run out after four days, but Wal-Mart receives 5,000 pairs late on Day Four. And not just 5,000 pairs of any jeans, but the "hot" stock—the sizes and styles that sold on Day One. Wal-Mart sells out again on Day Five. Since Day Two's sale of 5,000 jeans triggered alarm bells with Levi Strauss, 5,000 more jeans arrive late on Day Five. And so on.

Meanwhile, at our store, we know we won't see any more jeans for five weeks! We don't know how, but Wal-Mart has sold 5,000 pairs of jeans every day for the first five days. We know the store began with only 20,000 pairs. We begin to panic. All our customers are flocking across the street to Wal-Mart. We get on the phone, call the manufacturer direct, eliminating the step of ordering through head office. We pull strings, and place a special, one-time volume order. At the end of Week Four, we celebrate because 120,000 pairs of jeans arrive. Hallelujah! But in the intervening four weeks, Wal-Mart has sold 5,000 pairs of jeans a day—120,000 pairs in all—and few people in our area will buy jeans in the next three years. Now we really have a problem because we're stuck with $250,000 of dead inventory. The head of the clothing department is fired for incompetence.

And what happens to the jeans manufacturer that supplies our store? The manufacturer is plagued by stop/start problems created by our ordering pattern. When the manufacturer was pressed to produce 120,000 pairs of jeans in two weeks (in addition to meeting the needs of all its regular customers), the extra overtime shifts that were required cut into profits. And for the next several years, the manufacturer receives no further orders from our store as we work to flog the slow-moving jeans. Thus the manufacturer goes from boom to bust. Erratic production increases manufacturing costs. The "ordering system" does not allow the manufacturer to optimize production runs and thereby lower costs.

But the failure is a systems failure. As Peter Senge, in *Fifth Discipline: The Art & Practice of the Learning Organization*, points out, we need "systems thinking."

Increasingly organizations have to compete on speed and organizational capability not just product, price and positioning.

> **Opportunity comes to pass, not pause.**
> Dr. Michael Smurfit, CEO, Jefferson Smurfit Group

Lower Prices

Real-time information technology helps make Wal-Mart a desirable customer to its largest suppliers. Every night, Wal-Mart pays Levi Strauss by electronic funds transfer (EFT) for products sold that day. Most retailers pay their suppliers in 30 days, if then. With these payment terms and its high volume of orders, Wal-Mart can negotiate very favorable deals with its suppliers.

Basing orders on up-to-the-minute information means the manufacturer produces only what the fashion market is demanding today—not last year, last quarter or even last week. And the orders are by region, so even if wide-leg, stone-washed jeans are the rage in New York and boot-cut jeans the craze in Texas, Levi Strauss still ships exactly what is needed to each regional Wal-Mart distribution center. Information technology allows Wal-Mart to lower its prices because it ends up with less "dead" or slow-moving inventory. Thus the technology has created an alignment between retailer and supplier interests: the retailer sells more, the supplier sells more. The retailer does more inventory turns. The supplier doesn't have to deal with erratic ordering and can therefore reduce manufacturing costs. The retailer keeps on top of current fashion trends, whereas buyers for other retailers are expected to predict the fashion trends and place orders a year in advance! The manufacturer isn't pressured to take back dead inventory. There isn't any because it produced only what was selling in the first place. For the retailer, there is little negative cash flow and dead inventory; for the manufacturer, there is payment the day the inventory sells. Both organizations know exactly what is and isn't selling.

Increased Profitability

Once an organization uses real-time information technology, the possibilities for analysis are endless. For example, with its IT system, Wal-Mart can analyze profit per square foot of floor space. A store manager might think she should dedicate more floor space to Christmas trees in December and perhaps put on a local promotion. But Wal-Mart's system allows the store manager to analyze costs and margins. She discovers that the store makes only a $4 profit per square foot of floor space dedicated to Christmas trees. After investigating further, she finds that another hot-seller around Christmas is Nintendo games. These take up only a few inches of shelf space, can be stacked 10 shelves high and net a $38 profit margin per square foot. Rather than dedicate more floor space to Christmas trees, the store manager puts up a huge Nintendo display and launches an aggressive local flyer promotion.

The system also allows for profit maximization. Many retailers are competing blindly, they can't tell you what their true costs, margins or number of inventory turns are. They have an idea, a feeling about it, but IT transforms the hunch into a science.

Computers in the future may weigh less than 1.5 tons.
Popular Mechanics, 1949

Competing with Wal-Mart and Opportunity Cost

Wal-Mart's information technology analyzes which *existing* stock items *did* and *didn't* sell. But for items the company has never stocked, the system can't predict which items *would* sell if the company carried them. Wal-Mart works to offer the broadest range of merchandise possible to attract the widest segment of society. While Wal-Mart stocks over 70,000 SKUs in an average store, there are still hundreds of thousands of items the company *doesn't* stock. Items that would sell if Wal-Mart stocked them represent a lost *opportunity* for sales.

Opportunity cost is the cost of losing potential business and it is rarely measured. Opportunity costs are larger than just the lost potential sales. In the Wal-Mart example, if a retailer doesn't stock a product that a consumer wants, it drives that customer to search for the product at a competitor's store, where the consumer is likely to buy other items. If this occurs frequently, the consumer will come to think of the other store first when shopping.

Opportunity cost is difficult to measure. First, because the retailer can't analyze the sales data for items it doesn't sell. A competitor is not going to share its own analysis of which of its SKUs are the hottest-selling items. Suppliers are the sole source of information, but they only have data about their products or category, not comparative data for all SKUs.

Auditors measure what exists: existing sales, existing inventory, existing inventory turns. But how can you measure what doesn't exist? The sales you could have made if you had carried the item? The inventory turns you could have had? The profit you could have made?

How can accountants get some idea of what people would buy at, say, a Wal-Mart but are not able to? Conduct exit interviews with shoppers to discover what they would have purchased had the store carried it.

As you recall, when Wal-Mart executives "trait" a potential site for a new store, they study the surrounding area. If fishing is nearby, the store will stock fishing gear. But Wal-Mart doesn't have the widest selection of items in any category. Instead, the company stocks only the fastest-selling items.

Wal-Mart's fishing bags may sell for $19 but have only two pockets, while in specialty fishing stores fishing bags with 16 waterproof pockets sell for $99. In its effort to offer the lowest prices, Wal-Mart may cut back too far on features that anglers want. The optimum bag may be one that has eight watertight pockets and it would sell quickly at $49.

To compete with Wal-Mart, retailers must work to find the holes in Wal-Mart's merchandising selection and meet consumers' unmet needs. Some of these niches will be highly profitable. Niche retailers can also compete on the depth of selection in a category. Wal-Mart will only carry one or two types of fishing bags, whereas a specialty retailer may carry three or four, or fishing bags from every manufacturer in the category.

All organizations need to examine the opportunity costs of not changing, not creating new products and services, not having EDI capabilities.

No customer ever wrote to Nissan asking for a sleep warning device. No customer wrote to Chrysler asking them to introduce the minivan. No one asked Alexander Graham Bell to invent the telephone.

Similarly, no one at IBM was ever fired for not inventing the computer notebook. Toshiba took the honors. No one at Lotus was fired for not creating a *Windows*-based spreadsheet, until it was too late. What is the opportunity cost of not being creative, innovative and first to market? This is rarely discussed in organizations and never measured.

Can't Measure? Can't Manage!
Imagine going through school and receiving no marks on your tests, essays and final exams. At the end of the year you receive one mark. How much value would that mark have?

You would have no way of knowing which tests you did well in and which you failed, which essays were good and which were poor, what studying paid off and when going to the pub the night before really cost you. You wouldn't even know which subjects you did well in and which you didn't. How could you improve? Your mark would be totally meaningless. In business, if you can't measure your performance, you have no way of knowing how well you're doing in meeting customers' needs and company goals.

In most corporations, employee evaluations may be done annually, audits are conducted annually, inventory is taken semi-annually, projected and actual budgets are compared annually, with the real emphasis put on quarterly financial reporting. Imagine if my body gave me biofeedback only once a quarter, and I walked into the kitchen and put my hand on a red-hot burner. I'd have toast for a hand before I even knew I had a problem. It is impossible to think of our bodies working in anything but real time.

Let's say you are responsible for hiring a pay-and-benefits consultant to help your organization. You are choosing between two companies. Both have 80 staff located in your city.

I am a consultant working at Hewitt Associates. Hewitt has 80 consultants in your city and 3,200 consultants worldwide. I come to see you knowing nothing about your business. But I listen intently while you discuss your challenges and I ask a lot of questions. I return to the office, type up a case study and send an e-mail memo to 150 Hewitt specialist consultants in nine countries who work in this field, asking what they have done in similar situations. By the next morning, I have 15 responses, each 10 pages long, detailing specific case studies. On the third day, I send you a 50-page report outlining a number of possible approaches.

Now think of a consultant at the other firm, which also has 80 consultants. When he arrives to assess your problem, he also has no knowledge of your exact industry, but neither does anyone else in his office. Which consultant will you hire? By hiring Hewitt, are you hiring 80 consultants or 3,200?

Information technology enables new working relationships within organizations. Colleagues can be anywhere in the world. But introducing new IT structures without changing management structures will not give an organization any competitive advantage. For instance, if Hewitt's promotion, recognition and compensation systems were all based on increasing revenue in local offices, why would consultants take any time from their schedules to work on a proposal from a foreign office? In other words, the management structure is just as important as the IT structure for enabling new relationships within organizations.

The information flow can be global. Some companies are outsourcing a great deal of computer programming to India and Pakistan. Former barriers to business, including national borders, time zones and even language, are now broken.

Computers have become the central nervous system of organizations, giving them the ability to respond to a changing market in real time, and become learning organizations.

I have some friends who are computer programmers. I think programmers are genetically different from the rest of us. One friend says he does his best work at 3:00 a.m. But organizations are stuck in an old paradigm of production, where workers were required to be physically present at the production line at certain times. From Alvin Toffler's perspective this bias comes out of a second wave—industrial revolution bias. Peter Senge points out that workers were actually known as "hands."[3]

IT Enables New Relationships

The power of information technology isn't only in automating old processes but also in enabling new relationships. American Airlines' Sabre reservation system is a case in point. A survey of travel agents conducted by American Airlines revealed that agents had a strong tendency to book the first available flight. So American developed the Sabre reservation system and gave free terminals to a test group of travel agents. When agents made on-line inquiries about available flights, the system always listed American Airlines flights first. American experienced a 40 percent growth in bookings and a 40 percent surge in profitability from the test group. So after refining the system, Sabre launched the system throughout North America, giving all travel agents a free terminal. American's profit surged.

Other airlines soon caught on and began the two-year process of developing their own reservation systems. Two years later they went to travel agents offering free terminals and on-line access. But most agents said, "Thanks, but no thanks. It took us two years to get used to Sabre, and we're not going to go through that again." This example raises an important point: it's better to have a new product 80 percent right and be the first to market it than 99.9 percent right and two years late.

Sabre forged strong ties with travel agents through IT, "locking" them into a new relationship. Once this new relationship was well established, Sabre approached the other airlines and said, "Look, up until now we've been providing you with a free service by listing your flights. We're going to charge you for it now and if you don't pay we'll drop you from the listing." Today, Sabre generates more profits from American Airlines' competitors than American does from flying its own planes!

Sabre subsequently expanded. When you book a hotel with your travel agent, it's done through Sabre. When you book a car rental, it's done through Sabre. With each booking, Sabre takes a cut. At some point, American Airlines may get out of the airline business altogether.

American Airlines' use of information technology enabled the company to create a powerful new relationship with travel agents. At the time, no other airline had developed a system that enabled the agents to offer something new to their customers — the ability to instantly ascertain flight availability and offer advance-booking, discount fares.

California-based computer maker Sun Microsystems touts the slogan, "The network is the computer." Taking this slogan one step further, the Sabre case study shows that, "The network is the business."

When I say "encyclopedia," what comes to mind? "Large." What else comes to mind? "Many volumes." What else? "Britannica." Yes! For over 200 years *Encyclopaedia Britannica* defined the standard for encyclopedias. First published in 1768, it is the oldest and largest English-language general encyclopedia. The 15th edition first published in 1974 consisted of 32 volumes. Updated every five years, it was sold primarily through direct mail and from door to door for $1,599 a set. It has approximately 33,000 pages and weighs 128 pounds.

But during 1994, a company that had never published or sold encyclopedias became the number-one vendor. Microsoft. In 1994, computer retailers began giving away a free copy of Microsoft *Encarta* to customers buying a new $2,000 computer. Imagine that in your industry another company begins giving away a competing product as a premium!

Encarta integrated color illustrations with sound and video clips. Microsoft redefined what an encyclopedia was. Instead of taking up a whole shelf, you put *Encarta* in your pocket.

Production costs of *Encarta* were a fraction of those of *Encyclopaedia Britannica* and the product was updated quarterly. But it wasn't just *Encarta* that killed Britannica's markets overnight. Parents who could afford it used to buy a set of encyclopedias for their children's education. But today parents buy their kids a multimedia PC. The multimedia computer, not just the CD encyclopedia, led to the demise

> When you're a kid and you're learning, it's OK because a lot of things are confusing, and you persevere.
>
> Bill Gates, chairman, Microsoft

of the old encyclopedia market. As Don Tapscott writes in *Digital Economy:*

> In response, Britannica has taken a bold and innovative strategy. It has taken the next logical step and put its encyclopedia on the Net, charging a daily fee for those who "subscribe." The set of books has become a subscription service. The potential impact (and opportunities for the company) go far beyond the CD-ROM model. Rather than updating every decade or every year – or even every three months as the competition does, the encyclopedia on the Net can be updated hourly! Obviously the amount of information available is much greater than can be held on a CD. In fact, the amount of information is limitless. But most important, because it is on the Net, Britannica becomes something much greater than an encyclopedia. . . . There are "hot links" enabling the reader to instantly link to related subjects contained on other Web servers around the world. It becomes a directory to all human knowledge that is electronically stored!
>
> By embracing interactive multimedia, Britannica has been transformed from a mere publisher of books to a company providing access to all human knowledge.
>
> Encyclopaedia Britannica is changing its customer base. Rather than selling simply to individuals, Encyclopaedia Britannica is now making licensing agreements with institutions. By September 1997, about 800 colleges and universities were subscribing to Britannica Online, and almost 40 percent of U.S. undergraduates have access to the service through their institutions. A few dollars of each student's tuition goes to unlimited access to Britannica.
>
> Encyclopaedia Britannica is a case of a company that changed their product (from book to subscription service, compilation of human knowledge to a digital directory); changed their distribution channels and market place (from physical to digital); and changed their customers (from families to everybody, including institutions). This kind of corporate action goes far beyond the process of reengineering. It is transformation for the digital economy.[4]

What happened to *Encyclopaedia Britannica* is frightening enough to give most people a knot in their stomach. Literally everything about the company had to change – its product, how it was delivered and sold. Ultimate security comes from changing.

Dr Terry Paulson, a U.S. speaker, notes:

> Everyone knows the importance of lifelong learning, but how simple it is to settle for the easy learning opportunities. Anyone can quickly copy what you learn easily. As adults, we are often so afraid of being wrong that we play it safe when we need to be going for the uncertainty and the unexplored territory that will give us a sustainable strategic advantage. Relearn your childhood excitement of difficult, demanding, and challenging learning that will again require you to persevere through to skills worth learning. The difficult learning you and your team do will produce useful knowledge that others will have a harder time copying. Target your learning in the areas where you can strategically benefit you and your organization. Once you have mastered a new strategic competence, start looking for your next difficult learning opportunity. In short, the intent to seek knowledge in difficult areas may be your most important habit to ensure you and your organization's survival in the future. What difficult areas have you been avoiding that just may be the best place for you to start learning?[5]

New Banking Relationships

IT is not just more efficient, it's radically different. It enables new relationships and creates new markets. If, through ATM machines, I can get money any time, anywhere, in any currency, why do I need traveler's checks? I don't! Does that mean the ATM network enables the banks to compete with traveler's check companies such as American Express and Thomas Cook? Absolutely! The technology has allowed the banks to grow into a new market. With Interac and CIRRUS, information technology has blurred the whole concept of competition in banking. Information technology can change who your competitors are.

The Interac system is an example of "co-opetition." It requires the cooperative efforts of all banks. When I withdraw money in Florida, I'm doing it at a bank I've never even heard of. Co-opetition allows all banks to compete with traveler's check companies.

The development and spread of the inter-banking system is self-financing. When I withdraw $100 in Florida, I pay a $1 fee for the privilege of doing so. I am willing to pay the premium for the convenience, time saving and the one percent fee I avoid paying for traveler's checks.

In both the Sabre and Interac cases, the systems started small. As revenues increased, the companies reinvested in expansion. In the case of the airline industry, by the time competitors woke up, it was too late and the investment required to catch up was too great. The competitors were cooked. The same is true of Wal-Mart. Today, Wal-Mart invests millions of dollars a year in IT and the annual investment is growing. The catch-up costs are prohibitive.

One of the lessons from the Sabre case study is: start small. Growth should come from continually reinvesting from cash flow. It's organic growth as opposed to forced growth. Paying the price, learning from small mistakes and refining and developing the corporate culture around the new IT support new relationships.

Individuals and corporations need to continually ask, "What are the 'impossible' things that are holding us back from dramatic performance improvements, both personally and organizationally? A number of processes foster creativity (Chapter 6). The goal of creativity is to make the "impossible" possible. Always question paradigms. Always think conceptually.

All Relationships Must Change

Information technology on its own does not give an organization an advantage. For instance, if I have a Pentium computer on my desk but don't know how to use it, what advantage does it give? If everyone in the culture but the executives know how to use e-mail, how much use will e-mail have? To achieve a strategic advantage, the organization's culture as a whole must support the newly enabled relationships. Everything in the organization, including human resource systems and corporate training, must be oriented to the new paradigm.

As the investment in information technology grows, so must the corresponding investment in people. That is why 63 percent of the cost of maintaining a PC is hidden (Chapter 8). It is informal training and support for the end users!

The employee-employer relationship has to change as IT advancements enable new relationships. Increasingly, work requires creativity, ingenuity and thinking. As in the earlier example of the computer programmer who worked best at 3:00 a.m., some people are most productive at times other than nine to five. Organizations need to create systems and structures within the workplace (and workplace may not be the office, it may be in a client's office, in the car or at home) that support people working when it is best for them. All organizational structures and relationships need to be re-evaluated.

The Mobile Office and Hoteling

Ernst & Young International (E&Y) spearheaded an interesting program. Executives at E&Y, the second-largest accounting firm in the United States, noticed that their best consultants were spending the least amount of time in the office. Consultants with the highest billable hours were always out at their clients' offices, leaving their beautiful window and corner offices vacant. It followed that most consultants would be more effective if they were encouraged to spend more time in the field. In cities where the cost of real estate is high, large office complexes seemed an extravagant waste. As a result, the Mobile Office Project was begun. Ernst & Young decided to support consultants by giving them a notebook computer, a cellular phone and cellular datafax modem. These were seen as perks by the consultants; from the company's perspective they were productivity enhancers, allowing the consultants to perform more work in the field and enabling them to communicate with support staff and customers. The company was able to reduce its total office space, realizing net savings in the millions of dollars.

The mobile office is not to be confused with the home office. Obviously, while the home office offers gains in reducing real-estate expenses, it does not promise any significant improvement in face-to-face contact with clients. The mobile office addresses both needs.

Ernst & Young's New York and Chicago offices pioneered the practice of "hoteling." Under the "hoteling" system, a consultant in transit calls ahead to the office to reserve office space. By the time he or she arrives, his or her personal phone number will have already been transferred to the office phone and a name-plate will have been inserted in the slot beside the office door.

Executives who were initially reluctant to forsake their personal office space have been won over to the system by its financial benefits. Unnecessary office space ultimately increased overhead. As the bottom line improves, the firm can continue to invest in technology and training. Thus the firm becomes more competitive and job security is increased for all employees. Employees are less likely to defend their territory once they realize that their offices often amount to a $10,000 to $20,000 per annum luxury. The Mobile Office Project will eliminate half of E&Y's total office space in the United States![6]

Many employees have raised concerns about the arrangement. Some believe that reduced time spent in an office complex can be detrimental to team productivity and hence achieving corporate goals. Because communication between staff members is a valuable resource, it has required some discipline on the part of employees to maintain fruitful interaction; otherwise, access to "second opinions" might decline and ultimately result in them making hasty, inappropriate decisions.

Ernst & Young continues to explore alternative means of communication to address the detrimental aspects of the Mobile Office initiative. These systems are encapsulated under the banner of "EY/Link." The EY/Link has four components: e-mail, the global telephone network, database on-line discussion groups (which enable employees to work collaboratively on documents across a computer network) and desktop videoconferencing. Ernst & Young hopes that in maximizing information technology, it can maintain interpersonal cohesiveness within a more virtual corporation.

Whenever I cite a case, there is a countercase. Microsoft does not allow its programmers to work off campus, even though they are technically literate and could easily telecommute. Why does Gates demand that they be physically present on the Redmond, Washington, site? Well, first of all, because it is such a workaholic culture that programmers live in their offices, pizza boxes are stacked to the roof.[7] But second, Gates wants programmers to be physically present because of the informal synergy that occurs among programmers.

Human Potential: What Are People Capable of?
What are people capable of achieving? Outside of work, we raise families, negotiate $250,000 mortgages, decide which car to buy from a dozen competing makes, travel all over the world, deal with complex relationships and pursue many interests. But some organizations don't give employees the authority to buy $1.19 worth of paper clips. Few companies are tapping the full potential of their employees.

The goal of empowerment is to unleash the potential of employees; to provide the training, knowledge, physical, financial and human resources necessary for employees to learn, grow and thrive.

The new IT paradigm is dramatically changing information flow within organizations. The new IT enables employees to have information at their fingertips. Some companies are adopting open-book management or full disclosure, allowing employees to access any information about the business.

If we ask a construction crew to develop ideas on how to reduce construction costs, but then refuse them access to the blueprints, costs and profit margin figures, we won't get very far. We need full disclosure if we are to allow employees on the front line to make "moment-of-truth" decisions; otherwise, they could give away the store in the name of customer satisfaction.

Thirty-five days after I bought it, I returned a $300 inkjet printer to an electronics superstore. (A sign says you can return goods with the sales receipt for 30 days after purchase.) I had prepared myself for a fight, expecting to be refused by the clerk, then having to appeal to the manager, being turned down again and then having to start a letter-writing campaign directed to the president. I arrived at the store, I looked at the 18-year-old clerk and boldly stated my position. She looked at me, asked for my phone number and said, "I would be happy to give you a refund."

I was stunned. Where was the fight? You see, after she keyed my phone number into her terminal, the system pulled up my customer history. She could see my total cumulative purchases to date and knew that I had bought $7,000 of goods from the store in the past year. She decided on the spot to give me a full refund. Her action met the best interests of both the customer and the organization because the $50 profit from the sale of the printer was not worth losing a $7,000-a-year customer. And I am certain that she didn't have an MBA from Harvard or know how to calculate the lifetime value of a customer in net present dollars.

The clerk may or may not have received training about the importance of customer service, or have known that it costs five times as much to attract a new customer than to retain an existing one. She didn't consult a manager. The IT system gave her immediate access to the information she needed to decide how to best meet the company's and store's mission in a moment of truth.

The rapidly changing market environment demands that all participants in an organization be empowered to make these kinds of choices. No more can we afford to centralize decision-making or isolate management from the experience of workers in the field. There must be a free exchange of knowledge among all departments. New technology provides us with the means to give each member of the organization real-time access to the evolving corporate blueprint.

What Are the True Costs of IT?

The real-time revolution is being driven by technology that is becoming dramatically smaller, cheaper and faster. The price-performance ratio of microprocessors is driving a shift from mainframe computing to client/server computing, based on workstation and micros. The cost per MIPS (million instructions per second) varies depending on the type of processor. Mainframe costs have only recently fallen below $100,000 per MIPS (see graph on next page).[8]

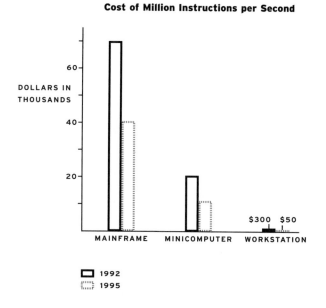

Cost of Million Instructions per Second

□ 1992
▥ 1995

As you will recall, Gordon Moore, co-founder of Intel, devised Moore's Law (Chapter 3, page 36). In a 1965 issue of *Electronics Magazine*, Moore speculated that the number of transistors per computer chip would double every year for 10 years while staying at the same price point. This became known as Moore's Law. In 1975, he revised his prediction, suggesting the pace would slow to a doubling every two years. However, the ingenuity of engineers has kept the pace doubling every 18 months. The effect of this compounding of computing power has been phenomenal.

The explosion in computing power has been driven by the miniaturization of transistors. In the 1950s, a computer with the power of a 286 took up an entire room and consumed tremendous amounts of power. These computers were based on vacuum tubes and wires. In the 1960s, engineers learned to make these same circuits on single, small pieces of silicon. Silicon-based computers were much faster and consumed almost no power compared to their predecessors. Moore's Law has held true. The number of transistors per chip has doubled every 18 months since 1961; 1961 — four transistors per chip; 1971 — 2,300; 1982 — 134,000; 1991 — 1.2 million and the Pentium II 300 MHz, released in 1997, has over 7.5 million transistors.

Explosion of Intel Processor Power

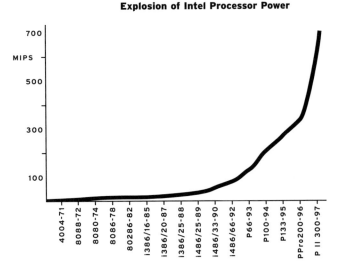

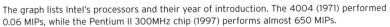

The graph lists Intel's processors and their year of introduction. The 4004 (1971) performed 0.06 MIPs, while the Pentium II 300MHz chip (1997) performs almost 650 MIPs.

Chip makers have been able to increase the number of transistors per chip by manufacturing smaller and smaller circuits. In 1961, the circuits of the 4004 chip (1971) were 10 microns wide. The Pentium II 300 (1997) line widths are 0.35 microns. In April 1997, Intel unveiled its new 0.25 micron manufacturing process. (To give you an idea of how small 0.25 microns is, a single human hair is approximately 3,000 times larger.)

Manufacturers will shrink circuits to 0.07-micron widths, allowing transistor counts to continue soaring.

As the circuits get smaller they can be manufactured closer together, minimizing the distance that an electron must travel. As a result, electrons move faster through the circuits, increasing the overall processor speed.

Processors with 0.25-micron circuits are 30 percent faster than 0.35-micron chips. The 0.25 micron also consumes 42 percent less power, even at higher speeds. Lower power consumption means longer battery life for mobile end users.

The corollary of Moore's Law is that the cost of a given amount of computer power drops 50 percent every 18 months. Whenever this happens, demand for computers increases because all sorts of new applications become economically feasible. By 2007 it will be possible to cram the power of today's supercomputers onto a chip costing a few hundred dollars.

What applications become possible? Traditional economics assumes a stable environment. Inputs such as land, machinery and labor were assumed not to change. Labor is labor. Markets mature eventually. But the microchip industry invalidates traditional economic theory. By doubling power every 18 months at the same price point, the semiconductor industry is creating a non-linear future. If I can buy the power of today's supercomputer on a $300 chip in 10 years, what will the size of the market be for those chips?

The rapid shrinking of circuit width can't go on forever. There are fixed limits to how tiny transistors can become. But physical limits won't end computing's increasing speed and falling costs.

Symmetric Multi Processing (SMP) computers harness the power of up to 30 microchips to produce mainframe-comparable performance. For instance, in 1996, Sun Microsystems launched a family of servers that have up to 30 chips producing throughputs equal to the largest mainframe! Microsoft's *Windows NT* (New Technology) operating system allows Intel chips to work in tandem and similarly produce mainframe-like performance. Does this mean that Sun and Microsoft have become competitors of mainframe manufacturers? Paradigm shifts redefine the very nature of competition.

In many cases, the capital costs of client/server solutions are less than the annual maintenance costs of mainframes. For instance, a company may be paying $50,000 a year to maintain a mainframe that will cost only $100,000 to replace with a new UNIX RISC-based system. While the numbers appear very attractive, they are misleading because the hardware is only a small part of the cost of a system. In the old mainframe environment, companies were locked into a dated way of doing business because the cost of changing programming was horrendous and changes took years to implement. In the new paradigm, programming development cycles are dramatically shorter and costs are much lower. But change requires hardware and software expenditures, new programming competencies and a new corporate culture to support the newly enabled relationships. Hardware savings are insignificant compared to these costs.[9]

There are other significant training questions around IT. When we know that 80 percent of the technology that we will use in 10 years has not yet been invented, how can we design training programs that will prepare people for the future? The only way is to create a learning culture. We need to enshrine lifelong learning as a corporate value.

Given that no individual or organization can accurately predict the future, the IT structure itself must be fast, flexible, focused and friendly. When determining the IT architecture, executives and IT professionals must ensure that it can be rapidly re-architected, that the selected languages allow for applications to be built and altered quickly and that the selected suppliers are forward-looking and continue to invest aggressively in research and development.

Plan for a Radically Different Future

The progress in computer technology is not linear, it's exponential. An incremental approach won't work when planning for the future. For instance, here is the assumption Microsoft makes when planning for the future: the size of your hard disk today will be the amount of RAM in the average new PC in five years. By mid-1997, the average hard disk was two gigabytes (GB). What kinds of applications could be enabled if you had two gigabytes of RAM in your computer? The future is not just a linear extension of the past, it will be a radically different future. PCs will deliver 10,000 MIPS by 2000 (in 1997, Pentium II 300 MHz chips were delivering over 600 MIPs) and bandwidth costs will have fallen substantially, allowing for richer, two-way interactive content.[10] Using these assumptions, people at Microsoft plan for a different kind of future than the average person can "see" today.

Doom, one of the most popular computer games, is driven by a powerful graphics engine that draws pictures so quickly, you think the motion is instantaneous. The engineering behind it will eventually be the basis for virtual reality on the Internet. The software engineers who created the game, when asked which competitor they feared most didn't answer, "Microsoft, Sega or Nintendo." They replied, "Two guys in a garage, working in total obscurity. Those are the guys who are going to come up with the stuff that will blow us out of the water."[11]

Investing in IT

Technology has changed forever the retailer-supplier relationship. When making IT investments, Sam Walton, founder of Wal-Mart, always challenged IT professionals to prove the financial case for their proposed investment. IT investments were not made for the sake of investing in technology. In fact, Sam was, in his own words, "cheap." He consistently turned down requests to invest in IT. He would send the IT team back to the drawing board to find a cheaper way. And, as the old saying goes, "Necessity is the mother of invention." Having to constantly go back and work out a less expensive architecture forced the IT team to find the best and least expensive way of achieving corporate objectives. Investments were made only when the IT team could prove the technology would lower costs, raise profits, increase inventory turns, increase margins, reduce dead inventory or create better management tools. The investment was made based on business strategy, not IT strategy.

Wal-Mart's success can't be copied just by duplicating the technology. First, few organizations can afford to make a one-time investment equal to Wal-Mart's investment over the years. Few companies can even match Wal-Mart's annual IT investment. Wal-Mart has been investing heavily in IT for years. Competitors can't hope to catch up overnight. Moreover, the systems and the corporate culture have to be developed together. Information technology is only a tool. People design the systems, people implement the systems and people make the systems work.

Investing in information technology for its own sake is wasteful. What bottom-line impact will IT investments have by enabling new or better business practices? What cultural changes are required to enable new processes?

This chapter ends with an overview of the evolution of computing and the new promise of the fifth era that we are just entering. The fifth era represents a profound paradigm shift. We will have to let go of all our prior assumptions about computing. Until now EDI (electronic data interchange or inter-enterprise integration), as demonstrated in the Wal-Mart/ Levi example, has only been pursued by large organizations because implementation costs run in the millions. But the fifth era of computing will make EDI a possibility for all organizations through the World Wide Web.

Paradigm Shifts and Punctuated Disequilibrium

Stephen Jay Gould has another way of looking at paradigm shifts. He describes biological evolution in *Wonderful Life*, calling it "punctuated equilibrium":

> Over millions of years, species adapt to fill every imaginable niche. Then along comes some external force — a volcano, an asteroid, an ice age — that changes all the niches and launches a mad scramble for survival. Evolution favors new forms of life that, through a sort of biological lateral thinking, can find a whole new way to thrive. Wings, legs, lungs: all were revolutionary mutations once. Life down the ages has tended to evolve in sudden great leaps, separated by long periods of slow change. The same is true for technology, though the time scale is compressed.[12]

The computer industry has gone through a series of stable periods punctuated by disequilibrium.

Fifth Era of Computing

IBM created the first era of computing by introducing the mainframe. Mainframes were kept in hermetically sealed, air-conditioned rooms. Only IT professionals had access to the computer. There was only one operating system and the IT department controlled it. Programs were written in lines of code. Users worked on dumb terminals and had only periodic or batch access, which meant you ran your program and got the results hours later. The first era created the Information Technology (IT) professional. IT professionals assumed a stature comparable to the Wizard of Oz.

Digital Equipment Corporation upset the mainframe world by making mainframe-type computers, called mini-computers, available at a fraction of the price. This was the second era of computing. Competing proprietary languages were introduced. Vendors took their clients hostage because the cost of conversion, once systems were implemented, was horrendous. Different operating systems would not interchange data so there was no integration among organizations.

Apple ushered in the third era of computing by introducing the personal computer. This was a radical break from the mainframe mindset. Subsequently, IBM introduced the personal computer, which was based on a microchip made by Intel and an operating system from Microsoft. The personal computer took the world by storm, allowing users to work independently Individuals gained control over computers. The PC was a democratic force, giving power to the people. But with the freedom of choice came chaos.

This department had Macintoshes, that department had IBM-compatibles. Incompatible operating systems and incompatible programs meant people couldn't share information even within the same organization. PCs couldn't communicate with the mainframe. The resulting proliferation of operating systems and applications created tremendous problems for IT professionals. The cost of ownership of computers increased tremendously as IT professionals were expected to manage the complexity of layers of incompatible software as they integrated new hardware with old.

Despite this chaos the third wave of computing brought forth tremendous innovation and wealth creation. John Doerr, a Silicon Valley venture capitalist, calculates that the introduction of the PC caused the greatest creation of wealth in the history of the planet.[13]

The personal computer was just that – a personal computer. All your applications, files and contacts were stored in one place. To gain access to your data, you could only use your computer.

The fourth wave of computing brought forth the workstation, which was based on microprocessors like those used by PCs, but with power rivaling minicomputers. Workstations introduced multiple processing where up to 64 microprocessors worked together (called symmetrical multiprocessing). Now, microprocessors working together like a 16-cylinder engine could reach performance levels rivaling minis and mainframes. Today, even some mainframes are built using small processors in an architecture called Massively Parallel Processing, where up to thousands of microprocessors work together.

The fourth era saw the rise of networked computers, where powerful workstations (clients) were connected to servers. In a client/server model some computing was done on the client and some on the server. While there was unprecedented growth in networking within organizations, a proliferation of different operating systems created challenges and meant that total cost of ownership was many times the price of the hardware (Chapter 8).

Finally, we are entering the fifth era of computing. It promises an unprecedented amount of freedom to users while significantly reducing the cost of computing.

Imagine that I could only use the telephone at my desk or that I had to carry that same telephone with me wherever I went because I could never use another telephone. Sound crazy? Well isn't that what we do with our computers?

Think about the telephone network. I can walk up to any telephone in the world, dial a sequence of numbers and reach any other telephone in the world any time of day. This is made possible by standards.

How much value would the telephone network have if each country had a different set of standards, such that telephone calls originating in one country could not be answered in another? Would telephones have become so widespread if telephones produced by one hardware manufacturer could not communicate with another's? If AT&T's network could not communicate with Sprint's or MCI's, would the value of telephones be greater or less? Or imagine that one individual in your organization bought a new telephone and it required every other person in the organization to buy the same new telephone. Sound ludicrous? Well, that is exactly what we have been experiencing in the computer world.

The fifth era of computing is based on the rise of the Internet and the World Wide Web. The Web is all about networking between organizations, regardless of their operating system. It is truly an "open" system, allowing the interchange of information between people anywhere in the world, using any operating system and any hardware. It is a revolution that will have a more profound impact than the introduction of the PC. While the Net is still in its infancy, its promise is tremendous.

Netscape's Web browser will run on any computer operating system. It is platform independent. Java, a new computer language created by Sun Microsystems, is driving the new paradigm (see below).

We are in the early stages of the fifth era. Imagine you could walk up to any computer in the world, log on to the World Wide Web, key in a password or stick a smart card into the computer, and access all your files. Sound far off? Applications already exist that are proving this promise. For instance, a service called hotmail (www.hotmail.com) allows users to send and receive e-mail using any computer in the world that can log on to the World Wide Web. As of August 1997, hotmail had four million users.

What are the benefits of the fifth era? The value of the Internet increases with each new user. How much value did the first fax machine have? None, because it could not communicate with any other fax machine. Now that everyone has one, you would be at a business disadvantage if you didn't have one, too. The value of having a fax machine increases as the number of individuals and organizations that have fax machines grows. The same is true of the Internet and computers. With each new computer that is hooked up to the Internet, the value of the whole network increases.

Why? Don Tapscott has coined the term prosumer[14] to refer to people using the Internet who are both PROducers and conSUMERS of content. Each individual who begins to use the World Wide Web increases the total value of the Internet. The growth of the Internet is driven by such open standards as Netscape and Java.

The Promise of Java

Hardware represents roughly 20 percent of the total cost of a personal computer or workstation (Chapter 5). Software compatibility and training, on the other hand, eat up at least 40 percent of the costs. With the rapid changes in hardware and the continual releases of software upgrades, IT professionals are in a constant state of crisis as they attempt to manage these costs.

Software has become bloatware. *Windows 95*, for instance, has 11 million lines of code. The larger the programs, the more complex they are, the harder to develop, the more bugs they contain and the more potential conflicts they are likely to create with other programs and hardware.

Java introduces a new paradigm of computing: IT professionals have to maintain only the server applications and end users just access Java programs—called applets—across the network on a need-to-use basis. Suddenly, an employee, like a bank teller, requiring only limited functions, no longer needs to run a program like *Windows* with 11 million lines of code.

Java is platform independent, meaning it will run on an IBM-compatible or a Mac or a Unix platform. So IT professionals do not have to worry about maintaining the software for many different platforms. Similarly, developers only have to develop for one platform. One of the largest costs of software development is maintaining multiple platform versions.

Java, while still in its infancy, has ignited excitement in the software developer community. Developers know that just as Netscape created a phenomenal market for itself using the World Wide Web, Java applets are both the product and the marketing channel. Developers can sell their applets to anyone in the world using the WWW. Therefore, the language unleashes the get-rich hopes of developers all over the world and means that a lot of development activity will occur in this new language. It also means that developers do not have to depend on making a deal with Microsoft, which many worry will over time only extend its dominance of software development.

The fifth era brings together the best of all the other eras as MIS departments regain control of the operating systems. In large organizations, MIS professionals will no longer have to spend time upgrading the software on thousands of end-user workstations (clients). They will only have to update the software on the server. By using platform-independent standards, MIS professionals will not have to spend large amounts of time solving conflicts between different layers of software.

Finally, users will have increased freedom and functionality because they will be able to access their data from any workstation in the world. Just as I can use any telephone in the world and reach anyone else. The good news for small organizations is that Web-based EDI will enable them to experience the same benefits that Wal-Mart enjoys.

To Summarize:
- Electronic Data Interchange (EDI) enables real-time analysis, which dramatically reduces cycle times, making organizations faster and more flexible, capable of responding rapidly in a dynamic, changing market.

- Fast, flexible organizations outperform their competitors by:
  - bringing new products and services faster to market
  - "locking" their customers into new relationships
  - detecting and correcting errors faster
  - enhancing individual and corporate-wide learning, and becoming "learning organizations"

Workshop Questions and Exercises:
- If your organization implemented EDI over the Web, what new relationships would be enabled:
  - within the organization (within teams, between departments and divisions, between different levels of the organization)?
  - with customers?
  - with suppliers?
- What would be the effect on cycle times?
- What new products or services might be enabled by the new paradigm?
- How would such a shift change your perception of your competitors?
- Would such a shift change your competitors' perceptions of your organization?
- What are the "impossible" things that are holding your organization back from dramatic performance improvements?

Reflection:
- What is the key learning/insight for me in this chapter?

Action:
- What one action shall I take tomorrow to move learning into action? And over time repeat, to move action into habit?

CHAPTER 11

The Internet Revolution

In 1997, for the first time in history, the number of e-mail messages in the United States exceeded the total number of addressed letters carried by the U.S. Postal Service! This fundamental shift will shake every business to its foundation.[1]

E-mail-enabled corporations are radically different from traditional companies. Hierarchies fall as information is freely shared. The need-to-know philosophy of the past is crumbling. Sun Microsystems employees send up to 1.5 million e-mail messages to one another every business day. That's 120 messages per person! Such a high-performance culture is fast and flexible. Product development is blistering—95 percent of Sun's revenues come from products that were not commercially available 18 months before! No wonder Sun is one of the fastest-growing companies in the history of the world.

But the Internet revolution is still in its infancy. As it matures, it will radically transform the very nature of business and many aspects of our society. Companies such as Intuit, Netscape, Microsoft, Sun Microsystems and Intel are rewriting the rules of business. The speed of change boggles the mind.

Worldwide buying and selling on the Internet, which totaled $132 million in 1995, exceeded $2.6 billion in 1996,[2] is projected to grow to over $8 billion in 1997,[3] more than $220 billion by 2001[4] and to as much as $1 trillion by 2005.[5] But the promise of the Internet is not just that it will increase sales, it will also reduce operating costs, shorten cycle times, compress the value chain and most importantly, enable radically new relationships between organizations and customers. Consider the possibilities:

> The Internet runs on dog years.
>
> James Gosling, VP Sun and creator of Java

- The Internet will enable the growth of on-line banking and electronic funds transfer.

- The Net will put heavy pressure on long-distance telephone rates, which over time will fall dramatically. New technology allows end users to make long-distance telephone calls over the Internet at local rates. Many companies have eliminated long-distance, interoffice faxing by using e-mail.

- E-mail cuts costs by eliminating the need to re-key data.

- Videoconferencing technology is readily becoming available on the desktop.

Of course, this new medium also raises disturbing questions for industries:

- As on-line banking evolves, will the public come to associate banking with such companies as Intuit, Netscape, Sun and Microsoft? Or will they think of traditional banks?

- How will phone companies and long-distance re-sellers survive if individuals and organizations are increasingly able to make phone calls, send faxes and videoconference over the Internet using local phone calls instead of paying long-distance rates?

- If executives can videoconference, how will airlines that rely on high-margin business travelers remain profitable?

- How will travel agents survive as more and more travelers realize that they can check timetables, availability of flights and book tickets over the Internet?

The Force Shaping the Future: The Net

The Internet was originally designed by the U.S. Department of Defense to interconnect military and university computers so that communications networks would remain intact in the event of nuclear attack. If one computer was knocked out of the network, communication would be routed around it through the network of connections.

For decades, the Internet remained the domain of researchers and techies because of the user-vicious, cryptic commands required to communicate. This has all changed with the introduction of easy-to-use, *Windows*-like software.

In November 1990 at the European Laboratory for Particle Physics, researchers built a prototype of the World Wide Web (WWW) that linked documents located anywhere in the world on the Internet. This allowed academics to cross-reference or "hyper-link" their research to other documents on other computer servers at different locations. Just click on a word that was highlighted in a color other than the normal text and you were taken to the other document. The Web was born.

The World Wide Web is the fastest-growing part of the Internet. Netscape, Sun Microsystems, Intuit, Microsoft and Intel are competing to set the standards for the new medium. The stakes are high as the Web will become the key to commerce in the future. The company that defines this new medium will be the dominant company of the twenty-first century.

Netscape: Born of the Web, Mother of the Web
In the fall of 1995, the stock market valued Netscape, a small, one-year-old company with annual sales of $16 million, at $2 billion on the first day of its Initial Public Offering (IPO). The news stunned markets and marked a turning point. Business began to take note of the potential of the Web. The Web ushers in a new reality that will change the way all companies will work. Netscape, which has become synonymous with the Web, is a new platform, just as the personal computer spawned a revolution in 1981.

In the early 1990s, Marc Andreessen was an undergraduate at the University of Illinois, making $6.85 an hour writing computer code for the National Center for Supercomputing Applications. He and fellow student Eric Bina became intrigued by the potential of the World Wide Web. But the Web lacked a simple graphical user interface (GUI)—an intuitive way for people to unearth the vast amount of material stored on the world's interconnected computers. In a manic burst of coding in the winter of 1993, Andreessen and Bina wrote the basics of a graphical Web browser called *Mosaic*. Almost overnight, their work turned the Web into the business and pop culture phenomenon it is today.

Mosaic was the first GUI for the Web. Internet users could download the browser for free. By the fall of 1994, it had become a fundamental tool for three million Web surfers and was growing at a rate of 600,000 new users per month.

Technical merit seldom determines who wins and loses the competitive race. Being first is more important than being best. And *Mosaic* was first.

Venture capitalist and entrepreneur Jim Clark, who founded Silicon Graphics, contacted Andreessen early in 1994 and suggested that they talk. Using Clark's capital, they founded Netscape with the idea of becoming the Microsoft of the Internet.

By November 1994, *Mosaic* accounted for 60 percent of all Web traffic. In December, Netscape launched its first commercial Web browser, *Navigator*. In four months, with no advertising and no sales in retail outlets, a stunning six million copies of *Navigator* were in use. By the spring of 1995, 75 percent of Web surfers were using *Navigator*. *Mosaic's* share had plummeted to a mere five percent.

Netscape redefined the standard. To succeed, speed is of the essence. Netscape is a pressure-cooker, workaholic culture where brilliant, best-of-breed programmers live in their offices, continually crunching code. Output is valued in the extreme.

"The medium is the message," said Marshall McLuhan. Netscape uses the Web to create a market for the Web. Netscape operates in a fundamentally different way than other software companies:

> If Netscape relied on standard retail distribution, the physical acts of manufacturing disks, shipping them across the country, advertising their arrival and waiting for customers to make their purchases would take months rather than minutes. If Netscape relied on traditional market surveys, the process of mailing disks to testers, following up with questionnaires and waiting for and sorting through returns would take months more. At Netscape, working off the Web translates into unthinkable delays.
>
> For most companies unthinkable delays are called business-as-usual. Consider Microsoft's August 24 [1995] launch of *Windows 95*. Microsoft had its final code on July 14. Why wait six more weeks? Because Microsoft had to organize a dozen manufacturing plants and 500 trucks to produce and deliver the software to 20,000 retail outlets. Life off the Web is awfully messy.
>
> There are, to be sure, risks to life on the Web. To an extraordinary degree, Netscape has opened itself up to the competition. Engineers from Spyglass, America Online, or any other company can log on to Netscape's user groups and see what its customers are saying, what its engineers are promising, what glitches are raising a ruckus. It's as if Pepsi published the results of its taste tests in a public forum that Coca-Cola could visit every day.[6]

Microsoft Wakes Up

Until December 7, 1995, it looked as if Microsoft was going to become irrelevant in the Internet age. While Microsoft dominated the PC software market, Bill Gates, who is widely seen as a visionary guru for the

PC industry, was completely blind-sided by the rapid rise of Netscape and the Web.

In May 1993, Gates approved a plan to launch a proprietary on-line service called *Microsoft Network (MSN)* to compete with America Online, CompuServe and Prodigy. The plan called for developing and bundling a browser that would be bundled with *Windows 95*. In February 1994, Steven Sinofsky, Gates' technical assistant, e-mailed his boss, informing him that the Internet was abuzz with *Mosaic*. On April 4, 1994, Netscape was founded. The next day, senior management at Microsoft held a retreat to debate the importance of the Internet. By this time work on *MSN* had been under way for a year. This focus prevented a shift in strategy. The decision was made to continue with *MSN*.

Throughout 1995, Microsoft was focused on the launch of *Windows 95* and *MSN*. The company was also offering to buy Intuit, and was involved in a number of inquiries with the U.S. Department of Justice.

By October 1995, Version 2 of Netscape *Navigator* was being downloaded across the Internet for free. At yet another Microsoft retreat, Benjamin Slivka, who was in charge of *Internet Explorer*, proposed that Microsoft give away the software on the Net, just as Netscape was doing. Gates dismissed the idea saying, "What do you think we are, communists?"

On August 8, 1995, Netscape's Initial Public Offering sent a shock wave through the consciousness of the business world. On the first day, the stock offering, which was priced at $25, rose in trading to $75. Amid the subsequent blaze of publicity, no one could ignore the power of the Web. On November 16, Goldman Sachs stopped recommending Microsoft stock for purchase because of Internet concerns.

Having realized the profound importance of the Web, Gates was swift to turn Microsoft around. The Internet Platform & Tools Division, created in February 1996, by the end of 1996 employed over 2,500 people—more than Netscape, Yahoo! and the next five Net upstarts combined. Microsoft's catch-up efforts have been swift and intense. While millions of copies of Microsoft's *Internet Explorer* have been shipped, usage studies show that over 70 percent of Web surfers use a Netscape browser.

Netscape's demise is greatly exaggerated. By January 1997, Netscape sold its one-millionth Internet/intranet server. "It took Lotus *Notes* seven years to get a million seats, and in our case, it took us a year to get a million servers, not even counting the seats," said Srivats Sampath, Netscape's vice president of server marketing.

Netscape's growth is being driven by two factors. First, an "anything but Microsoft" fear that exists in the software developer community. Microsoft dominates the industry. Microsoft's 1996 profits totaled $3.45 billion. The next nine largest PC software makers' combined profits totaled $523 million.[7] Microsoft has used its near-monopoly practices with a ruthless competitiveness that borders on bully-boy tactics. Second, Netscape has great products and a blisteringly fast product development cycle.

This case study highlights the importance of being first and why organizations are not just competing to create a new product, but to create the market standard by which all competitors will be measured. For Microsoft, which would have been better, throwing 50 people at the opportunity early in 1994, setting the standard and creating the market, or having to pay 2,500 people to try and catch up in 1996? The leverage of time is immense.

Leaders Are Only Human
Paradigm shifts can be like watching a sunrise. The black night sky sprinkled with stars slowly gives way to gray. The stars fade, the East turns pink and eventually yellows. Finally, the sun rises, breaking above the horizon. But awareness of the dawn has come long before. At what time did it dawn? Changes are subtle and incremental.

No leader is omnipotent. No leader can perfectly predict the future no matter how successful or brilliant. No one company has exclusive insight into new products or services that will excite and delight customers. Ultimately, complacency kills. Even the best and brightest individuals and organizations must continually question the way they see the world.

While this book cites examples of corporate strategies, it is important to remember that these strategies work today — not forever. At some point in the future, changes in circumstances will invalidate some of them. Therefore, it is important to think critically about all the concepts presented.

"One size fits all" solutions do not work. A strategy that works for a company at level four of business development (video game) may not work at level seven. In fact, applied at level seven it may cause the demise of the organization. What works for a manufacturer may not work for a service company. Instead, the cases and strategies cited are meant to provoke thought. Debate the issues within your organization. See how the strategies apply. For every case I cite in this book, there is a countercase.

Internet Explosion

Before Netscape's IPO, most businesses ignored the Net. Even after Netscape's IPO, some market commentators dismissed the Web as frivolous because of the relatively small volume of commercial activity and the lack of business applications. Few businesses can ignore the Net now.

By mid-March 1997, Dell was selling $1 million worth of computer equipment per day over its Web site. Selling over the Internet is a powerful tool: 80 percent of people buying from the Web are new customers.

By August 1997, Dell was selling over $2 million worth of products a day over the Web. But according to Scott Eckert, director of Dell Online, that's just a pilot. Ninety percent of Dell's almost $9 billion of sales are direct to businesses. In August 1997, Dell went live with corporate intranet sales.[8] Dell will put a custom store directly on its customers' intranet, with custom corporate configurations and pricing.

> Business on the Net is "a zero-variable cost transaction. The only thing better would be mental telepathy."[9]
>
> Michael Dell, CEO, Dell Computer Corporation

An intranet is a computer network within an organization that uses Internet protocols. The benefit to the company is that it can cut software costs by using the same software for external communications (Internet) and internal communications (intranet). Similarly, employees only have to learn how to use a single piece of software, the browser, to access information inside or outside the company.

Internet sales not only cost less, but they also save time as customers can answer their own pricing queries and create their own configurations, saving Dell money. People on the phone who visit the Web site before calling are 1.5 times more likely to buy than those who cold-call the toll-free number.

Cisco is selling $4 million a day of network products across its Web site. That's $1.5 billion a year! According to Cisco Chief Information Officer Peter Solvik, Internet sales saved the company $250 million last year, cutting expenses by 14 percent. Thus, companies can reach more customers with fewer staff while raising the quality of service to 24 hours a day, 365 days a year with relative ease, not to mention the huge savings on the phone bills.[10]

Companies are using the Web in very creative ways.

PC Flowers

PC Flowers, launched in January 1990, allowed users of such on-line services as Prodigy to order flowers. At that time the company ranked last among the 25,000 Florists' Transworld Delivery (FTD) Association's U.S. members.

FTD is the largest retail trade association of florists in North

America. Founded in 1910 to facilitate the exchange of floral orders among florists, it has grown to an affiliation of more than 50,000 florists in 160 countries.

By May 15, 1990, PC Flowers had become the tenth-largest FTD florist in America and by 1997, it was the second largest.

In December 1994, the company launched its PC Flowers & Gifts service on the Internet (www.pcflowers.com). One year later, the company launched its "Internet Consumer Incentive Traffic Program," linking major Web sites and on-line services to the PC Flowers & Gifts Web site. The consumer traffic is tracked and PC Flowers pays the on-line services and Web sites a percentage of each sale. Orders placed with PC Flowers are transmitted directly into the FTD order processing.

E-mail Reminder

PC Flowers' Web site features an e-mail reminder service. Customers can enter important dates—wedding anniversary, family members' birthdays, Mother's Day—and the service will send you an e-mail to alert you well in advance of the event. Of course, this gives you plenty of time to choose the flowers or gift you want to send from PC Flowers.

A Small Company Can Create a Big Presence

The first financial institution in the world to approve loans on-line was a small Canadian financial institution called Bayshore Trust. The company was so successful that in 1996 Trimark Financial Corporation bought it and renamed it Trimark Trust.

Bayshore Trust had only eight branches in 1995 when it launched its on-line loan service. For less than the cost of opening one new branch, Bayshore developed a Web site offering instant loan approval and the ability to buy financial products on-line. The stand-alone site did not integrate with Bayshore's database, so security was not an issue (http://www. trimarktrust.com).

The site lists Trimark Trust's loan rates along with those of competing banks. Trimark Trust's rates average one full percentage point below the banks'. The Web site takes visitors through the buying process. The Web page asks, "Want to know how much Trimark Trust will SAVE YOU over the long haul?" Click on the text and it takes you to a little questionnaire. I answered the questionnaire as follows:

How much do you want to borrow?	$300,000
How many years do you want to pay it back?:	5
Enter Trimark Trust's interest rate:	8.75
Another financial institution's rate:	9.75

The next screen comes back with, "Okay, here are the facts. When you borrow from Trimark Trust, you can expect to pay less. For a loan of $300,000, your monthly payment with Trimark Trust will be $6,191, compared to $6,337 with the competition. Over the five-year term of your loan, this means you will save $8,766 in interest. It's money that stays in your pocket, not ours. The total interest cost with Trimark Trust will be only $71,471, while the other guys will charge you $80,237. Right now, on-line and totally secure, you can apply for a loan with Trimark Trust."

Thus the Web page takes customers through the buying process, proving the financial benefit of taking out a loan from Trimark Trust rather than one of the banks. The site spurs customers to act. A customer can then fill out a financial questionnaire. The customer enters all the data rather than a Trimark Trust employee having to take the time. By hitting a button, the customer submits the form. On the back end, the information goes to the credit bureau to approve the credit. Approval takes as little as 60 seconds. The company couriers to the applicant the legal documents for signing. Once Trimark Trust receives the documents back, the money is deposited into the customer's account within 24 hours. The whole process can take less than two days.

As the CEO points out, "Trimark Trust now has a branch anywhere that a customer can log on to the Web." In fact, the first loan that the company approved was to an individual who was thousands of miles away from the nearest branch. The Web site now generates more loans business than the eight branches combined! And it has attracted an entirely new demographic of customers. The average customer before the Web site launch was over 50 years old. The average customer currently using the loan facilities is thirty-something.

Free Phone Calls Across the Net

In 1995, Israeli-based VocalTec Communications created a new market by introducing the *Internet Phone*. It works this way: you speak into your PC's microphone and the software digitizes and compresses the sound into data packets that are sent over the Net. Using the same software, the PC on the receiving end decompresses the data, turning them back into sound. End users typically pay $20 a month to hook up to a local Internet Service Provider (ISP) for unlimited access. *Internet Phone* means that long-distance calls are essentially free. Users of early versions of the software had to tolerate poor voice quality and long delays. And they had to take turns talking. But quality has greatly improved.

According to International Data Corporation (IDC), the market grew to $3.5 million in its first year as 500,000 active users began dialing for dollars on the Net. VocalTec captured 94 percent of the market it created.

VocalTec's *Internet Phone 4*, released in March 1996, combines business phone features with such capabilities as whiteboard/ document conferencing and voice mail. It retails for $49.95. The $149.95 VocalTec *Internet Conference* introduced in 1996 allows real-time collaboration among users working with such applications as Microsoft *Office*. VocalTec's other core products include the *Telephony Gateway* server and the *Atrium Conferencing Suite*.

IDC predicts VocalTec will keep the largest share of the Internet telephony market and estimates that it will grow to $560 million and 16 million active users by 1999.

A study by telecom research firm Frost and Sullivan shows that VocalTec held on to almost 79 percent of the market revenue in 1996.[11] The study predicts that the market will grow at 149 percent compounded annually, reaching $1.89 billion by the end of 2001.

At an industry conference in 1997, a panel of industry executives concurred that as early as 2002, and by 2007 at the latest, at least 50 percent of the telephone traffic will go over the Internet rather than through telephone companies' lines.[12]

Low-cost, Internet-based, long-distance calls for the masses are frightening the telcos. Internet telephony boldly challenges the existing telecommunications regulatory paradigm. Until 1997, *Internet Phone* was a small niche product appealing to hobbyists, Internet enthusiasts and a core group willing to suffer poor quality in return for free long-distance calls. But quality is improving and demand exploding. Gateway devices, which VocalTec also produces, are allowing traditional telephones — not just PCs — to be used on one or both ends of the call.

Recently, Internet software providers have been able to offer traditional telephone features, including call waiting, caller ID, conferencing and hold. Valuable business applications such as whiteboard teleconferencing and the ability to upload and download files while speaking are making Internet telephony attractive to corporations.

The phone companies are feeling so threatened that in March 1996, over 130 of them acting through the American Carriers Telecommunication Association (ACTA) petitioned the Federal Communications Commission (FCC) to define VocalTec and other software vendors as telecom carriers. This would subject them to tariffs, and ACTA further argued that until the FCC decides the case, VocalTec and other companies should be prevented from selling their products. (Such a move is unprecedented for the FCC and therefore unlikely.)

It is easy to see why the telcos are upset. Internet Service Providers buy data lines from the telcos and resell them to end users for a monthly hook-up fee, typically $20. In the end, the telephone traffic is going across the phone companies' lines, but as data, not voice, at a fraction of the revenue to the telco.

In July 1997, Motorola signed a licensing agreement with VocalTec to bring the full range of its Internet telephony software to mainstream corporate customers. Using Voice over Internet Protocol (VoIP), corporations can move traffic off the telephony infrastructure and on to the data intranet/Internet. Most companies' existing computer network infrastructure connects to the Internet, allowing them to consolidate data, voice, fax and video traffic and send it all over the Internet, eliminating long-distance charges and cutting travel costs by enabling distant users to work together in real time. The new technology also increases productivity by providing richer interfaces for collaboration. This strategic relationship between Motorola and VocalTec will bring IP telephony to the mainstream much more quickly.

In 1997, USA Global Link in Iowa launched a service to let customers make cheap long-distance calls over the Internet using phones instead of PCs. It will charge 25 to 50 cents a minute for calls to 120 countries, saving up to 80 percent on international rates. Customers call the company's network, then dial the number they want to reach. Global Link converts the call into digital format and transmits it over the Internet, bypassing the international phone system. It's converted back into sound (analog form) by a USA Global Link computer at the other end and transferred to a local phone network. USA Global Link is spending $500 million to install its own Internet computers in 120 countries.

USA Global Link's new service is enabled by VocalTec's *Telephony Gateway*, the company's most powerful product. Priced at about $1,400 per line, the current eight-line version works with the voice processing board and requires a dedicated Intel Pentium 200MHz PC running Microsoft *NT 3.51* or *4.0*. Companies are also buying this product to switch telephone networks to the Internet, while at the same time keeping the public phone system as a back-up.

And it's not just one rebel telco. Jumping on the bandwagon in January 1997, MCI introduced its *Vault* system, which enabled MCI to switch voice and data calls to the Internet.

It will be common to make international phone calls over the Internet in 1999, says Merrill Lynch telecommunications analyst Daniel Reingold. "It will start with international and go to domestic long distance." The Internet is encroaching on the profitable long-distance phone business. There is not going to be an overnight exodus, but the Internet is a threat to the long-distance rates that phone companies enjoy.

As more and more customers begin using Internet Phones or sign up with services that digitize their normal phone calls and send them over the Internet, companies will save money on toll-free numbers. Companies can already integrate call centers with the Internet. For example, a national catalog sales company accepting orders via a toll-free voice line can also accept voice and e-mail orders from buyers browsing its interactive Web-based catalog, capturing sales more quickly and cost effectively.

VocalTec plans to develop future capabilities to let users hold two-way videoconferences, send a document to or receive a document from a fax machine, exchange messages with two-way, wireless pagers, or place calls to or receive calls from standard and cellular telephone sets anywhere in the world. The company is also planning to ship a video phone and introduce a new product, V-mail, which features audio-based messages rather than the text-based e-mail.

Virtual Meetings Replace Real Ones

Wayne Seifreid, a NorTel manager, pointed out to me that he can have a virtual meeting with someone 30 miles from his office for free using the Internet. To have a real meeting requires him to have a car or take a taxi, go on the highway for 45 minutes, pay for parking, have the meeting, then take 45 minutes to get back to the office. The real meeting costs at least $50. If he was "meeting" someone in Hong Kong, a virtual meeting would still be free while the real meeting would cost more than $2,500. Eventually, most meetings will be virtual. The virtual meeting isn't actually free because NorTel had to make a capital investment in its computer network and videoconferencing software. Once this investment is made, however, the operating cost of having a meeting is next to nothing.

In the future, reality will be too expensive for businesses.
Wayne Seifreid, manager, Multimedia, NorTel

Currently, virtual meetings are the privilege of the elite. Companies must invest in their systems, create secure firewalls that link to the Internet and manage the network. At the individual level, users have to have the patience to configure their modem, work out the conflicts in the hardware and software, deal with logging on or hire a computer technician to do it, and have the courage to go through the learning curve. So for now, the virtual experience is for the elite, while the masses have only the real experience.

However, in the future, as the price of desktop videoconferencing plummets and hardware and software become easier to use, the virtual experience will be for the masses while the real experience will be for the elite.

Andy Grove, CEO of Intel, addressed the 1995 National Speakers Association conference in Minneapolis. Andy was very polite to speak to us for 15 minutes. I say polite because in 1995 Intel revenues were $16.2 billion. Assuming Andy works 50 hours a week — or 2,500 hours a year — the company revenue divided by his number of hours ($16.2 billion divided by 2,500 hours) gives a figure of $6.5 million per hour. Thus Andy should be focusing each hour of his time on activities that are of significant enough importance to generate $6.5 million over the long term. So why would Andy Grove fly to Minneapolis, take a taxi to the hotel and address 2,000 professional speakers who have little to do with his industry? The answer is that he won't. The real experience would take at least eight hours of his time for 15 minutes of speaking. So instead, Andy addressed us from his desk using Intel's videoconferencing system. The total experience took 20 minutes out of his day. He still was generous with us and did it for the public relations opportunity.

When will Andy Grove conduct a face-to-face meeting? When he is working on high-leverage activities that have a profound effect on the future of Intel, meeting with Intel's senior design engineers, scientists and executive team, meeting with industry partners and talking to a software developers conference or Wall Street analysts. For senior executives whose limiting factor is time, the virtual experience is already the way they communicate with most people.

Charles Schwab Revolutionizes Stock Trading

Charles Schwab allows its clients to buy and sell stocks, options, mutual funds and bonds 24 hours a day. Clients can also short stocks, place limits or stop orders, good 'til and cancel orders. They can get real-time quotes, independent analysts' picks, choose from 6,700 company reports, create a personalized news clipping service, check their order status, review and download transactions, trace interest and dividend payments, and organize tax schedule information — all from the comfort of their home or office. Clients also have the freedom to choose how to access this information: Web-based trading, PC-based trading, automated phone trading or talking to a broker.

Schwab was the first brokerage to offer on-line trading, introducing a *DOS*-based software in 1984, and *Windows*-based software in 1993. In 1995, the company introduced an "all electric account" called *e.Schwab*, giving investors real-time quotes, news and research, and trading at Schwab's lowest commission rates. Customers pay just $29.95 for stock trades up to 1,000 shares and $.03 a share for trades over 1,000 shares. *e.Schwab* clients do all their business electronically and have almost no interaction with people at Schwab. In 1996, the firm introduced its Web-based *SchwabNOW!* Any customer can use the site to place trades and access account data and investment information. Clients who normally place trades over the phone with brokers at Schwab receive 20 percent off Web trades. In 1996, the company also introduced the industry's first speech recognition quotation service, providing real-time quotes on over 13,000 stocks, mutual funds and market indicators. It complements Schwab's automated phone system, which allows clients to access account balances and make trades.

Schwab's aggressive and strategic investments in new technology have given its customers the widest range of choice on how to access information and trade. As a result, Schwab has created an effective monopoly in the market. As of December 1995, no other brokerage offered a *Windows*-based trading system. Schwab has grown quickly:

Charles Schwab & Co., 1990-1997

Year	# of accounts (millions)	average # daily trades in '000s	Revenue (in $M)
1990	1.4	13.1	387
1991	1.6	17.9	570
1992	2.0	23.6	750
1993	2.5	35.3	965
1994	3.0	43.5	1,065
1995	3.4	56.3	1,420
1996	4.0	78.0	1,851
1997 (to Q2)	4.5	100.5	1,066

Schwab's PC-based electronic services (excluding phone-based) accounted for 30 percent of Schwab's 21 million trades in 1996 and over half of the company's 97 million calls. By June 1997, on-line services accounted for 36 percent of all the company's trades.

As of July 1997, Schwab had over 908,000 active on-line users with over $66 billion in on-line customer assets. According to Forrester Research, this represents 50 percent of the on-line market in both accounts and assets, and makes Schwab the leader in on-line brokerage.

By comparison, e*trade in 1996 reported 140,000 accounts and approximately $3 billion in assets. While e*trade has experienced great growth (as of July 1997, e*trade has 300,000 accounts), Schwab still dominates this rapidly growing market. Schwab offers "multiple-channel" capabilities for investors, including 250 branches, Internet, PC-based, telephone, and round-the-clock service.

"Our on-line growth is directly related to investors' comfort with being able to get through to us many different ways, regardless of market volatility," notes Tom Taggart of Schwab. "This is something that Internet-only brokers just can't deliver. The chat-rooms are littered with disgruntled investors who have tried to get through to their Internet broker on a busy market day."

Schwab's heavy investment in IT has lowered the cost of transactions, allowing the company to deal profitably with small investors who were unprofitable for other brokerages and therefore considered a nuisance.

"In the traditional brokerage, clients are controlled through a commission broker," comments Taggart. "But we empower clients with a lot of tools without trying to control the relationship. What used to be the exclusive domain of brokers is now available on-line to Schwab clients: Dow Jones News Retrieval, S&P Market Scope, Reuters Money Network, company reports, analysts' reports and independent research."

Schwab has added features with each release of its software. "Our clients wanted more mutual fund information," notes Taggart. So Schwab introduced *FundMap for Windows*, allowing clients to compare, select and track 1,300 different mutual funds from 194 different fund families, including 750 of Schwab's *OneSource* (no-transaction-fee mutual funds).

Schwab wants to give clients a compelling reason to consolidate all their assets. "People don't want the hassle," Taggart states. "Instead of receiving a monthly statement from each mutual fund that they own, we provide clients with one consolidated statement listing all their funds and access points 24 hours a day."

Schwab's revenues rose 30 percent to $1.9 billion, and doubled the 14 percent industry-wide gain in 1996 in retail commissions. Customers' assets exceeded $250 billion in December 1996 and $300 billion by June 1997. Despite this rapid growth, Schwab still has less than eight percent of retail brokerage commissions and only nine percent of the total assets in money market and no-load mutual funds. Federal Reserve data shows that total consumer investable assets in the United States reached $13 trillion in 1995. If Schwab continues to anticipate and meet its customers' needs, and grow at the same pace as it has from 1990 to 1997, the company will reach $500 billion in assets and five million customers by 2000.

Chairman and CEO Charles Schwab's vision is to build one of the greatest financial services companies in the world. In the highly dynamic brokerage business, successful firms must be able to prosper in good and bad markets. By increasing operational efficiency, Schwab ensures its cost structure will be far lower than traditional brokers', giving it the capital required to further invest in technology and offer investors better investment tools and greater choice. In 1996, revenues grew more than twice as fast as staff. And despite record trading volumes, Schwab's high-tech, high-touch philosophy kept customer satisfaction levels up at 95 percent.

"With all this technology you may wonder why we need branches," notes Taggart. "While many customers enjoy doing business over the phone or PC, most customers bring us new assets in person at our office, where they can get personal service and convenience you simply cannot match with a machine. Most investors want both high-tech and high-touch service, depending on their needs at the moment. This requires a difficult balancing act."

Schwab maintains 250 branch offices in the United States, Puerto Rico, Britain, the Cayman Islands and Hong Kong. Schwab shatters paradigms on more than just the technological level. Who would have thought you could get a Visa card or checking account from a broker?

Schwab's strategy is attracting a new generation of investors. Some of the estimated 75 million baby boomers who are entering their wealth-building years are more concerned than ever about their financial future, paying for their children's education, managing their parents' health care and planning for their own retirement. This group doesn't want a traditional relationship with their broker. Many are Net-literate and know how to access the same information. A traditional broker sending annual reports to them by snail mail insults their intelligence. They can read corporate reports on-line, have stock prices running across their computer screen at the office or home continuously, and read the same Reuters and Bloomberg news service announcements as fast as traders can.

Baby boomers, a large number of whom are new to investing, are turning to Schwab in record numbers. In 1996, Schwab opened nearly one million new accounts.

Schwab has also developed a strategy for first-time investors who may be overwhelmed. There are now more funds to choose from than there are stocks on the New York Stock Exchange. Investors want guidance. For investors who do not want or are unable to hire a personal financial advisor for ongoing investment management, Schwab's investment specialists evaluate a customer's investment profile using computer-based tools and then recommend several simple approaches to mutual fund investing.

In 1996, Schwab, for the first time in its history, began offering customers advice, but not the way traditional brokerages do. Traditional, commissioned brokers are in a conflict of interest, because their companies often expect them to sell stock placements that the firm is underwriting. Clients can't be sure whether a broker recommends a stock because it truly is a good investment and fits with their investment strategy or because the firm expects the broker to sell a certain amount of the stock. Second, traditional brokers are only paid upon the buying or selling of stocks. This creates an incentive to "churn" accounts—buy and sell stocks just to make commissions. Therefore many investors don't trust advice to buy or sell. They wonder, "Is it based truly on my interest or the broker's interest in a commission?" Schwab investment advisors are paid for their advice, regardless of the client's action. Therefore the advisor, not seeking to make money, does not bias the advice.

Technology Is Accelerating the Rate of Organizational Learning

A number of technology trends have been discussed. As the cost of technology falls, more organizations can afford to deploy IT to accelerate the distribution of information and decision-making.

Four million years ago in Africa, humans first stood up on two limbs. Two million years ago, they began making tools. Only 35,000 years ago, cave paintings appeared. Just 12,000 years ago, humans began domesticating plants and animals. Starting only 10,000 years ago, most languages and vocabulary were developed.[13] So it took humanity almost four million years to create language. These days most children can speak by age two. If children were isolated from any contact with people, they would not develop language on their own. Language learning comes through interaction with others.

The Sumerian language is the oldest written language. It emerged around 3100 B.C. As written language spread, only an elite group could read and write. It wasn't until the invention of the Guttenberg press in 1450—just 550 years ago—that reading and writing became more widespread. In western society we consider reading and writing to be essential skills, and most children have learned these by age five. Children today stand on the shoulders of millions of years of human development by the time they are six. And we take it all for granted.

While learning occurs best through interaction with others, accelerated learning results from increasing interaction.

As more and more organizations adopt leading-edge technology — e-mail, computer networks, the Internet, intranets, videoconferencing and Electronic Data Interchange — employees are able to learn faster and make better-informed decisions, through access to more information, than ever before.

Factors That Will Propel the Web Explosion at Higher Velocity

The Web will grow even faster as certain restraining forces are removed. Six factors slowing the Internet's explosive growth are: 1) competing hardware/software standards; 2) ease of use; 3) bandwidth; 4) perceptions about security; 5) tools to exchange cash; 6) copyright. As these are removed, the Web's impact on organizations will increase.

Standards

The phrase "competing standards" is an oxymoron. But in any new industry, until standards emerge the industry can't reach its full potential. As an example, in the early 1800s there were over a dozen different gauges of railway. The gauge is the distance between the rails. A train traveling on a narrow-gauge railway track could not travel on a wide-gauge track. Eventually, a standard gauge emerged.

The absence of standards will always be a problem for the Internet until competing companies cooperate and set common ones, or until one company dominates a market segment and creates the de facto standard. Standards need to be established in the areas of audio- and videoconferencing, Internet addresses, chat services, Internet advertising and more. These will emerge over time.

Ease of Use

The user-vicious computer industry is its own worst enemy. The combination of configuring a modem, installing and getting the software working with the hardware, the challenges of logging on to an on-line service for the first time are still too much of a challenge for most users. In July 1995, only four percent of U.S. households were on-line. While 40 percent of *Windows* users had modems, only 10 percent subscribed to an on-line service. The untapped market is huge. To develop mass markets, user-friendliness has to be the most important dimension not just for using software, but for the whole process of getting on-line — purchasing and installing the modem, configuring and operating the system, trouble-shooting hardware-software conflicts and logging on to the Internet.

Bandwidth

To get on the Internet you must have a connection to it, and the speed of your connection will determine the speed at which you will get information and the kind of applications you can run. Bandwidth is currently a challenge, but there is such an intense focus on the solution to this limiting factor that by 2002 it will not be an issue.

Bandwidth is like a plumbing pipe that carries water. A one-inch pipe with a steady flow of water passing through it will have a certain amount of water flow through it over a period of time. A pipe four inches wide at the same pressure and over the same period will transfer four times greater volume. The principle is the same when transferring data across the Internet. The faster the connection to the Internet (the wider the pipe) the more data you can get instantly and the richer the applications.

Regular phone lines called POTS (plain old telephone service) are like a narrow pipe. The standard modem speed for 1997 — 33.6 to 56.6 kps (kilobytes per second) — is great for transferring text. However, pictures and audio are slow, and video is unacceptably slow. Modem technology is pushing the limits of what it is possible to transfer by standard phone lines.

Telecom companies also offer ISDN (Integrated Services Dedicated Network), which is like having four phone lines rolled into one, and there is an even faster connection called a T1. Only companies can afford to install and pay monthly charges for this type of bandwidth. Unless the price falls substantially, the market will find other ways to increase bandwidth.

Cable television companies are beginning to convert their one-way systems (delivering TV programming from the cable company to your home) into interactive, two-way systems. Using a cable modem in your PC, you will then be able to transfer data at rates that are 10 times faster than 33.6 kps modems. All of a sudden, new applications become possible. These speeds are fantastic for transferring photographs and audio, but still slow with video.

Finally, satellites can provide broadband, two-way communication, but are prohibitively expensive. All these mediums are racing to provide more bandwidth. One thing is certain: as the cost of bandwidth plummets, demand will increase exponentially.

Security

In March 1996, Visa and MasterCard announced a joint standard for processing secure payments across the Net. The companies participating in developing the standard include Intuit, Netscape, IBM, Microsoft and others.

The purchasing of goods and services on the Internet has been stalled by the *perception* that Internet transactions are insecure. Many people have been unwilling to type their credit-card number into their terminal and e-mail it out into cyberspace. But the problem is perceptual, not technical. As the figures of commerce across the Net already indicate, people are becoming more comfortable in their perception of how secure this new medium is.

Cash Transferring Tools

Ultimately what will explode e-commerce is the proliferation of tools allowing consumers to send and receive money across the Internet. Currently, I can buy across the Internet by typing in my credit-card number when I am on a secure server, but as a consumer I have no way to receive money from someone else across the Internet.

Receiving money across the Internet could be achieved if the credit-card companies changed the way they saw their product. Imagine that credit cards really lived up to their name, allowing cardholders to receive money and have their accounts credited. This way, at month's end, Visa or MasterCard might owe you money and pay you interest for the time the money sat in your account! Now that's a paradigm shift!

Copyright

The Internet is the world's largest printing press. Anyone hooked up to the Net can distribute information globally to millions of on-line users at no cost. Digital information can be sent instantly to any number of on-line users. The Net is also the world's largest photocopier. Hundreds or millions of users on the Internet can choose to make copies of a file that is posted on a public site.

At the heart of copyright issues is the question of who should control the expression of ideas. Since we can't physically restrain or control thought, companies making money from copyrighted materials have worked to control the containers that thoughts come in: compact disks, books, videotapes and software diskettes. Essentially, companies have sought to control the packaging.[14]

The purchasing of goods and services on the Internet has rendered this process obsolete, because no physical container is required when information is digitized.

For the explosion of commerce in copyrighted materials, new methods need to be developed that pay a royalty to the author and publishing company every time a document is accessed, a song played or a piece of software downloaded. In 1996, Digital Equipment Corporation announced that it was developing such a tool. The ability to transfer small increments of cash will be available by the year 2000.

Proprietary Walls Are Falling to Open Systems

In September 1997, America Online, with 8.6 million subscribers,[15] bought CompuServe (and its Internet subsidiary SpryNet), with 5.4 million subscribers, making it the largest on-line service provider in the world.[16] Meanwhile, the Internet has been growing exponentially. According to the Internet Society, which measures traffic, there were 100,000 hosts in 1989, 1 million by 1992 and close to 10 million by the end of 1995. The number is projected to grow to 100 million by 2000![17] Although no one knows for sure, conservative estimates put the number of Internet users at 1 million in 1990, 50 million by the end of 1995 and over 1 billion by 2000!

Proprietary, on-line services have stagnated, by contrast. New York investment banking firm Veronis, Shuler & Associates predicts that by 1999 commercial services such as America Online, CompuServe, Prodigy and Microsoft Network—services that provide proprietary content to paid subscribers—will be abandoned by users. Instead, users are turning to the Internet with its vast, non-proprietary reservoir of free content.[18]

Microsoft has a huge, installed base of more than 160 million users worldwide. Imagine that Microsoft decides to bypass retailers and sell its own software directly to end users across the Internet. Eliminating the intermediary, Microsoft could sell its software at current retail prices, while doubling or tripling the profitability of each transaction for the company, and simplifying the entire purchasing process for the customer.

Imagine logging on to the Internet, surfing to Microsoft's Web site, browsing through various menus of software, making a selection, keying in your Visa number, confirming the selection and then watching as the software immediately downloads onto your system and automatically configures itself on your hard disk. You wouldn't even have to leave your desk!

Over time, Microsoft could include remote access software in its operating system. Under such a system, an on-line Microsoft technician could take control of your PC across the Internet and solve any configuration problems. Microsoft could either include free support for the first 90 days in the price of the software or charge a support fee.

For the customer, it would be better service and less hassle at the same price as retail. Within the first year of selling software directly to end users, Microsoft would likely become the world's largest retail vendor of software and experience a corresponding surge in profit.

With the launch of *Windows 95*, Microsoft had planned to include *Office 95*, its product suite — *Word* (word processor), *Excel* (spreadsheet), *PowerPoint* (graphics), *Mail* (mail client) and *Access* (database) — on the CD-ROM version of *Windows 95*. CD-ROMs have about 650 megabytes (MB) of storage space and *Windows 95* only takes up about 100 MB. Customers would have gone to the retailer, paid roughly $100 to buy a copy of *Windows 95* on CD and installed it on their system. The software then would have asked them, "Would you like to install *Office 95?*" Users wanting to purchase it would have been prompted to call a toll-free number, whereupon a Microsoft representative would have taken their credit-card number and given them a unique numeric key to unlock and install *Office 95*. Under the plan, Microsoft would have received the secondary sale without any portion going to the software retailer. Rumors of this plan so frightened a group of U.S. software vendors that a number of them banded together to bring anti-trust action against Microsoft.

Netscape has already bypassed the retail channel by allowing anyone to download *Navigator* for free from its Web side. However, to get support, users must purchase a copy by keying in their credit-card number. Netscape has produced the software on diskette for purchase in retail stores. But why bother when you can get it for free?

In the software business, sales are one-off, with upgrades every year or two. By contrast, utilities such as Bell Canada receive monthly payments that generate huge cash flow. Utilities experience ongoing and ever-increasing revenues as more and more individuals and organizations subscribe. Microsoft, Netscape and Sun Microsystems want to become utility companies.

On-line Flight Reservations

American Airlines has its own Web page that allows travelers to compare flights from different airlines, select flights by schedule, or price or look at existing reservations (www.americanair.com).

The Sabre reservation case (Chapter 10) highlighted how redefining the relationship between the company and customers shifted the very nature of competition. American Airlines, by offering a free reservation system to travel agents, created a new business: real-time, on-line reservation systems for travel agents. But the explosion of the Net now threatens travel agents, as American and other airlines can make bookings directly with customers. Sabre is also threatened, as the reservation market is once again open to competition.

If you are interested in on-line information and reservations for airline travel, visit http://www.itn.net/airlines. The site lists every airline in the world, along with information on frequent flier programs. Visitors help update the site, and it is the most comprehensive listing of information on air travel that I have seen.

On-line Commerce

In 1994, Microsoft announced its intention to buy Intuit. Intuit's *Quicken for Windows* is one of the most user-friendly pieces of software on the market today. It is a simple program that allows individuals and small office/home office businesses to perform accounting easily and painlessly. Microsoft's plan to buy Intuit was stalled by the U.S. Justice Department, and Microsoft eventually withdrew the offer. Microsoft's own product, *Money*, has not matched *Quicken's* ease of use, functionality or popularity, despite Microsoft giving away 450,000 free copies of the program to users who downloaded the software from Microsoft's Web site.

Imagine that by using a package such as *Quicken* you were able to send money to any other individual or organization on the Internet, or similarly receive money, such that when both parties confirmed the transaction, the money was automatically debited from one bank account and credited to the other. Imagine being able to instantaneously receive funds owed to you—no delays due to the payment being in the mail or having to clear the banking system, but instant credit to your account! This could be banking of the future by the year 2000. If this scenario transpires, the Net would become the largest clearinghouse of banking transactions in the world.

Some U.S. banks were so worried about this that they banded together to complain to the U.S. Department of Justice about their anti-trust concerns with Microsoft—to prevent it from buying Intuit. But the market, as described, doesn't exist yet! How can there be antitrust action against dominance in a market that doesn't exist?

What about the Banks?

Some banks have been building branches—although banking in the future will have more to do with keystrokes, mouse clicks and phone lines than visiting buildings. How much of research and development budgets at North America's largest banks have been dedicated to developing PC-based, on-line banking software since 1990? Not much. To do so would have been in their own interest. It costs a bank over one dollar to process, manage, store, reconcile and audit a physical, paper-based payment, but it costs less than seven cents to do the same with an electronic transaction.

Why then have few banks been active in this field? On-line banking will change the industry more fundamentally than ATMs did.

The explosion of the Net won't be driven by current applications. What will explode the Net is real-world, commercial applications that make life significantly easier for people.

This leads me to conclude that banking is essential but banks are not. We need to separate form from function. The form that banking takes in the future will not be the same form as it is today.

Imagine Some of These Possibilities

Imagine visiting a car dealership, test-driving a new General Motors model, then going home, logging on to a Web site and viewing the custom features of your choice on-line. You could choose the color, air conditioning, sunroof, stereo, leather or fabric seats, five-speed or automatic transmission, with or without cruise control — and watch how each option affects the price and see the car rotate three-dimensionally. You could then punch the purchase button using your mouse. After a series of confirmations, your selection would be automatically conveyed to the assembly plant, where, through flexible manufacturing processes (see appendix on flexible management), your custom car would be produced and delivered to the dealer or even directly to your home two weeks later.

All these services would become possible with the service provider or credit-card company guaranteeing the security of payment across the Net. The only limiting factor in this paradigm shift is imagination.

In 1994 for the first time North Americans bought more PCs than televisions. In fact, more PCs were sold than any other consumer appliance. Of the 40 million PCs sold in 1995, more than half were sold to households. Now 35 percent of all North American households have PCs.

Banks of the Future

Intuit (the world's leading provider of financial software and electronic financial services) and America Online (AOL — the world's largest on-line service), announced in November 1995 that they had signed a strategic agreement to jointly provide electronic banking. Starting in 1996, AOL members gained access to their checking, savings, money market and credit-card accounts at participating banks and financial institutions. They are able to check their balances, download complete account statements, transfer funds and pay bills electronically from within their AOL account. AOL has six million subscribers. In 1995

In real estate the axiom used to be location, location, location ... perhaps now it should be location, bandwidth, location.

Real estate broker attending a conference

Intuit announced strategic partnerships with 22 leading U.S. financial institutions to allow customers to pay their bills on-line.

As of March 1996, Intuit's *Quicken* had eight million devoted users, versus two million for Microsoft's *Money*. By contrast, Netscape *Navigator* had an estimated 15 million! Banks and these software vendors are engaged in a life-and-death struggle to determine the future of banking. The banks are scared to death of the comparatively small software companies.

Banks Move to e-commerce[19]

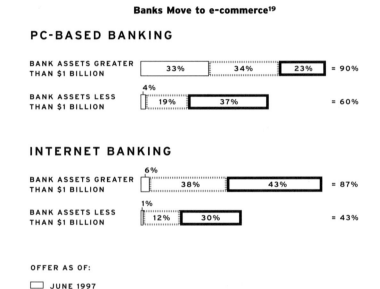

PC-BASED BANKING

BANK ASSETS GREATER
THAN $1 BILLION   33%   34%   23%   = 90%

4%
BANK ASSETS LESS
THAN $1 BILLION   19%   37%   = 60%

INTERNET BANKING

6%
BANK ASSETS GREATER
THAN $1 BILLION   38%   43%   = 87%

1%
BANK ASSETS LESS
THAN $1 BILLION   12%   30%   = 43%

OFFER AS OF:

☐ JUNE 1997
▥ JUNE 1998

The hallmark of banks is to create a perception of security, stability and solvency. Banks are big, have indestructible steel-doored vaults and solid names built on words such as National, America and First. Customer loyalty is based on the psychology of trust.

As the number of on-line transactions soars, banking steadily migrates into the turf of software developers. The banks realize how little they know about this business, and that's why they're concerned.

Software companies want us to view banking as just another form of information processing, and money as just another form of information. They want to transfer customer loyalty from the trusted bank to the preferred software application. Financial institutions would become low-margin, invisible providers of services whose main feature would be low cost.

The company that controls the standards of on-line banking wins. That's why Intuit, Netscape, Microsoft, a host of technology companies and banks are scrambling to own the standards, and consequently the future, of on-line banking. Banks don't know how to compete in this new environment.

A 21-member consortium of American banks and technology companies will launch the Electronic Check Project by 1998 making Internet-based checking available.

Predictions

I predict that by 2001, the banks in North America will cut their staff to as little as half of 1994 levels. There is little security in being a bank teller. New jobs will be created, but they will require far different skill sets than that of a teller.

The demographic shift to those using on-line banking will closely parallel the usage of ATMs. People born before 1950 have a predisposition not to use an ATM and those born after 1950 have a predisposition to use one. Likewise, consumers born after 1960 will be more likely to use on-line systems.

Given demographic and technological trends, a large shake-up in banking systems and market share is inevitable. Only time will tell which banks will survive. One or two companies—a credit-card company and/or software company—could emerge as major winners in defining new banking standards.

To Summarize:

- The Internet is the fastest-growing social and business phenomenon of this century. Its impact will be more significant than the invention of the Guttenberg press.

- Barriers to the explosion of commerce across the Internet will fall as consumers adapt to the new medium.

- Companies that thrive in this new medium will create the tools of commerce of the future.

Workshop Questions and Activities:

- If you were starting a company today to serve your customers, what technologies would you use to simplify the industry? What advantages would these give you versus your current practices? Why isn't someone doing this?

- One of the characteristics of the Internet is that it eliminates the physical distance between buyer and seller. A search for drill bits may yield suppliers from Taiwan, Canada, Germany, and the United States. While this effectively brings new competitors into your markets, it also opens the world to you. How will your business deal with the implications of global market access by all competitors, including the small start-ups on other continents?

- What will be the role of your Internet presence? Many shoppers use the Internet solely for gathering product information, but many observers feel that this is because of nervousness using the Internet for transactions. Should your role on the Net be that of information provider, or will you use the Net as a completely new channel of distribution for your company?

- Remembering that everyone, including your competition, has access to your site, how much information should you make available?

- Many grocers are treating companies such as Peapod with the same indifference that local drugstores treated the entry of Wal-Mart into small towns during the 1980s. Not many small drugstores are left. What new technologies or new players are likely to hurt your business over the next few years? How can you offset these effects?

- Suggest ways your company teams can understand the problems that prevent the organization from increasing its operational efficiency.

Reflection:
- What is the key learning/insight for me in this chapter?

Action:
- What one action shall I take tomorrow to move learning into action? And over time repeat, to move action into habit?

CHAPTER 12

Business and the Environment

As we enter the next century, nothing will have a greater impact on business than the environment. While the media's focus on the environment appears to have waned since the 1980s, researchers note it has become a core issue, a non-negotiable concern. The public expects corporations and governments to protect the environment.

Enlightened corporations know that what is good for the environment is also good for business.

"Green is not a new product line or a new sector, it is a new way of doing business. It is not something to do as a legal obligation, as a contribution to society or the planet," says Wayne Roberts, co-author of the environmental handbook *Get a Life*. "It is a way of doing business that comes automatically."

The shifts that individuals, organizations and society as a whole will have to make as a result of the environmental imperative are more confounding than any other changes discussed so far.

At the core of most organizational problems are faulty paradigms. One of these is the concept of control and power. Paradoxically, the more leaders cling to power, the less powerful their organizations are. The more they control, the more out-of-control their organization. Hierarchical, top-down companies can no longer compete in this rapidly changing environment. The loss of market share, increased competition and the speed of change are causing a great deal of pain for individuals in organizations. Out of this pain comes the search for new ways of working.

This book is written to help people understand the forces that are driving change and to bring about greater freedom of action for individuals within organizations. Once individuals can more freely interact to shape the mission and vision of their organization, companies and society will be in a better position to address the environmental problems we currently face.

Politicians often say it's an issue of jobs or the environment. This is a false dichotomy. We can't have one or the other, it must be both. We need a new way of thinking.

Good for the Environment; Good for the Bottom Line

On March 25, 1989, the Exxon *Valdez*—an oil tanker three football fields in length—ran aground in Prince William Sound, a sensitive marine area off the coast of Alaska. The tanker spilled 200,000 barrels of crude oil.

What was the true cost of the disaster to the company? Not only did the clean-up cost Exxon $2 billion, the bad publicity resulted in the loss of thousands of customers, many of whom wrote to the company, saying they would never again buy gasoline from Exxon.

Research shows that for every customer who complains, four or five feel the same way but won't take the time to call or write to complain. The loss of market share for Exxon was huge. Being a corporate polluter cost the company billions of dollars.

While they weren't even directly involved, French wine makers paid heavily for their government's policy of nuclear testing in the South Pacific. French wine companies admit that the international boycotts cost them $150 million in lost sales in 1995 alone.

> Not everything that counts can be counted and not everything that can be counted counts.
> Albert Einstein, physicist

By contrast, companies and industries that are good to the environment are winning market share. Black's Photography in Canada is a case in point.

Federal government regulations on pollution are often stated in terms of acceptable parts-per-million. Before 1991, Black's would dilute certain toxic, photo-finishing chemicals, then release the effluent into sewers. Then-president Eddie Black, realizing that this practice was unacceptable, began a drive to eliminate discharges. The result was *System Crystal*, a closed-loop process that separates the chemicals from the water, purifies both and then reuses the photochemicals. Today, nothing goes down the drain.

Black's reduced water usage by over 90 percent—from 13 million gallons a year to less than two million. In 1992, other photo finishers' chemicals, one way or another, ended up in the sewer system and eventually in the drinking water.

The problem is that it costs less money to pollute than to deal with waste properly. Despite conserving so much water and saving on recovered chemicals, Black's environmental approach actually costs the company more. The new process, though, was a winner with employees and customers. Employees take pride in being environmental leaders, and Black's increased its market share by three percent in a stagnant market after introducing *System Crystal.* The response of some of Black's competitors was to send scientists to lobby legislators, claiming that diluted photochemicals in our water pose no health hazard! Others saw a good thing and copied the revolutionary process.

The End of Work

Jeremy Rifkin in *The End of Work* argues that new technology is ushering in an era of workerless production. Rifkin predicts that by 2020, blue-collar work will have been completely eliminated and that three-quarters of all current white-collar work will be lost to automation. If Rifkin's predictions come true, society as a whole will have to redefine the concept of work. Work weeks will be significantly shorter, allowing for more quality of life. Participation in the volunteer sector will rise steeply. With fewer people making money at work, there will be less disposable income for the purchase of discretionary goods. GNP may begin an annual descent.

With three-quarters of all North Americans out of work, how will individuals be able to maintain a sense of self-worth when society and individuals currently place so much value on jobs? How will companies stay in business if 75 percent of former consumers are unemployed and have little or no income? How will society hold together? If Rifkin's predictions transpire, it will shake the very foundations of our faith in organizations and government. It will force us to question the purpose of the individual in society and business, and the role of government. It will require a complete rethinking of what it means to be "successful." If Rifkin's predictions prove correct, the consequences could be the most disastrous or the most liberating shift in the world's history.

New Economic Measures of What Counts

Gross National Product (GNP) measures monetary transactions, not value. For instance, when the Exxon *Valdez* sinks and spills oil all over the Alaskan coast, GNP goes up. Why? Because the company has to spend $2 billion on clean-up. Similarly, wars are great stimulators of GNP. But never would people argue that these events were good for society, people or the environment.

We need a new economic measure. We need to start looking at what

Thomas Berry, co-author of *The Universe Story*, calls GEP — Gross Earth Product. It's a genuine progress indicator. When we clear-cut a forest, GEP decreases because we encroach on the natural habitat of plants and animals. Animal and plant populations decrease, sometimes to the point of extinction. When the Japanese and other whaling nations hunt certain species of whales to extinction, GEP decreases as the diversity of life on earth is decreased and the food chain is imperiled.

As Berry says, "The earth economy is primary, the human economy derivative. Anything that hurts the earth economy will eventually hurt the human economy. We need to be wary, because the earth economy is showing signs of bankruptcy."

The Canadian government shocked the world when it banned cod fishing off the Atlantic Grand Banks in 1994. An area once teeming with fish, the stock was so depleted by over-fishing that the government took this unprecedented measure. As a result, East Coast fisheries shut down and thousands of people were thrown out of work in a region dependent on fishing. The costs to the government — make-work programs, grants and social assistance — ran into the hundreds of millions of dollars.

Economic growth can only continue if our material impact on the earth is dramatically reduced. Fortunately, the new economy offers hope (Chapter 7), as our economy shifts from being materially based to mentally based. Computer hardware and software, entertainment and the arts generate far more jobs and have little negative impact on the environment, while strip mining and clear-cut logging generate few jobs and have very negative environmental impact.

Our economy may grow, but our material consumption must decrease. In other words, GNP can increase, but only if GEP is stable or preferably increasing. If we think of the world as a one-time capital endowment, we can live off the interest, but never the capital. There is enough for our need but not our greed. To behave responsibly is far from limiting. It offers exciting possibilities for the enterprising mind.

For example, the dominant belief within most North American electric utilities is, "We exist to produce electricity. Increased economic growth is good. Increased economic growth requires increased electricity production. So increased electricity consumption is good."

However, North Americans consume more energy per person than any other people in the world. If everyone else in the world consumed as much electricity as we do, the resulting environmental damage would be catastrophic. The production-oriented mindset is dangerous. We can't have infinite material-based economic growth on a finite planet.

Consumers don't want electricity or gas, they want cold beer and warm showers. How they get cold beer and warm showers is relatively unimportant to them. Why couldn't a utility lease the best available energy-efficiency equipment — hot-water heaters, refrigerators — to consumers that use 80 percent less electricity? The average electricity bill would remain the same, but 80 percent of the payment would be for leasing appliances and the remaining 20 percent for electricity.

Unless the utilities can adopt such a mindset, their competitors will be energy-efficient appliance companies. How can a company make more money by selling less of its product or service? Only by dramatically changing the way it looks at its business. Such shifts, however, would be good for the environment and good for business.

Loblaw: G.R.E.E.N. Is Gold

Loblaw, one of Canada's largest food retailers, launched an exclusive line of environmental G.R.E.E.N. products with the endorsement of Pollution Probe, an environmental group. Initial advertising showed the president of Loblaw and the president of Pollution Probe jointly endorsing the products. Some environmental groups condemned the launch because disposable diapers were among the products. These are not truly "green," they argued, since cotton diapers are the preferred choice of environmentalists. But which is more important, progress or perfection? It is necessary to strive for the highest ideals, but it is also important to recognize progress. Progress is more important than perfection, because rarely will we get it right the first time.

Loblaw began a promotion of compact, fluorescent lightbulbs with the provincial electricity utility in 1990. Anyone buying an energy-efficient bulb received a five-dollar rebate from Ontario Hydro. Loblaw, just one supermarket chain in one province (Ontario), sold more compact fluorescent bulbs in a three-month period than the combined sales of all retail outlets in North America the previous year! Loblaw moved the market, changing forever business perceptions of the potential for energy conservation products.

Loblaw's experience also shows that it is worthwhile for companies to follow environmentally friendly practices within their own operations. Patrick Carson, vice president responsible for Loblaw's G.R.E.E.N. products, claims in *Green Is Gold* that there are only 100 truly green companies in North America. Companies that do not join the movement, says Carson, will ultimately suffer decreased profits.

He makes a number of powerful points to prove his views. For instance, energy efficiency has become a major profit center for the grocery chain. Every $100,000 a year that Loblaw saves by retrofitting its stores with energy-efficient lighting has the same bottom-line impact as increasing grocery sales by $10 million! This is because in the grocery business margins are only one percent (for every $100 worth of groceries sold, the company makes a profit of one dollar). Once retrofitting is done it will continue adding to the bottom line every year to come. So $100,000 of energy savings over 10 years has the same impact as increasing sales by $100 million over the same period! A one-time expenditure produces a lifetime saving.

Social Marketing: Cost Effective and Elegant

Black's, Loblaw's G.R.E.E.N. products, The Body Shop and Ben & Jerry's Ice Cream are all examples of social marketing.

Markets are fragmenting as highly focused niche players carve out high-margin business, while large warehouse/discount chains carve out price-sensitive mass markets.

Similarly, advertising media are increasingly fragmenting. As we move to 500 TV channels and then thousands of channels with the rise of the Internet, advertisers can no longer reach consumers with one message advertised in one media.

Social marketing creates products that are in alignment with the consciousness of consumers. It offers no-cost advertising in the form of consumer support and media coverage, and creates consumer insistence. In other words, consumers insist on buying your products or services.

For instance, The Body Shop does not spend one cent on advertising yet receives millions of dollars' worth of publicity every year. The company sends out executives, store managers and franchisees to organizations to talk about social responsibility. The Body Shop products are not tested on animals and the company works to return part of the profits to the communities in which its products are made.

Being responsible about the environment doesn't cost these companies anything, and the publicity far exceeds the reach of buying advertising. The only costs are the product development expenses, which are a necessary investment anyway.

Ben & Jerry's Ice Cream

Ice-cream maker Ben & Jerry's generated tremendous publicity in 1994 when the state of Illinois prevented it from selling anti-rBGH-labeled products. Recombinant Bovine Growth Hormone, known as rBGH, is a bioengineered hormone that stimulates a cow's natural body processes to "trick" it into producing more milk than is natural. Environmentalist and organic farmers argue that rBGH increases the risk of dairy cows contracting a variety of diseases including udder infections, which require increased amounts of antibiotics to treat. Opponents argue that milk from rBGH-treated cows has not been proven unsafe for human consumption.

Despite objections, the FDA approved rBGH for use in November 1993, but the agency did not require foods containing rBGH to be labeled.

The state of Illinois and the city of Chicago forbade Ben & Jerry's from anti-rBGH labeling under threat of seizing all the company's product. Vermont-based Ben & Jerry's, along with natural food manufacturers, producers and retailers, launched a court case. The suit, filed in May 1996 against the state of Illinois and the city of Chicago, charged that prohibiting anti-rBGH labeling was a violation of the company's First Amendment right to honestly inform customers about the contents of their products amid a controversial political issue.

"The use of bio-engineered growth hormones in dairy cows is inconsistent with everything we stand for," said Perry Odak, CEO of Ben & Jerry's. "Consumers should have a right to information that allows them to make an informed choice."

Ben & Jerry's received tremendous publicity from the initiative. The news stories about the issue gave the company tremendous name recognition, which had a far greater impact than any advertising campaign could ever have had.

CFCs and Lily Ponds

The ozone layer prevents most of the sun's ultraviolet (UV) radiation from penetrating the earth's atmosphere. Chlorofluorocarbons (CFCs) are used in refrigerators, aerosol cans and in many manufacturing processes. Their release into the atmosphere is destroying ozone, resulting in the thinning of the ozone layer. The "holes" in the ozone layer, as they are known in the media, are allowing increased levels of UV radiation to reach Earth.

Those who hear not the music think the dancers mad.[1]
Dr. Janet Lapp, professional speaker

A CFC molecule that is released into the atmosphere rises 30 miles to the stratosphere where the ultraviolet rays will shatter it, releasing a chlorine atom. Each free-floating chlorine atom will destroy 100,000 ozone molecules over a 25-year period. The destruction of the ozone layer will continue for 25 years from the day the last CFC is released into the atmosphere.

As the ozone layer thins, the increasing levels of UV radiation are causing increases in incidents of sunburn, eye cataracts and skin cancer (melanoma). Increased UV levels also affect the food chain, reducing the amount of plankton in the seas, which in turn reduces the number of fish that feed upon it, and so on.

The United Nation's Montreal Protocol on Substances That Deplete the Ozone Layer (known as the Montreal Protocol), signed on September 16, 1987, calls for the elimination of all CFCs in industrial processes by 2003.

"Environmental crisis" may appear to be a misnomer. "Sure, there are problems," some say, "but there is still a great deal of time to prevent them from growing to the crisis point." Recall the lesson of the lilies and the pond. Today, a few people are running around shouting warnings of impending doom, that our pond is about to be covered over by lilies. When so much of the water is still open, the casual observer can be easily forgiven for dismissing these warnings and thinking, "These people are crazy."

When not addressed, exponentially growing problems become enormous very quickly. That is why it is so important for individuals, organizations and governments to pay attention to the early warnings. Environmental security can only come from a willingness to question the wisdom of current ways of working and to change our personal lifestyles and business practices based on a new understanding of our interdependence with nature.

Thankfully, more and more corporations are making decisions based on long-term ecological viability, not just short-term profitability. Northern Telecom (NorTel) used to be one of the largest industrial users of CFCs. The Montreal Protocol calls for the elimination of CFCs from industrial processes by 2003. When it was signed, the company could have spent millions of dollars hiring lobbyists and public relations firms to oppose it. Arguments could have been advanced that the agreement was unfair and that thousands of people would have to be laid off as the company was forced to shut down plants that used CFCs in the manufacturing process. Veiled threats could have been made to politicians that their parties and campaigns would no longer receive financial support. Politicians could have been told that the company would blame them, their parties and the government when the plants in their ridings closed down unless they worked to repeal the protocol.

Instead, NorTel chose to be proactive. Rather than fighting the agreement, the company decided to embrace it. And rather than waiting until 2003, the company decided to do something immediately. Three task forces were struck.

The first task force asked, "How can we immediately reduce our CFC use through better conservation techniques, better CFC-recapture methods and slight modifications to the process so that the need for CFCs is reduced?"

In the telecommunications industry, CFCs were used to "clean" circuit boards. After the boards had been soldered, CFC solvents were sprayed on the boards to dissolve the excess flux. This first task force was able to reduce CFC usage by 50 percent within a year, through simple conservation techniques and modifications to the production processes.

The second task force looked at redesigning the industrial process by asking such questions as, "Are CFCs necessary at all? Can some other substance remove excess flux? Do we have to use solder at all or can we electronically join points without soldering? If we have to solder, could it be done in such a way that no flux is left over at the end? Is there a way to solder that does not require cleaning?" Every assumption of the process was questioned.

The third task force looked at partnering, asking, "How can we partner with our customers, our suppliers, the government and even our competitors to help us in this process?" NorTel shared its challenge with suppliers, including the solder supplier. They asked customers if they could accept greater amounts of flux left on the board as long as it did not compromise the performance of the board. They even asked competitors what solutions they had come up with.

In the end, NorTel, working with its material and equipment suppliers, developed an entirely new manufacturing method. The process uses low-solid flux while soldering in a nitrogen atmosphere, leaving little residue on the board and therefore requiring no cleaning, which eliminates the need to use CFCs. In the process, NorTel has saved $50 million a year since it no longer has to purchase or pay to dispose of CFCs. Over a decade this translates into a $500-million saving—half a billion dollars! Rather than a threat, environmental sensitivity has been a bottom-line blessing!

The engineers in NorTel were excited, galvanized by the challenge. There is nothing an engineer likes more than a really formidable problem. The task forces were excited by the process of questioning the manufacturing process.

NorTel did not rest on its laurels. The company recognized its corporate responsibility and immediately began transferring the technology to its competitors around the world. The company made all the technical information available to anyone and any company worldwide interested in learning the details of the redesigned industrial process.

In addition to saving $500 million over 10 years, NorTel's actions increased the pride that employees feel in working for a company that is a world leader in social responsibility. It is difficult to estimate how much pride, trust and loyalty the company's actions created for

NorTel employees when the corporate policies were aligned with their personal values. The company won wide praise for meeting the Montreal Protocol ten years ahead of schedule. If the company had failed to act, it is difficult to estimate how much resentment, anger and fear it would have generated from employees, customers and suppliers, environmental groups and the public had it continued to participate in the destruction of the ozone layer.

Perception is Primary

How individuals or organizations perceive problems determines the solutions that they will propose. Because of the billions of dollars that change hands every day in the stock and money markets, that industry attracts the best and brightest minds. In his book *Market Wizards*, Jack Schwager quotes one broker saying, "We have been thinking about this problem for a long time [10 years]. Half the work in solving a problem is finding the right way to conceptualize it. It took us years before we figured out the right questions to ask."[2]

This is powerful and instructive. How much time do we spend thinking about how we perceive the problem, compared to the time spent trying to solve it? Most people tend to jump in and try to solve it.

Seven Environmental/Business Operating Principles

Businesses can save the planet while bettering the bottom line. Environmental principles are simple, elegant and can be implemented immediately. Here are the operating principles:

1. Do More with Fewer Natural Resources

Businesses need to do more with fewer material resources. Decreasing raw inputs is good for business. Low raw-material costs actually promote inefficiency because material resources are not identified as a limiting factor. Therefore, an organization's intellectual capital is not focused on reducing or eliminating certain material inputs (as in the case of the CFCs with NorTel).

Doing more with less does not mean doing more with fewer people. People are the engines of the new economy. In a downturn, few companies sell off their capital equipment. But many companies lay off people, their only producing asset in the new economy. People alone add value by redesigning production processes. Creativity, ingenuity and innovation come from people alone. They are the producing capital assets in new economy companies.

The three R's (Reduce, Reuse, Recycle) need to include Rethink and Repair: Rethink, Repair, Reduce, Reuse, Recycle. The order is important. A tremendous emphasis has been placed on recycling, but in the order of the five Rs, it is last. We first need to rethink. Do we need to use this product at all? If we do have to use it, how can we reduce its use, then reuse, then repair, and finally, recycle? There is an imperative that business can no longer ignore: we have to decrease our material consumption per person because the earth cannot sustain growing levels of demand. Two thousand years ago, there were only 250 million people on earth. The number has grown steadily to 500 million in 1640, one billion in 1850, six billion today and is currently doubling every 39 years. The greater the earth's population, the greater the pressure on the natural ecosystems as humans clear more land for farming, catch more fish and mine more minerals. The individual actions of six billion people have a powerful collective impact on the earth's ecosystems.

The earth appears to be such a vast place from our individual perception that it is very difficult to understand the severity of our human impact. Here is a simple but significant fact: more people are alive at this moment than all humans who have died throughout history combined.

Emerging nations aspire to our lifestyles in the developed world. Explosive population growth coupled with exponential per capita material consumption is a recipe for disaster. We need to significantly decrease our per capita consumption of resources in developed nations.

Fortunately there is hope. Amory Lovins, the world's leading energy-efficiency expert at the Rocky Mountain Institute, has proven how North Americans could reduce their energy consumption by three-quarters and still maintain their current standard of living! All it would take is using the best available technology.[3]

Amory Lovins and William Browning prove that energy savings of 75 to 80 percent are possible from the use of efficient lighting, advanced window glazings, better heating, ventilation and air-conditioning system (HVAC) design for buildings even less than five years old![4]

Lovins cites the case study of retrofitting Boeing Aircraft's office-building lighting, reducing lighting costs by 90 percent with a less than two-year payback! The goal was achieved by redesigning the building, increasing the number of skylights and windows, and by using special window glazings, which allow in 75 percent of visible light but keep out 50 percent of the heat. Lighting levels were increased, and over-heating, which occurs even in winter, was reduced. The 90 percent cost savings from lighting came not just from the lighting cost reduction, but also the large savings in the reduced capital and operating costs of significantly lower air-conditioning requirements.

Lovins promotes life-cycle costing, where lifetime capital and operating costs are taken into account. For instance, baseboard heating is cheap to install, hence it is used in public housing projects for people with low income, but it has the highest operating costs. When capital and operating costs are added together, it is the most expensive home-heating option.

2. Align Systems with Environmental Principles

An organization is nothing more than a collection of individuals. And yet individuals within organizations often behave differently than they would in their personal affairs. Within some organizations, decisions are made based on values that are contrary to the values that govern employees' personal lives.

Deming believed that systems and structures determine behaviors. If companies are not performing in the best interests of all stakeholders — and the health of the environment affects us all — it is not due to bad people, it is due to bad systems and structures. But we must remember that people create systems and structures in the first place.

In many jurisdictions non-returnable pop bottles and cans are cheaper than returnable ones. So most consumers buy the cheaper ones. But if landfill and garbage-hauling costs were added into the equation, in other words, if full-cost accounting was performed, it would be cheaper to use refillable bottles.

It is the responsibility of all individuals in an organization or in society to work to change the systems and structures to create greater alignment with their values and environmental principles.

3. The Learning-Based Economy Has Arrived

The new economy gives the world hope because it is not as intensive in its use of raw materials as the old economy. Value is added principally through knowledge, creativity and innovation. Physical commerce will not disappear as humans will always have physical needs such as shelter, food and clothing. But an ever-increasing percentage of rapidly expanding and high-value companies are learning-based. The stock market values software companies in the billions of dollars, but these firms work exclusively to produce non-physical products and services.

The new economy is not limited to western nations and does not recognize national boundaries. India and Pakistan have large communities of computer programmers, working remotely for western corporations.

4. Be Proactive

While environmental activism may have seemed more prevalent in the 1980s, it is not an issue that will ever go away. The environment will remain a priority as long as it is under serious threat. The problems are getting worse, not better.

Occurrences of cancer and other diseases are rising at an alarming rate. Many researchers are pointing to increased chemical contamination of our environment as the source. And the impacts are greater than just cancer.

As the baby boomers (people born from 1947 to 1963) become more conscious of their own mortality, they are questioning their values and searching for meaning in their lives. They are concerned about such issues as fertility. Studies now show that sperm count in men has been falling by 2.1 percent a year between 1976 and 1996 in industrialized countries. This trend is blamed largely on chemical pollution.[5] The boomers are concerned about the health and welfare of their children. As the boomers' values shift, putting the environment on the business agenda is good business.

We tend not to appreciate how quickly paradigms can shift. If in 1980 I had said, "An imprisoned black revolutionary leader will become the president of South Africa and that apartheid will end; the Berlin Wall will crumble when people tear it apart with their bare hands; the Soviet Union will dissolve," you would have thought I was crazy. The future is not a linear extension of the past.

5. Resource Poverty Forces Innovation Richness

Resource-poor companies and countries, if they are to succeed, must be more creative than their competitors. Many environmentalists have tremendous, simple and financially sound solutions to problems.

Challenge, as in NorTel's case, can help an organization. Higher resource prices force companies to be creative. Resource-rich companies often experience an ingenuity void.

One of the benefits of having high raw-material costs is that companies are forced to become efficient very quickly. Japanese steel manufacturers became energy-efficient in the 1980s because electricity costs were higher than those of North American steel makers.

6. Leveraged Partnerships and Creating Synergy

Cooperation is the dominant law in nature, not competition. Ecosystems work together in symbiotic relationships. The challenges we face in business and the environment are so large that no one company can solve all the problems or create all the opportunities. Leveraged partnerships will be key in the future and they will not necessarily involve cash. We need to be more resourceful, not more gluttonous, with resources.

When intellectual capital replaces financial or physical capital as the primary means of generating wealth, a whole new series of laws come into place. Synergy is achieved through attraction. To attract intellectual capital, people must have a stake in the project emotionally, mentally and spiritually.

This is the age of emerging spirituality. People want to know, why? What is the meaning of life? Why am I here? What is my contribution? One of the significant benefits that NorTel's employees experienced was the increased pride in working for an environmentally responsible company, and avoiding negative feelings of guilt in working for a polluting company. Employees want to make a difference.

There are numerous examples of employee-driven, environmental programs saving thousands of dollars while increasing morale. Many actions are simple things, like eliminating disposable cups in the cafeteria and using mugs. North Americans use and discard enough disposable cups every year to circle the Earth 40 times! Employees want to make a difference, and they will if allowed and encouraged by the corporate structure.

7. Leadership

At times, leadership requires tremendous courage. We have reached a point in human history where environmentalists can now say, "The emperor has no clothes." Our current business system is leading the world to the brink of collapse. To stand up among business peers and deliver such a message requires tremendous courage—the kind of courage and conviction Columbus had to display when everyone believed the world was flat.

Given the depth of their concern over the seriousness of the crisis, some environmentalists come across as shrill and alarmist. But what do you do if you are watching the lily pond? We need the courage to hear the truth about the environmental crisis we face, and then speak out within organizations. We also need creativity to address these challenges in a positive way that brings environmentalists and business leaders together. Blame, guilt, finger pointing and anger will not bring about a better world. Environmentalists actually need entrepreneurs to create market demand and sell new concepts to consumers. Likewise, business leaders need environmentalists because of the low-cost, simple, elegant solutions that they devise, which can significantly improve the bottom line and win market share.

The Future of Business

Business will not be able to operate if the earth's economy is bankrupt. The earth economy is primary, the human economy a derivative. Business leaders and environmentalists must work together to find creative and practical solutions to the environmental challenge. Business leaders and environmentalists, by assuming leadership roles and forming partner-ships, can forge a new society.

To Summarize:

• An irresponsible environmental record is a public relations death knell.

• Companies that are good to the environment are winning market share.

• By acting in an environmentally responsible manner, businesses can attract top-quality professionals and consumer support.

Workshop Questions and Activities:

• How important are environmental issues to your employees?

• What is your "worst nightmare" in terms of your company's potential impact on the environment? What would the newspapers look like the next day? How would you feel about this personally? What can be done now to prevent this?

Reflection:

• What is the key learning/insight for me in this chapter?

Action:

• What one action shall I take tomorrow to move learning into action? And over time repeat, to move action into habit?

Kanban: Flexible Manufacturing

With retailers requiring just-in-time (JIT) delivery (as in Wal-Mart's supplier, Levi Strauss), manufacturers are adopting fast and flexible production processes—producing only what is needed, when it is needed, and guaranteeing delivery to where it is needed within three to five days. Kanban is the Japanese philosophy of flexible production that manufacturers are using to meet retailers' JIT demands.

Camco Inc., a 51 percent–owned subsidiary of General Electric Canada Inc. is the largest manufacturer, marketer and servicer of home appliances in Canada. Production facilities of its core products are located in Hamilton, Ontario, and Montreal, Quebec.

Camco introduced "make-to-order" production in 1990, allowing its manufacturing teams to respond rapidly to customer demand by reducing production-cycle times from months to days. This improved product availability while reducing inventory levels. Camco's closing inventory of $38 million at the end of 1996 was the lowest in the company's 20 years of operation. Prior to the implementation of "make-to-order," Camco's inventory levels reached as high as $97 million on sales over $550 million.

The Hamilton facility manufactures over 700 different styles of ranges and refrigerators under such popular brands as GE, Hotpoint, Moffat and McClary. In addition, it produces private brands for major department stores.

Camco simplified its inventory requirements. In the Hamilton plant, 95 percent of all parts used in products are the same, regardless of the model, brand or style. This allows for predictability in the ordering of parts.

Using this philosophy, manufacturers can reduce the number of suppliers to create stronger, long-term relationships where quality and guaranteed delivery are ensured.

The final five per cent of unique parts are designed to be as inexpensive as possible, and the differentiation between different models and makes is made as late in the production process as possible. And it's far less expensive to keep inventory in the form of parts than finished goods.

With this modified version of Kanban, Camco maintains enough inventory of common components to manufacture and ship any customer's order within five days of receiving it.

The production line runs continuously for 16-cubic-foot and 18-cubic-foot refrigerators. The refrigerator line will produce twenty 16-cubic-foot refrigerators followed by thirty 18-cubic-foot refrigerators. The first appliance of the new batch carries an order tag alerting employees to the unique parts it requires. Production runs can be as short as a single unit!

Often in workshops executives will say, "All this theory is great, but you don't understand. We are unionized and the union is unwilling to change."

Camco's hourly employees are members of the Canadian Auto Workers (CAW). People who work on the production line are cross-trained to work at other stations. This has a number of benefits. The work is more varied and therefore more interesting. There is less risk of sustaining injuries due to repetitive motion. The line is not brought to a halt if one person is off work sick. And when demand is high, the company can put on extra shifts and run at a higher capacity.

As Camco has gone through its turnaround, workers have seen inventory levels falling. In the past when inventory was too high, work stopped as the company worked to sell existing inventory into the distribution channels. Quality has also risen. With a make-to-order philosophy, sales have been increasing. As a result, union members, who get steady and varied work, have a positive attitude toward the change.

The retailer, distributor, manufacturer and suppliers, including the metal-stamping company and steel maker, comprise the value chain. Each company adds value to the final product as it moves through production and distribution.

As the expression goes, a chain is only as strong as its weakest link. The value chain is interdependent. The whole production process is halted if one supplier fails to deliver parts that are needed for production on time. As such, Camco has established strategic relationships with selected suppliers. These suppliers are often integrated into the company's manufacturing operations and participate in decisions relating to quality, design and new materials.

Manufacturers and suppliers are going through "inter-enterprise integration," as organizations in the value chain begin to act as though they were one organization.

The human body is an example. Even though the body has separate limbs and organs that perform different functions, they are integrated. The whole body needs to work as one system in real time. The manufacturing value chain needs to work in the same way to be efficient.

Kanban shifts manufacturers from pushing products into the retail channel to allowing the end consumer to pull them. It's the difference between pushing and pulling a string.

We don't know what we don't know
We can't act on what we don't know
We won't know until we search
We won't search for what we don't question.
We won't question what we don't measure.
Hence we just don't know.[1]

Mikel Harry, author

Reflection:
• What is the key learning/insight for me in this appendix?

Action:
• What one action shall I take tomorrow to move learning into action? And over time repeat, to move action into habit?

Reactions
From Leaders and Authors

Everett Anstey
President
Sun Microsystems of Canada Inc.

How do organizations create? How do they learn and get smarter? Only by fostering an atmosphere of trust, one where employees are encouraged to share information, exchange ideas and solve problems.

As *The Learning Paradox* notes, technology — specifically networks — are allowing organizations to communicate and innovate like never before. This is a belief that Sun Microsystems has espoused since its founding, when Sun coined the phrase *The Network Is the Computer.*

Sun Microsystems is committed to helping connect people together regardless of where they are, allowing them to share information, to exchange ideas and to create new products and services. And only out of that sharing will innovation occur.

The shift to network computing and the utilization of the Internet is occurring faster than anyone thought. This shift is accelerating the availability of higher bandwidth, as we are seeing with the development of high-speed modems, ATM (Asynchronous Transfer Mode), cable modems — all of which will allow people to access information faster, and will give rise to new applications such as real-time videoconferencing. Businesses are now writing their applications for the network, not the desktop.

Network-centric computing requires companies to look at computers in a new way, as communications and collaboration tools. We've reached a point where computers must be able to communicate and share information over a network seamlessly, regardless of operating system or hardware platform. Today, customers are looking for simplicity and lower total cost of ownership of technology.

Java Computing addresses these needs. It shifts the computer's functionality from the desktop to the network, where the company can better control costs, security, application deployment and administration. According to industry analysts, companies implementing Java Computing in the enterprise can save more than 40 percent on the total cost of ownership each year.

The savings can be measured in other ways as well. Freeing companies from feeding the admin-intensive PC network means faster time-to-market, more opportunity to concentrate on breakaway business strategies and a marked competitive edge.

Java Computing is changing the face of computing as we know it. Leading operating system and browser purveyors are building Java into their next-generation system, and major development tool vendors and application providers are supporting the move. Meanwhile, Java is becoming so ubiquitous that it will soon be embedded in such devices as pagers and cellular telephones—all joined by the Internet and the network.

That's what Java makes possible. Its platform-independence frees software developers from the operating system lock, giving them the choice to create products for every major platform, whether it's a desktop computer or a handheld device. Write Once, Run Anywhere. Soon, accessing the network or the Internet may become as simple as plugging your telephone into the wall and dialing. And because Java "thin client" devices can co-exist with PC, Mac and UNIX machines, they can be adopted incrementally, on the back end, with little impact on cost.

Just as Java is changing the way people think about computing, the incredible power of the Internet is forcing companies to re-evaluate the way they do business.

Businesses are recognizing the power of partnerships. Companies that connect with other organizations have the real competitive advantage. They gain by the innovations of each other. It's network computing that will enable that kind of dialogue to take place.

Increasingly this dialogue is extending into the world of electronic commerce. *The Learning Paradox* notes that electronic data interchange (EDI) is a powerful tool that makes "organizations faster and more flexible, capable of responding in a dynamic, changing market."

Attainment of a widespread electronic economy will require more robust security, which is advancing rapidly, and continued adherence to standards and open systems. The Internet is a platform-independent mechanism, and public and private organizations wishing to succeed in electronic commerce will need to support existing and emerging standards.

The payment phase of electronic commerce requires certification and authentication mechanisms to ensure the security of customers' transactions. Visa and MasterCard, for example, are promoting a standard, called SET, for secure on-line transactions. Network-layer encryption technologies also help secure the Internet for data transmissions such as EDI.

Extranets, too, allow companies to effectively communicate with each other and share ideas. Extranets allow companies to link their intranets — including databases and other information resources — and share them with suppliers, partners, resellers, and other organizations with which they do business.

Technologies such as Java are available for implementing smart EDI and other elements of successful extranets. Of course, companies must consider their own cultures and practices when building extranets. Companies accustomed to dealing openly with third parties may have few or no problems in adapting to the extranet model of doing business. Other organizations may need to rethink their stance on certain business issues, such as data sharing.

Provided that security and related issues are adequately addressed, extranets offer organizations a new, lower-cost method of doing business with their partners and customers.

Today's employees are gaining access to information like never before. They are proving that the key to competitive advantage is innovation, accomplished only through the sharing of ideas, experiences and knowledge. A key facilitator to this process is the network. The network is the catalyst for this change. Network computing is making a reality out of what was once only a dream.

Charles S. Coffey
Executive Vice President
Business Banking, Royal Bank

The Learning Paradox presents innovative ideas and strategies to help leaders learn more about lifelong learning. Gaining security in uncertain times is a significant challenge at all levels of an organization, especially when fear and constant change remain the norm in most environments. It is clear that sending out the right leadership signals on a consistent basis is both key and even critical. The right signals need to be learned over the long term.

The Learning Paradox does a superb job of positioning the process of summarizing, reflecting and taking action. It is a thinking and doing process to be noted and practiced. As a result, the book drove home many principles re the learning economy:

- Experiences that come from encouraging challenge and providing feedback represent the most effective means of learning.

- People will support emotionally what they have helped to shape.

- Learning is the ultimate corporate signal. Successful leaders effectively create and sustain enterprises because they are obsessed with actively and visibly sharing their vision. We repeat. We listen. We empower. We ask questions. We generate action and gain commitment. We communicate clearly. We build teams through trust. We make mistakes and fix them. We encourage win/win solutions. We continuously learn.

Leaders create value and learning paradigms. They also recognize that the intellectual resources of their organization remain their primary competitive edge.

The New Information Technology Paradigm

The Learning Paradox reinforces that information technology is becoming the driving force behind learning and change. The electronic revolution is putting information in the hands of organizations and consumers. Greater learning is creating higher expectations and increased demand for better products and services. Customers are insisting on greater selection of goods, a wider choice of services and more convenience when conducting transactions. These are impotent changes they know today's technology can give them.

At Royal Bank Financial Group, we, too, recognize the value of information technology and the role it has played and will continue to play in our society. Our ongoing investment in emerging technologies, such as telephone banking as well as PC and Internet banking, allows us to provide seamless delivery channels for customers who want broader access to their financial services. It also opens the door for our account managers to deliver higher end customized financial solutions that meet the specialized needs of business and retail clients.

Companies, including ours, need to be more efficient and more flexible. We all require better working relationships with our suppliers and we must be able to meet the unique needs of each and every customer. Only those businesses, large and small alike, that adapt quickly to these realities will make the cut. Electronic commerce has arrived and is here to stay.

As readers, we are made acutely aware that electronic commerce is the enabling technology for achieving change and staying competitive in the future. Those who pursue it half-heartedly, as an add-on to their existing business practices, will only be partially successful. It is critically important that strategic application of technology become an integral part of all business plans. Technology has the potential to transform Learning.

There is no doubt that the intrinsic value of electronic commerce is beyond question. Companies that do business on-line, primarily in the manufacturing sector, are already selling hundreds of millions of dollars' worth of goods and services. Like most paradigms, striking a balance between technology and corporate strategy will separate the novices from the learners.

The Internet Revolution

Again, *The Learning Paradox* acknowledges the fact the impact of the World Wide Web cannot be denied. Almost single-handedly, the Web is changing the very nature of doing business. Markets are literally being transformed. Companies have adopted the Internet as a fourth channel—supplementing face-to-face meetings, mail and phone for conducting their business and trade. As a result, business is booming. As the Internet continues to evolve, a broad subculture is beginning to emerge. Virtual communities are leveraging the capabilities of the network to bring people together. On-line businesses have an exciting opportunity to build new and dynamic customer relationships. As the Internet grows, virtual communities are set to become an integral part of the new culture of business. Bridging the gap between the old and the new will be the single greatest challenge companies will face in the coming year. Businesses will have to reinvent themselves. They will need to question their preconceived notions of value and service to learn how value and service is created, captured and delivered in the new economy.

In the long term, this book points out and illustrates that we are going to continue applying technologies to proved real-time information and value-added services through the Internet. As the learning economy takes hold, companies will need a successful formula for managing their businesses in the digital age, as well as the courage and determination to put it in place. The question remains, where does the learning economy take us?

In the spirit of *The Learning Paradox*, what one action will I take today to move leaning into action and to move action into habit?

I will demonstrate communications leadership by finding one opportunity each day where the right signals assure the questioning, change, support or recognition of decision-making and behaviors. It will mean learning security by example, ultimately changing the way we do things while enhancing shareholder, employee, customer, supplier and community value.

Bill Foster
Managing Director, Publications Division
Richard Chang Associates, Inc.

Over the past decade, individuals and organizations have been presented with some very difficult challenges — from global competition to the ever-increasing expectations of customers. Today, leaders are faced with a more complex playing field in which to compete, including a world that is open 24 hours a day, rapid technological advances and organizational changes that are occurring at an exponential rate. Yet, through it all, the fact remains that people continue to be an organization's most valuable resource. Given that, how can you gain the advantage in the twenty-first century?

The advantage will belong to those with a commitment to continuous learning. Whether on an individual basis or as an entire organization, one of the key ingredients to building a continuous learning environment is the ability to find and utilize credible and insightful learning tools. *The Learning Paradox* is an ideal learning tool if you take the time to apply the principles within.

One highly effective learning tool that is often overlooked is the mentoring process. A mentor is a trusted tutor or guide who plays an active role in the development of an individual. Within your own organization, is there someone who can become a mentor for you or the people you work with? Learning new knowledge and skills from someone else who has already been down the path before you is an excellent way to accelerate learning. And, it can be equally rewarding for the mentor.

Effective learners rethink everything they "know" about management, leadership, customers, markets and suppliers. They question and shift their paradigms. Great organizations need great management. However, on its own, great management does not make for a great organization. Great organization must also have great leadership. With competent leaders, everything else falls into place. That is, organizations with competent leadership tend to have better customer service, produce higher-quality products, commit fewer errors, maintain a more motivated workforce and enjoy superior financial performance.

Those who believe that continuous learning and growth are important know that they have to change the way they think and behave. "If you keep doing what you've always done, you'll keep getting what you've always got." For instance, everyone in an organization may look up to the leader because his or her drive and talents built the business. What if, however, to survive and thrive, the organization has to leave behind the legacy? Can the leader let go of what was the cause of the success? For example, not even the best buggy business survived when the automobile came along. Astute business leaders question their business at a fundamental level and are willing to reinvent themselves as they reinvent their business.

Some of the best companies today have had to turn themselves upside down. That is, they've discovered that the old top-down pyramid-style management doesn't work. So they've flipped the pyramid over, giving employees and customers more say in what goes on. And it works, as evidenced in improved sales and earnings. The new organization challenges employees to come up with their own better ways to do their jobs. The new organization seeks out ideas from everyone, not just those who have a direct involvement with the job. Sometimes good ideas come from unlikely sources. The new organization treats employees with honesty and respect. Authority is shared so as to empower employees to take responsibility. The new organization is structured to create greater alignment and enable the process of creating a common vision, where employees from across the whole organization not only understand the vision, but are committed to and excited by it.

The new paradigms of leadership challenge us to think differently, ask the tough questions and change the way we've done things in the past. And we all know how difficult and even painful change can be — when the change is forced upon us. Often we believe that change will leave us damaged and defeated. Yet we all know that nothing ever gets better until someone or something changes.

Researchers conducted an experiment with grasshoppers. They discovered that if you catch a bunch of grasshoppers and put them in a glass terrarium with a screen cover on it, the grasshoppers will try to jump out. After a while, the researchers discovered that the grasshoppers get tired of bashing themselves against the screen and learn to jump just as high as the cover and no higher. Once the grasshoppers learned that the screen constrained them, the researchers removed the cover and the grasshoppers did not jump out. This is called *assumed constraint*. The grasshoppers assumed — based on previous experience — that they are being constrained and thus can only jump a certain height. However, once the constraint was removed or altered, the behavior remained the same. What we need to do in our organizations today is think of ways to remove the lids to change and create opportunities for people to challenge their assumed constraints.

When change comes, it's natural for us to want to hold on to what we have, to cling to our current reality no matter how difficult or painful. We choose to hold on to what we have because it is familiar and comfortable. To let go of the familiar and reach for what is new feels awkward and is difficult. Yet, we all know that without change, we take a chance that we may become extinct. How many times do we have to tell ourselves that the best thing to do is to let go?

This book talks about rediscovering the joy of learning. Change is also inevitable. And don't bother waiting for change to slow down. It won't. However, if we embrace change with an open mind, we are destined to learn and grow. It's our nature, our duty, and our destiny.

At times, our destiny changes course and forces us to alter our game plan, for the winds of change can be unpredictable. Like it or not, the game of life doesn't come with a set of instructions and the winds of change don't always come with a warning. With effort, planning and hope, we can set a course and alter our sail settings as wind directions change. The winds of change can be used to our advantage if we understand their purpose, direction and destination. Once we understand the wind's purpose, we can be supportive of it. Once we know the wind's direction, we can help guide it. And once we feel comfortable with the wind's destination, we can facilitate its journey. Only then can we take action to harness the energy of change and use it to our advantage.

For those of you in positions of management and leadership, it will be your job to coach others toward better individual and organizational performance. In general, the job of the coach is to help the team win. As coach, your motives, attitude and actions are all focused on winning. Coaches are motivators of people and teams. They inspire others to work hard and continually improve. They are the consummate observer and subject-matter expert. The task of a coach is to help others perform better. If you subscribe to the theory that leadership is *doing the right thing* and management is *doing the thing right*, then perhaps coaching is *helping others to do the right thing right*.

With a continued focus toward ongoing learning, the role of a coach is simplified, but still not easy. However, if you follow through with your plans and keep your commitments, improved performance is guaranteed. Show people that you are honest in everything you do. Be a change agent—welcome change, and plan for it in a proactive manner. Inspire your team members. Give them the desire to become peak performers by developing them each and every day. And, finally, don't stop learning, yourself. Never stop learning and be the best you can be. It's not enough to just learn the tricks of the trade—learn the trade!

Bill Foster can be reached at Richard Chang Associates, Inc. at (714) 727-7477

Jim Carroll
Author, *Surviving the Information Age*
Co-author, *Canadian Internet Handbook*

I spend a great deal of time working with organizations to help them focus on the change being wrought on our social, economic and business systems as a result of the emergence of what I call "the wired world"—that emerging economic system which is increasingly linked together and dependent upon the Internet.

It's a complex task—after all, I find that many executives are overwhelmed by the rate of technological change around them, and can all too often become complacent about its potential to wreak havoc on their business organizations. That's why Jim Harris' book is an important one — for it will help you to realize that complacency toward change is no longer an option — in fact, it is a death sentence.

Why would I make such a bold statement? For this reason — the fact of the matter is that coping with technology-induced change is about to become even more challenging in the future than it is today. If you don't believe that, you should take note of some estimates which indicate that 80 percent of the technology that we will use some 10 years from now has yet to be invented.

Take pause for a moment, and look around your office. Now imagine that a lot of the things that define your day-to-day work patterns will be replaced by something completely different through the next decade. Your telephone, computer, daytimer, heck, maybe even your paper clips, are not going to be like they are today. The financial systems that you have in place will become integrated into a worldwide financial system. The thermometer on your wall will be replaced by some type of high-tech automatic weather station linked into a satellite some 22,000 miles overhead. Cleaning your rug? I dare not even think of what type of newfangled vacuum machine we will see!

Technological change, however, isn't simply about technology — it is the impact of new technology that presents the greatest challenge. And one of the most significant changes that is under way has to do with the way we access and utilize information.

Consider this statistic: researchers indicate that as much information is now generated each and every day as was produced from the beginning of time to the start of the 19th century. Others indicate that a student today will be faced with 50 times more information by the time they are 10 years into their working career.

That means that we are about to drown in the era of the information flood — and I am convinced that people who develop the skill to extract knowledge from the raging rivers of information around them will be those to succeed in the wired economy.

Certainly I've done what I can to develop this skill. One of the reasons I have managed to establish a thriving and profitable consulting practice is that I have mastered the ability of just-in-time knowledge — I can teach myself about anything by utilizing the global information networks that envelop me. To do that, I've equipped my home office with the best darn technology I could, since I am convinced that to be a participant in the wired world, I've got to have what it takes. Today, I can instantly research tens of thousands of magazines and newspapers, and can electronically scan developments affecting particular client projects that I might be involved in.

The information age isn't just about a lot of information floating about — it is also the fact that this wired economy is leading to entirely new, and very different, forms of corporate organization.

I believe that we are headed for an economic system in which companies will hire the best talent they can, regardless of where that person might be. Indeed, in the new millennium, where people work from won't matter, since you'll simply have to "plug in" to the global economy in order to take part. I see the emergence of a new type of "nomadic worker," one who will make career decisions that are based on lifestyle. They will have different attitudes toward life and work, and will reject many of the currently accepted norms of the corporate environment — and their attitudes will revolutionize the world of work.

I'm already there. Today, my office environment is indicative of the type of work quarters that many other people are establishing for themselves. My home features a separate office, and a high-speed local area network that extends to every room in the house, with up to six computers linked in at any one time. A high-speed connection to the Internet, three phone lines and other communication tools plug me into the world. I can service my clients, wherever they might be on the planet.

What does that make me? I'm already a nomadic worker, able to be a full participant in an economy that is becoming increasingly wired together. I'm no techo-dweeb, but a business executive carving out a highly lucrative, profitable and fun career in the wired world. The key thing that drives me? The realization that I'm living and surviving in an economy that will be completely different year by year, month by month, day by day.

I live with the reality that the future is characterized by an economy in which there is less job security, more career volatility and far less opportunity. The result? I've a new form of entrepreneurial aggressiveness, fueled by my mastery of technology — I'll do what it takes to survive.

Constantly enhancing my skills and capabilities, I already subscribe to the belief that learning is what most adults will do for a living in the twenty-first century.

For me, learning isn't a luxury — it's a survival skill.

Jim Carroll can be contacted at jcarroll@jimcarroll.com, or via his Web site at www.jimcarroll.com. The Web site contains many free articles and reports. As of October 1997, the new 1998 Canadian Internet Handbook *and the* 1998 Canadian Internet Directory and Research Guide *are in bookstores everywhere.*

Susan Jurow
Executive Director
College and University Personnel Association

For three years Jim Harris and I have kept up an ongoing, sporadic conversation about the contemporary workplace. It has been both stimulating and rewarding. The underlying question to which we have continually returned is: How can we create a humanistic workplace in the midst of instability and unpredictability? What constitutes a meaningful work experience in such an environment and what are the implications for leadership? How can we rediscover the joy of seeking, learning and growing despite all the challenges to be faced in today's workplace?

Instability, perception, change, learning and growth are the key issues that *The Learning Paradox* addresses so well. The premise of this book is that by becoming a learner, willing to constantly challenge yourself and the way you see the world, you will have the flexibility to make the most of your life in a constantly changing world. I agree. I also believe that an openness and a spirit of adventure will be the best way to sustain a satisfying, productive worklife in the twenty-first century.

Peter Vaill was the first to use the term "permanent white water" to describe our complex work environment. In *Learning As a Way of Being: Strategies for Survival in a World of Permanent White Water* (Jossey-Bass, 1996, p.16), he describes the work world as full of "surprising, novel, messy, costly, recurring, and unpreventable events" which lead to "feelings of lack of direction, absence of coherence, and loss of meaning." He argues that by trying to deal with "white water," we often create "white water" for others. We look for ways to try to gain control, to set direction and to establish accountability in new ways. In the process, we initiate change for others.

As a management consultant, I learned firsthand how painful change can be for some people. In every organization, there were those who either denied the need for change or denied that a change was about occur, no matter what the evidence was. There were also those who, once a decision had been made to make a change, put their energy into fighting it rather than working to improve the outcome. Their pain and their outrage were palpable.

Their resistance was seldom because they were old-fashioned or slow-witted, or had negative personalities. It was not resistance just for the sake of resistance on their part; it was a perceptual problem. These individuals did not see what others around them clearly saw. Evidence that did not fit into their well-honed world visions was dismissed as negligible, unimportant or overblown. We cannot embrace what we cannot see.

Unfortunately, managers and staff often see things differently because they read different books and magazines, attend different conferences and have their eyes on different aspects of organizational success. Sharing information and sharing the thinking process are critical in our new environment. Everyone must have the opportunity to hear the same facts and speculation, to test the same assumptions, to discuss the same possibilities and to debate the merits of myriad potential conclusions. If not, we will continue to misdiagnose looking past each other as just so much stupidity and wrongheadedness.

David Bohm tells a story about an anthropologist who lived with an American Indian tribe. They used to meet as a group and just talk for no apparent purpose. The group was leaderless, and the participants weren't making decisions. After a while they would just get up and leave. But after that, everyone seemed to know what they were supposed to do because "they understood each other so well."

A belief in the value of shared perception and understanding is at the heart of my appreciation for Jim's book. I believe that this is a great book for enlightened leaders to give to all their staff. It provides a framework for developing together an understanding of the complexities of the contemporary workplace. It gives managers and their staff a common platform to stand on. They can talk about their discomfort with uncertainty and about how they see the world they work in together. They can chart their change strategies together in ways that encourage risk, learning and growth.

Some of the resistance to change also comes from the recognition that growth itself can be painful. "Growing pains" is more than just an expression; we know that in childhood and adolescence fast physical growth can, in fact, cause physical pain. Managing the speed and intensity of a change can mitigate the worst of its negative effects. A focus on the value of the potential outcomes can turn the change process into something more akin to an exhilarating white-water river ride.

In the chapter "Leaders are Paradigm Pioneers," Jim broadens the definition of leadership to allow for each of us to see the leadership potential within us. He also defines new ways for managers to operate as leaders within their organizations. Wilfred Drath and Charles Palus move us from the concept of the individual leader acting with or on followers to the concept of leadership as a shared process. They define leadership as "the process of making sense of what people are doing together so that people will understand and be committed." This definition not only broadens the concept of leadership to make it more inclusive, it places experience and learning at its heart.

We tend to take learning for granted because we feel we have done it all our life. In truth, much of that learning was structured by others. From our scholastic experiences, we come to believe that learning has mostly to do with what someone tells us or what we read in a book. To truly become learners, we must recognize and accept the lessons of our experiences as well.

The College and University Personnel Association recently updated its strategic plan and wrote a new mission statement that says that we will "be recognized and valued as an essential higher education organization because people are the key to success". Organizations are not successful; it is the people within them who are successful. It is through curiosity, learning and flexibility, all the lessons of *The Learning Paradox*, that we can achieve the synergy to make our workplaces the stimulating, humanistic environments people crave and in which they thrive.

References

Bohm, David. *On Dialogue.* Ojai, CA: David Bohm Seminars, 1990. p.10-11

Drath, Wilfred H. and Charles J. Palus. *Making Common Sense: Leadership as Meaning-making in a Community of Practice.* Greensboro, N.C.: Center for Creative Leadership, 1994.

Vaill, Peter B. Learning *As a Way of Being: Strategies for Survival in a World of Permanent White Water.* San Francisco: Jossey-Bass, 1996. p.16

Jonathan Wellum
President & Portfolio Manager
AIC Group of Funds

1. Setting Goals

Successful management teams set goals. I have never encountered a successful business that is not characterized by goal setting. A management team must develop daily, weekly, monthly and yearly goals. Where is the business headed? If management has no vision, the company will definitely fall short. At AIC we only invest in companies that can lay out for us both a short- and long-term plan that is well thought out, rational and opportunistic. Goals often must be flexible and adaptable depending on the changing environment, although changing the fundamental goals of an organization must be taken very seriously. We admire the management team at Franco/Euro Nevada. When you sit down with them, they will lay out their exact goals for the next week, month, year and 10 years.

2. Strategic

A successful management team must be very strategic in achieving goals. The Loblaw Companies executive team, for example, has broken down each part of the business, challenging existing paradigms, in order to continually improve their delivery of household needs to Canadian consumers. From economies of scale in delivery, to branding their own successful line of products, they have consistently improved their business to the place where it is by far the best in its class. When you discuss the future, the management team will chart out their strategic initiatives over the next five years and beyond. They have analyzed their competitors' strategies and protect themselves from being caught off guard. The most successful companies have a focused strategy (as opposed to scattered) and clearly defined goals.

3. Discipline

Successful management teams are always disciplined. Unfortunately we live in an undisciplined culture and this is often imported into our corporate life. Management must not only lay out their short- and long-term goals, they must not deviate from them even if in the short run things are not going as planned. Trimark Investment Management, one of the companies we have a large position in, set out to cre-

ate a mutual fund franchise unified around the concept of value investing and making long-term investments. This requires the discipline of
adhering to the strategy when the market moves against you. Strong
investment businesses are not created overnight — they are created over
years as management tenaciously adheres to their fundamental goals
and principles.

4. Patience

The best management teams exercise a healthy degree of patience. This
does not mean they are lazy or inactive. There is a difference, sometimes you can be so patient that you let opportunities go by. The most
successful companies set their strategic goals and are patient enough to
wait for the perfect opportunity to strike. Sometimes this will mean
that they will wait for their competition to make a mistake and then
enter their competitors' market opportunistically and capitalize on the
error. In this current stock market environment, where prices are generally high, the best companies are not out buying other businesses.
Rather, many are building cash reserves to be well positioned if the
market turns down. If you have a disciplined long-term focus, then it
is much easier to be patient. The survivor and not the first out of the
gate often wins the game.

5. Persistence

Persistence is critical to success. I've talked to many leaders who started
out with nothing and created billion-dollar companies. The Asper
family company, CanWest Global, is an example. Starting from a little
station in Winnipeg, the Aspers now run a company worth over $3.5
billion that operates in three countries. Naturally they set goals, exer-
cised discipline and were strategic, but they were also persistent. They
never gave up, despite all setbacks. We at AIC struggle with this within
our own organization. How can we make our people persistent in their
efforts to achieve their goals? How can we create the stamina to persevere through the ups and downs of the market? Often it's through the
perseverance of a visionary management team that focuses the company on the long-term opportunities and rise above the short-term
challenges that becomes the dominant industry player. One of the key
attributes evident in successful management teams is a tremendous
degree of perseverance, regardless of what detractors might say.

6. Motivation and Passion

What motivates us each day? Do we have passion about our work? Is
it the desire to excel and do the very best job possible? I've never met

a successful person who is not passionate about their job or life in general. Successful people learn to challenge themselves, to motivate themselves, to excel at all they do. We live in society that is generally too satisfied with mediocrity. Successful people are never satisfied with the status quo. People must be motivated constantly and encouraged. Cash motivation is not enough. It must come from the heart — an inner passion to excel. One of the companies we have a large stake in that clearly exemplifies these traits is Newcourt Credit. The management team of this company is absolutely driven to excel and top their competition. How else could a company that started in the early 1980s by 1998 be the second-largest vendor finance company in the world if it was not driven by a highly motivated and passionate management team? Unfortunately, most people are not passionate about what they do and as a result have to drag themselves through life. What a miserable way to live! Rather, we should be those who take full advantages of the opportunities that come our way each day and run with them as far as we can.

7. Ownership
If you're confident in what you're doing, you're going to take ownership of your job. Successful management teams take charge! Warren Buffett exemplifies the manager who confidently takes ownership regardless of whether other people think he's right or not. He analyzes and reasons through all his decisions on his own and when he pulls the trigger by making a major investment, he doesn't fool around. Great managers develop confidence in themselves and in their skills. That translates into taking ownership of one's job and taking charge in terms of one's actions on the job.

8. Courageous, Independent Thinking
These attributes emanate from an individual who is confident and knows where they are headed. If you want to cultivate leadership, you have to be courageous in your decision making process. This often means being very independent in your thinking. You want to be a leader and not a follower. This often involves a paradigm shift. People that are great leaders constantly try to think outside the box. This is very tough in practice. In our own financial services industry, we have witnessed one of the major paradigm shifts of this century when we look at Charles Schwab. Here's a business that capitalized on both regulatory changes and technology changes and created a whole new method of distributing financial services products.

Through one of our U.S. mutual funds, we have a stake in this company because of the power of this franchise to distribute financial services electronically, which is clearly the wave of the future, and to continue to challenge existing paradigms and think in broader terms. Now with their extensive database leveraged into the latest technology, they are able to offer a greater number of services down their electronic pipeline.

We are never required to follow the institutional imperative and simply replicate the acts of others. We need to constantly challenge conventional wisdom. If Mr. Buffett just did what other money managers did, he would have a diversified portfolio of bonds and equities with a market value that would be a fraction of what he now manages. He would also not be one of the wealthiest individuals in the world. Instead Mr. Buffett chose to be different, to think outside the prescribed box! The result is well known!

9. Depth of Management

A successful management team builds depth. The larger a company gets, the more important it is to surround yourself with great people, people who will supplement and add to the overall management team. Find and attract other smart people who can provide valuable counsel, accountability and eventually fill your shoes. The best-run businesses build strong management teams over time. Good leaders should not be threatened by other good people around them.

10. Unified Philosophy

I believe that one's personal and business philosophy should be integrated. Each of us must go back to basics and ask the foundational questions: Why am I ultimately here? Am I accountable to my conscience? Do I adhere to a consistent worldview? What is my life plan? What am I trying to attain? These are tough questions to ask and even tougher to answer. As a Christian, the answers to these questions provide me with the foundation to live, to work my very hardest, to further the cause of humankind and honor my Creator. Ultimate motivation, drive and discipline must be rooted in the spiritual. The greatest leaders in history founded their ideals in the transcendental. Would-be leaders must come to grips with their own personal philosophy and integrate this into their life which includes their professional life.

11. Build Your Own Franchise

All the foregoing points can be summarized as *build your own personal franchise*. At AIC we buy only the best companies — ones that have differentiated themselves within their market. They sell value-added products, they have successfully branded themselves, and built their business on unique products that people demand and use on a regular basis. Leaders, teams and organizations must develop their own personal franchise. Each of us should ask ourselves the question, "What am I all about? Do the attributes that we have been discussing describe me?" As leaders we need to differentiate ourselves, brand ourselves, in terms of standing for something, making a difference where we work, where we live, enjoy life to the fullest and make the greatest contribution we can to our organization.

You can reach Jonathan Wellum or AIC Group of Funds by calling 1-888-7104AIC (4242)

Wayne Roberts
Author and environmentalist

The Learning Paradox offers business leaders a toolkit which equips them to participate in the greatest economic transformation of all time, the emerging green entrepreneurial revolution. There's no mistaking that this is where the information age is heading. Indeed, that's what the information economy is all about—displacing finite and often toxic materials with infinitely renewable and life-enhancing human talent. The deeper the process gets, the greener the economy becomes, by definition.

Of course, the transformation won't come about automatically. Entrepreneurs—people who "shift economic resources out of an area of lower and into an area of higher productivity and greater yield"—will lead the way. But to lead where no economy has gone before, they'll need to master new ways of learning, creating new products that are knowledge-intensive, rich in creativity and innovation—rather than material-intensive products, services and old ways of doing business.

The Learning Paradox puts this learning challenge front and center on the business agenda. New learning methods are how business leaders can work on what green business leader and author of *The Ecology of Commerce* and futurist Paul Hawken defines as the "design problem" which underlies environmentally destructive economies.

Most greens underestimate the scope of this design problem and learning challenge. That's why they blame pollution on corporate greed, and call on governments to limit the damage done by executives who put the bottom line ahead of the public good. But the fact is that the bottom line is a powerful motivating force for the green revolution. Being green can save companies millions of dollars. With few exceptions, almost any company can make more money enriching than despoiling the planet. It's been shown time and time again that when companies work creatively to cut pollution, they cut costs and capture new byproducts. That's only to be expected, given that pollution is just a nice word for managerial incompetence that results in wasted and misplaced resources. The heart of the pollution-reduction exercise is learning new ways to substitute competence for incompetence in dealing with resources. Greed has almost nothing to do with this changeover. It's a red herring.

It's not only greens who need to learn to be more charitable about the learning problem faced by corporations. Executives have to admit to their learning disability too. Business leaders are quick to denounce union rules that insist on strict seniority and narrow job classifications, for instance, and to point out that these rules actually threaten workers' employment security by undermining a firm's viability. To boot, strict seniority undermines the job rights of youth and minorities, by and large the last hired, first fired. And narrow job classifications undermine the dignity and variety of work. When it comes to unions, business leaders readily understand that sticking to old rules is counterproductive and ends up violating basic values such as employment equity and workplace empowerment. But business leaders aren't so adept at locating their own blind spots.

The business equivalent of insistence on strict seniority and narrow job classification is insistence on the seniority rights of established technologies and the narrow classification of corporate responsibilities to the society and environment which nurture them. Business lobby groups, law firms and public relations outfits make a fortune out of neurotic business fears about going up the learning curve. As a result, it's not uncommon for companies to spend more money and time battling environmentalists and community groups than productively solving problems.

The time has long since passed when executives should have learned that there is profit to be made in proactive change. And the time is fast approaching when those who say the change can't be done will be eating the dust of those who are doing it. This changeover will take place with lightning speed, as in the computer industry, because in the information age the only barrier to entry to the new ways of doing business is old ways of thinking about learning. Executives who take a fresh look at the challenges of environmental limits, treat them like any other limiting factors they learn to overcome, will find there's a seamless web linking the key concepts in *The Learning Paradox* — problem-seeing, visionary or paradigm leadership, value-adding innovations, customization, employee empowerment and superior first-to-market profits.

Take the example of gas and electric utilities, among the worst of the environmental bad guys in the minds of most people. A new paradigm for the energy sector comes from examining three truths. First, the utilities sell a product that causes a problem, pollution. There's no room to debate the extent of the pollution or the level of public concern. Second, no one, even the most loyal consumer, cares a fig about the product that utilities sell. No one jumps out of bed with excitement at the prospect of buying more gas or electricity that day. All people want is the service — hot showers, cold beer and comfy room temperatures. Third, utilities, by the very nature of their business, enjoy preferred access to customers' homes and preferred interest rates from money lenders.

A new paradigm for the energy sector is staring us in the face, as soon as utilities learn to reconfigure themselves as energy service companies.

You want a hot shower? Here's a water-efficient showerhead. It costs $30 retail, and pays for itself in water-heating savings inside of a year. If the electric or gas utility bought them in bulk for $15, installed them in your house for a total cost of $30, and charged you on your monthly utility bill such that the savings offset the lease payments for the equipment. Call it a pay-as-you-save plan.

You want cold beer? Here's an energy-efficient fridge, pays for itself three times over in electric savings over its 15-year lifetime. Again the utility could charge you a portion of your bill as lease payments which would be offset by energy savings. You want comfy rooms? The utility can sell windows that don't lose heat in the winter. Or energy-efficient lightbulbs. Touch one, it's not hot; it doesn't waste 90 percent of its energy creating heat rather than light. As your electrical bill for lighting goes down, so will your electrical bill for air conditioning. No need to pay $25 for every bulb. The utility can buy them bulk for $10, install them for a total cost of $25 and adopt the pay-as-you-save plan. In this scenario, the utility recognizes the true business it is in, selling an energy service, not a fuel product. It uses its access to customers' homes and confidence to sell high-cost, high- margin items. It uses its access to credit to arrange a lease that solves the problem of high up-front costs of quality fridges and lightbulbs. It makes more money selling energy-efficient showerheads, windows and lightbulbs than it makes selling raw energy — selling negawatts instead of megawatts, to use the terms of energy conservation expert Amory Lovins. This strategy reduces the burden of pollution and avoids all the political hassles of bringing new power sources on-line, and all the expenses of pollution control equipment for fuel that isn't needed in the first place. And instead of paying off longtime employees with $50,000 in severance packages, downsizing is avoided and the $50,000 goes to wages that yield productive results.

Customers also win because these energy services add value. Once there's no draft around the windows, chesterfields can be pushed back to the wall and the living room is expanded. The more the service is customized, the more value-added. The customer is thinking of planting a tree in the yard? The utility's service rep can suggest reputable landscapers, since mature trees lower summer temperatures by as much as five degrees and reduce winter heat losses by as much as 20 percent; the cost of the mature tree can be paid for by the same pay-as-you-save plan. The more empowered the service rep, the better the service rep knows the customer and can act on customer concerns, the greater the variety of products the utility can sell. And the value-added for the environment, which no longer receives unnecessary pollution, is beyond measure.

There isn't an industry that can't be transformed and greened by this kind of thinking and learning. There are three reasons why North American corporations have been slow learners when it comes to new paradigms that enrich themselves and the environment.

First, our governments are pushovers. Why bother learning a new way of doing business when a quick lobby can put the fear of layoffs into the politicians? Contrary to the advice of competition guru Michael Porter — who the federal government and business groups paid two million dollars for before burying his 1992 report — neither politicians nor business executives see government as being able to lead in innovation in the international competition in the quest for best practices. Second, our consumers are just learning to be tough customers. They're a far cry from the German shoppers who instigated comprehensive, industry-financed recycling by dropping excessive packaging in store aisles and telling store owners the garbage was their problem.

I wouldn't hold my breath waiting for these two factors to change. Not so with the third reason that has retarded North American corporate learning. Until now, big corporations haven't had much reason to lose sleep worrying about losing market share to green products. Until now, producers and marketers of enviro products have stuck pretty close to the counter-culture niche markets that gave them birth. That's changing, as I document in my book *Get A Life! How to Make a Good Buck, Dance Around the Dinosaurs and Save the World While You're at it.*

Moore's Law—coined by the founder of computer-chip maker Intel—states that the power of microchips will double every two years while prices remain constant. This law can now be applied to the field of green technologies and services. The power of energy conservation technology will double every two years while staying at the same price point. Small, green entrepreneurs now have access to all the information and contacts on the Internet. They can afford Internet real estate that's every bit as spacious and prestigious as the digs of the biggest corporations. On the ground, they can shorten the chain between producer and consumer—one of the features Jim Harris highlights as a hallmark of value-adding innovation. Community Support Agriculture (CSA) is an example of explosive growth. CSA links farmers directly to customers who pre-buy fresh, organic produce delivered to their door. Other green entrepreneurs have track records showing they can outperform conventional sewage and energy systems. These companies are on the edge of going mainstream just as a new generation of talented youth are looking for employment opportunities denied them in downsized conventional organizations.

The ability to learn is very democratic. It's equally dispersed in a way that the factors that used to govern competitive advantage weren't. This is the real challenge that Jim Harris puts to business. If you don't bring your traditional business skills to learn about the new paradigms, others will bring their new paradigms to learn about traditional business skills. Which skill set is faster to master or easier to contract out? For your own sake, as well as that of the planet, I hope you take *The Learning Paradox* themes to heart, and apply them to an exciting new era of business contribution.

Wayne Roberts is the lead author of Get A Life! How To Make A Good Buck, Dance Around The Dinosaurs And Save The World While You're At It. *He can be reached at 1-888-ECO-5444.*

Rick Broadhead
Co-author, *Canadian Internet Handbook*

Andy Grove, the CEO of Intel Corporation, was once asked to comment on the return on investment from his company's Internet ventures. Grove aptly responded, "What's my ROI on e-commerce? Are you crazy? This is Columbus in the New World. What was his ROI?"[1]

Grove's remarks are a sharp reminder of the cloud of uncertainty that hangs over so many executives when it comes to the Internet. But while the Internet remains an enigma for many managers, the future impact of this technology on the business world is a lot more pronounced than many executives realize.

Much of the current discussion of the Internet's potential as a business tool centers around its use as a sales tool. While the Internet won't replace shopping malls anytime soon, even the medium's staunchest supporters are impressed with how quickly consumers have embraced the technology. Take Toyota for example. The Internet generates more sales leads for Toyota than any other sales tool, including the company's 1-800 line.[2] Think carefully about that: *The Internet has surpassed Toyota's toll-free number as the number-one source of sales leads.* It boggles the mind, doesn't it? Through strategic use of the Internet, Toyota has managed to achieve a remarkable conversion ratio — at least 10 percent of customers who contact the company through the Internet convert into car buyers within three months![3] It's an earth-shattering statistic, especially when you consider that it's attributed to a consumer brand like Toyota and not to a high-tech marketer such as IBM or Microsoft. Indeed, Toyota's success with this medium has silenced many Internet naysayers and proven once and for all the Internet has clearly entered the mainstream.

An important component of Toyota's Internet strategy was the use of on-ine advertising to drive customers to the company's Web site. On-line advertising expenditures were close to $1 billion in 1997. Incredible as it may seem, if this growth continues, on-line advertising spending will soon eclipse spending on traditional outdoor billboard advertising in the United States, which reached US$1.3 billion in 1996.[4] This fact is even more astounding when you realize that only a couple of years ago, on-line advertising was frowned upon! The ability to serve up highly targeted ads to an increasingly mainstream audience is causing marketers and advertising agencies to take notice of the Internet like never before. While on-line advertising expenditures are still a tiny fraction of advertising spending on traditional media such as newspapers and television, the reach of the on-line marketplace is enormous. Consider America Online (AOL). With over 10 million subscribers, AOL has a higher circulation than the top 11 newspapers in the United States combined![5] And if that isn't powerful enough, consider that some Web sites already have a reach that is similar to, or exceeds, many television networks in the United States and Canada. For example, the ESPN SportsZone Web site attracts eight million monthly visitors[6] while Yahoo! is used by more than 15 million unique Internet users every month[7] (SportsZone is a popular site for sports news while Yahoo! is a popular site for searching the Web[8]). In comparison, some television networks, such as CBC Newsworld in Canada, attract less than 30,000 viewers per day. Over the long term, as bandwidth limitations disappear, ads on the Internet will be as glamorous and electrifying as those on television.

Anyone who has conducted a search on the Internet has experienced the frustration of sifting through thousands upon thousands of search results. This scenario poses a serious challenge to every marketer on the Internet: how to drive traffic to your Web site by making your firm stand out from among thousands of other search results. Traditionally, generating sales on the Web has required that people visit your Web site. For example, in Toyota's case, advertising banners were used to lure sales prospects to Toyota's Web site, where visitors were invited to fill out an on-line form and request a Toyota brochure. But is all of this about to change? Companies like Narrative Corp. of Waltham, Massachusetts, (www.narrative.com) are developing technologies that stretch the capabilities of on-line advertisements by allowing consumers to conduct real-time financial transactions and product demonstrations within the confines of banner ads. (A banner ad is a rectangular advertisement usually located at the top of a Web page). For example, a campaign Narrative developed for New Balance shoes allows customers to shop for shoes by answering questions such as, "Are you looking for a men's or women's shoe?" and "Are you a high or average mile runner?". All interaction with the customer is handled within the banner ad, and the customer only connects to the New Balance site once a specific shoe has been selected. Eventually, as this technology matures, customers will be able to purchase their shoes without ever leaving the banner ad. Hard as it is to believe today, such a technology could eventually diminish the importance of Web sites as banner ads take on functions (such as credit-card transactions) that only

Web sites currently support. Indeed, leading-edge firms like Narrative understand that success on the Internet is not measured by how many visitors come to your Web site but rather by maximizing the number of places on the Web where people can be exposed to your product or service. This line of thinking has already been successfully applied by industry trend setters such as United Parcel Service and Amazon.com, a virtual bookstore that operates on the Web. Amazon.com, for example has established an Associate Program that pays referral fees to other Web sites that sell its books. Amazon.com benefits by having thousands of points-of-sale for its products rather than just one.

Finally, the Internet will force many industries to redefine their roles as the Internet reduces the need for middlemen — a trend known as disintermediation. Professions threatened by the Internet include travel agents, stockbrokers, librarians, real estate agents, automotive dealers — anyone who makes their living by acting as an intermediary between the consumer and the manufacturer of a product or provider of a service.

Perhaps nowhere is disintermediation more pronounced than in the travel industry. While less than one per cent of travel reservations world wide are made on-line today,[9] more and more people are booking their trips on the Internet. Many people discount the role that the Internet will play within the travel industry, but the statistics are enlightening. The Travel Industry Association of America (TIA) found that the percentage of U.S. travelers who use on-line services to make travel plans or reservations jumped from 11 percent in 1996 to 28 percent in 1997. The TIA also found a 19 percent increase in the number of Americans who prefer the Internet for travel reservations, and a decline in the number of people who prefer travel agents. Airlines have been quick to cash in on this trend, setting up Web sites that make it easier for customers to purchase tickets on-line, while at the same time slashing the commissions paid to travel agents. Sounds like a great time to set up an on-line travel agency, right? On the contrary — the on-line travel industry may in fact be consolidating in the future. In an effort to protect their on-line turf, some airlines now pay *lower* commissions to travel agents if the tickets are processed on-line rather than through traditional channels, in effect penalizing travel agents for doing business on the Internet. The battle has become so cut-throat that American Express steadfastly refuses to process on-line reservations for United Airlines, Northwest Airlines and British Airways because the commissions paid by these airlines for on-line bookings have dropped to unacceptable levels. All this doesn't mean that travel agents are destined for extinction, but for travel agents to survive this new paradigm shift, they will have to continually strive to exceed the value offered to customers by their on-line counterparts.

Even doctors, as providers of health care, are middlemen, and hence face new challenges created by the Internet. As more and more health care information proliferates on-line, consumers are bypassing their local doctors and hospitals and accessing medical advice over the Internet. Recognizing the opportunity, a publicly traded company called Mediconsult.com (www.mediconsult.com) has opened up a virtual medical center on the Internet that provides Internet users with quick access to top medical specialists. For $195, consumers can receive a confidential report, including treatment recommendations, from a physician of their choosing. Full biographies and C.V.'s of participating doctors are available on the Mediconsult Web site, and the waiting time for an assessment is generally less than five days! Such a revolutionary, yet simple, approach to medical care will forever change our health care system and alter the centuries-old relationship between doctors and their patients.

Success on the Internet requires that business leaders continually question existing ways of doing business. Companies like Toyota, Narrative and Mediconsult share one trait in common — each is challenging the status quo. Unilever, the second-largest advertiser in the world, has committed unprecedented levels of funding to the Internet, in recognition of the importance of this new medium. When asked why the company was taking such a giant leap into new media, Unilever's chairman responded, "Yes, it is a significant jump but we need to do that because it is a very advanced market and many of our lessons will be learned there."[10]

Rick Broadhead can be reached at rickb @ sympatico.ca or via the Web at www.intervex.com

1. Survey of Electronic Commerce, *The Economist*, May 10, 1997.
2. Web Ads Start to Click, *BusinessWeek*, Oct. 6, 1997.
3. Online Ads Booming as Marketers Discover Web, *Reuters*, Dec. 4, 1997.
4. Ibid.
5. Ibid.
6. Ibid.
7. Yahoo Most Popular Web Site in Dec, *Reuters*, Jan. 12, 1998.
8. SportsZone is at espn.sportszone.com and Yahoo! is at www.yahoo.com
9. Internet No Threat to Agents, Yet, *The Toronto Star*, Oct. 21, 1997.
10. Unilever To Spend More On Internet Advertising, *Reuters*, Jan. 16, 1997.

Hope and Optimism

I would like to convey hope and optimism. Thriving in the future (for individuals, organizations and society as a whole) requires a willingness to being flexible and adaptable, and constantly questioning, learning and meeting new challenges. We can change ourselves, examine our paradigms, assume leadership and strengthen our relationships with others. By becoming comfortable with the fear and discomfort that we experience when learning new skills, questioning assumptions, developing new products and services, we develop a greater tolerance for ambiguity, uncertainty and paradox. As we gain experience by repeatedly passing through the learning paradox, the greater the faith we develop in our talents and abilities. Security and self-esteem develop. The more this occurs, the more power and knowledge an individual can share with others.

I would like to write a book about personal growth and call it *Being and Becoming*. I envision the cover having an acorn on it. The central question of the book will be: Is an acorn just an acorn or is it a potential oak tree? Who am I? Am I all I am today, or am I who I could potentially be? What is the purpose of my life? Why am I here? As I wrestle with these questions, I get a sense of who I could become. If I revel in this potential, if I continue to develop the sense of who I am and the commitment to live out of my potential rather than my past or present, I become who I am meant to be. I hope that this book serves as a catalyst for personal and organizational growth and success.

What lies behind us and what lies before us are tiny matters compared to what lies within us.
Ralph Waldo Emerson, philosopher

If you treat a man as he is, he will stay that way, but if you treat him as if he were what he ought to be and could be, he will become that bigger and better man.
Johann Wolfgang von Goethe, philosopher

Index

Endnotes

MAKING YOUR MARK

1. I am grateful to Janice McNally for suggesting that readers rip out the first page.

INTRODUCTION: GAINING COMFORT FROM DISCOMFORT

1. David Hurst, *Crisis & Renewal: Meeting the Challenge of Organizational Change* (Harvard Business School Press, Boston, 1995).

2. Stephen R. Covey, *How to Succeed with People* (Deseret Book Company, Salt Lake City, 1971), page 9.

3. George Hartman uses this analogy to make the point that an investment strategy needs to be custom-tailored for a client in *Risk is a Four Letter Word: The Asset Allocation Approach to Investing* (Stoddart Publishing, Toronto, 1994), page 9.

4. See Chapter 11: The Internet Revolution.

5. Sam Geist, *Why Should Anyone Do Business with You Rather than Someone Else?* (Addington & Wentworth, Markham, Ontario, 1997), page 305.

CHAPTER 1: SHIFT FROM SATISFACTION TO SECURITY

1. Robert Levering, *A Great Place to Work: What Makes Some Employers So Good (and Most So Bad)* (Random House, New York, 1985). Based on the polling work of Daniel Yankelovich who found that in the United States, only 27 percent of employees report that their work turns them on. Despite these figures, Yankelovich found most American workers still want to do a good job.

2. *Newsweek,* "The Hit Men," Feb. 26, 1996, pages 44-48.

3. *Fortune,* "Brands Rule," Mar. 4, 1996.

4. *Business Week,* "A Third Front in the Cola Wars: Private Label King Cott Launches a Blitz Against Coke and Pepsi," Dec. 12, 1994, pages 66-67.

5. Judith Bardwick, *Danger in the Comfort Zone* (American Management Association, New York, 1991).

6. Gary Hamel and C.K. Prahalad, *Competing for the Future: Breakthrough Strategies for Seizing Control of Your Industry and Creating the Markets of Tomorrow* (Harvard Business School Press, Boston, 1994), page 6.

7. Judith Bardwick, *The Plateauing Trap* (Bantam, New York, 1988), page 23.

8. Stephen R. Covey, *How to Succeed with People* (Deseret Book Company, Salt Lake City, 1971), page 23.

9. Aire de Gues is the former head of planning for Royal Dutch Shell. His new book *The Living Company* (Harvard Business School Press, Boston, 1997) is well worth reading. This quotation is from Peter Senge's book *The Fifth Discipline: The Art & Practice of the Learning Organization* (Doubleday/Currency, New York, 1990), page 4.

10. *Information Week,* "Only the Strong Survive: Top 50 Software Vendors," May 22, 1995, page 44.

11. All figures cited are in U.S. dollars unless otherwise noted.

CHAPTER 2: THE LEARNING PARADOX

1. This expression is from Kelly Smith of Key Consulting, Calgary, who specializes in organizational development. He can be reached at (403) 264-7200.

2. The diving story is told by professional speaker Martin Rutte, who discusses spirituality in the workplace. He is co-author of *Chicken Soup for the Soul at Work*. Martin can be contacted at (505) 466-1510.

3. Michael Hammer, "Reengineering Work: Don't Automate, Obliterate," *Harvard Business Review,* Jul.-Aug. 1990.

4. Michael Hammer quoted in *Fortune Magazine,* April 17, 1995.

5. M. Scott Peck, *The Road Less Traveled* (Simon & Schuster, New York, 1978), page 15.

6. Pritchett's Law by Lou Pritchett, *Stop Paddling & Start Rocking the Boat* (HarperBusiness, New York, 1995) page 39.

7. Don Tapscott, *The Digital Economy: Promise and Peril in the Age of Networked Intelligence* (McGraw-Hill, New York, 1996), page 3.

CHAPTER 3: THE BUSINESS OF PARADIGMS

1. Joel Arthur Barker, *Paradigms: The Business of Discovering the Future* (Harper Business edition, New York, 1993), pages 15-17.

2. *Forbes,* "Whither Moore's Law," Sept. 11, 1995, pages 167-168.

3. Sun Microsystems press release, Nov. 1994.

4. Henry Mintzberg, *The Rise and Fall of Strategic Planning* (Free Press, New York 1994.)

5. Don Tapscott uses this term in *The Digital Economy: Promise and Peril in the Age of Networked Intelligence* (McGraw-Hill, New York, 1996).

6. Michael A. Cusumano and Richard W. Selby, *Microsoft Secrets: How the World's Most Powerful Software Company Creates Technology, Shapes Markets and Manages People* (Free Press—Simon & Schuster, New York, 1995), page 169.

7. Figures provided by Jim Sanders, Director of Research at the Software Publishers Association (SPA). Figures are total shipments for North American retail market in millions of dollars. For more updated information, visit SPA's Web site at http://www.spa.org.

8. The SPA does not provide information on individual title sales. These figures are for total *DOS* vs. total *Windows* sales of spreadsheets. However, given that in the *DOS* paradigm *Lotus 1-2-3* enjoyed 75 percent of market share, while now in the *Windows* environment, Microsoft's *Excel* sold through the *Office* suite enjoys almost 90 percent market share of current spreadsheet sales, these figures provided by Jim Sanders, Director of Research at the Software Publishers Association (SPA) for the whole category can be taken to apply to *1-2-3* and *Excel.* Figures are based on total shipments for North American retail market in millions of dollars. For information on software sales, visit the SPA's Web site at http://www.spa.org

9. Cusumano and Selby, *Microsoft Secrets,* page 146.

10. This is a simple explanation of RAM and a hard disk. To use an analogy, a hard disk is like the physical size of a bookcase. The larger the bookcase, the more books can be stored. The size of the hard disk determines the volume of information that can be stored on a computer. The RAM—or Random Access Memory—would be like your capacity to read. If you can read one page a minute in this analogy, that would be equal to one megabyte of RAM, but if you are a speed reader and can read 16 pages

a minute, that would be equal to 16 MB of RAM. RAM (working memory) determines how much information the computer can work on at one time.

CHAPTER 4: LEADERS ARE PARADIGM INNOVATORS

1. Information provided by Dennis Jones, FedEx's CIO an interview.
2. Ibid.
3. I believe this is James Champy's quotation, but I have been unable to source it.
4. *Fortune*, "Service is Everybody's Business," June 27, 1994.
5. *Forbes*, Lincoln Continental advertisement, June 17, 1996, pages 256-257.
6. Information on booking two-hour or full-day seminars with the world's leading business thinkers can be obtained by calling Satellite Seminars at (800)491-6000 or (416)488-9265
7. *Fortune*, "Your Next Phone Call May Be Via the Net," June 23, 1997, page 139.
8. Gary Hamel and C.K. Prahalad, *Competing for the Future: Breakthrough Strategies for Seizing Control of Your Industry and Creating the Markets of Tomorrow* (Harvard Business School Press, Boston, 1994), pages 8-9.
9. Christopher Cerf and Victor Navasky, *The Experts Speak* (Pantheon, New York, 1984).
10. Roger Kay, International Data Corporation (IDC).
11. Stephen R. Covey, *The 7 Habits of Highly Effective People* (Fireside, New York, 1989), page 101.
12. 3.x is the convention used to signify Windows 3.0, 3.1 and 3.11. Collectively they are known as Windows 3.x.
13. This quotation is from Carl Jung's *Two Essays on Analytical Psychology*.
14. From a paper by Dr. Terry Paulson, "Tactics for Building Confidence and Teamwork in the Midst of Turmoil." Contact Dr. Paulson at drterryp@aol.com or Paulson and Associates (818) 991-5110.

CHAPTER 5: CREATING SUSTAINABLE ENTERPRISES

1. The origin of the Serenity Prayer is obscure. It may date back to Boethius, a philosopher who lived about A.D. 500 and was martyred by Christians. It is usually credited to Reinhold Niebuhr, a 20th-century theologian who in turn credited an 18th-century theologian, Friedrich Oetinger.
2. Wilfredo Pareto (1848–1923) was an Italian economist and political sociologist who devised Pareto's Law. Known as the 80:20 rule, it is the law of the trivial many and the critical few. The rule states that in any activity, 80 percent of potential value can be achieved from just 20 percent of effort, and that one can spend the remaining 80 percent of effort for relatively little return.
3. Pat Robinson is dean of health programs at Malspina University College in Nanaimo, B.C. She can be reached at robinson@mala.bc.ca, or (604)755-8779.
4. Robert Levering, *A Great Place to Work: What Makes Some Employers So Good (and Most So Bad)* (Random House, New York, 1985). (Based on the polling work of Daniel Yankelovich who found that in the U.S. only 27 percent of employees report that their work turns them on. Despite these figures, Yankelovich found most American workers still want to do a good job.)

CHAPTER 6: CREATING VALUE

1. David Osborne and Ted Gaebler, *Reinventing Government: How the Entrepreneurial Spirit is Transforming the Public Sector* (Addison-Wesley, Toronto, 1992), page 110.

2. This is a variation of a quotation from Adam Smith's *The Money Game*: "If you don't know who you are, the stock market is an expensive place to find out."

3. Robyn Allan is president of CYF Consulting Limited. When Ms Allan became president of the Insurance Corporation of British Columbia, ICBC had a projected $200-million annual deficit. Within 10 months, without downsizing, the corporation had a $150 million profit. She can be reached at (604) 685-4160.

4. Other fun oxymorons include airline cuisine, fresh frozen, criminal justice, military intelligence, pretty ugly, strategic planning, jumbo shrimp, air traffic control, great depression, competing standards, fresh frozen jumbo shrimp, gourmet pizza, mandatory option, first annual, relatively simple, unofficial record. Most of these come from Don Tapscott's Web page. For more oxymorons, visit www.mtnlake.com/paradigm/moron.html.

5. Ravi Vijh's of Moval International can be reached at (416) 730-8811.

6. Gary Hamel, "Killer Strategies" *Fortune*, June 23, 1997, page 72.

7. Ibid, page 74.

8. Ibid, page 73

9. Ibid, page 74.

10. Francis Aguilar and Arvind Bhambri, "Johnson & Johnson," Harvard Business School, Harvard Business Case Studies, 1983, page 5.

11. Dr. Janet Lapp is the author of *Plant Your Feet Firmly in Mid-Air* and *Dancing with Tigers*. She hosts the CBS affiliate TV series *Keep Well*. To find out more visit, www.lapp.com

CHAPTER 7: the new economy

1. Alvin Toffler, *The Third Wave* (Bantam Books, New York, 1981), pages 1-25.

2. Nuala Beck, *Shifting Gears: Thriving in the New Economy* (HarperCollins, Toronto, 1992).

3. Bruce Little, *The Globe and Mail's Report on Business*, "Tilting at Smokestacks," July 20, 1991.

4. Don Peppers and Martha Rogers, *The One to One Future* (Currency Doubleday, New York, 1993).

5. *Fortune*, "One Writer's Hunt for the Perfect Jeans," April 17, 1995. Levi's market share of jeans grew from 14.5 to 19.1 percent over the 1990-1995 period.

6. For the most recent figures visit, www.intel.com.

7. Figures from Howard High at Intel's investor and media relations department.

8. Justin Fox, "The Next Best Thing To Free Money" *Fortune Magazine*, July 1, 1997, page 52.

9. An interesting case highlights the value of employee experience. In Europe, General Motor's head of purchasing, Jose Ignacio Lopez, after saving the company $1 billion in just a few years, left to join Volkswagen. What was Lopez's value? GM successfully sued Volkswagen, after it proved that some of Lopez's lieutenants (known as "warriors") had stolen GM documents. The documents in question were lists of GM parts and suppliers, which have little value to Volkswagen. Why was this case so hotly contested? On a personal level, GM executives felt betrayed by a former col-

league. From a competitive standpoint it is even more upsetting that Lopez and a number of his team took their considerable knowledge to a competitor's camp. No book or course could replace the practical experience and inside information that the managers took with them.

10. Nuala Beck, *Shifting Gears: Thriving in the New Economy* (HarperCollins, Toronto, 1992).

CHAPTER 8: VALUING PEOPLE

1. Michael A. Cusumano and Richard W. Selby, *Microsoft Secrets: How the World's Most Powerful Software Company Creates Technology, Shapes Markets and Manages People* (Free Press — Simon & Schuster, New York, 1995), page 92.

2. *"Managing End User Computing,"* Multi-Client Research Study, Nolan, Norton & Co, 1992.

3. The Gartner Group, "Total Cost of Ownership: Reducing PC/LAN Costs in the Enterprise," Sept. 2, 1996.

4. Jean-Pascal Souque, "Training and Development Practices, Expenditures and Trends," Conference Board of Canada, 1996.

5. Visit www.astd.org/who/research/benchmar/benchmar.htm, ASTD's site, for more information.

6. The exception to this statement is the current demand for Cobalt programmers to deal with the year 2000 crisis. Old mainframe systems were designed with only two digits for the year — instead of 1997, the program reads 97. In 2000, the year will read 00 and the programs will not generate proper results. Companies will spend an estimated one trillion dollars between 1995 and the year 2000 fixing the year 2000 crisis! Estimates range from $600 billion (Gartner group) to $1.6 trillion (Capers Jones). Peter de Jager, a world authority on the Y2K crisis, estimates the cost at $1 trillion! To learn more, visit his site at www.year2000.com/

7. Michael A. Cusumano and Richard W. Selby, *Microsoft Secrets: How the World's Most Powerful Software Company Creates Technology, Shapes Markets and Manages People* (Free Press — Simon & Schuster, New York, 1995), pages 124-125.

8. Ibid, page 10.

9. On his deathbed Maslow actually refuted this claim, suggesting that the highest need is self-transcendence, working for some larger, worthier goal than just our own interests. Paradoxically, the only way an individual can achieve self-fulfillment is through service to others.

10. Robert Levering, *A Great Place to Work: What Makes Some Employers So Good (and Most So Bad)* (Random House, New York, 1985).

11. National Speakers Association 1995 Convention, Minneapolis, July 15-18, 1995.

CHAPTER 9: KEEPING CUSTOMERS

1. Jack Parr researches customer satisfaction. Contact Jack Parr and Associates, (913) 827-0404.

2. *Harvard Business Review,* "Realize Your Customers' Full Profit Potential," Sept.-Oct. 1995.

3. Gary Hamel and C.K. Prahalad, *Competing for the Future: Breakthrough Strategies for Seizing Control of Your Industry and Creating the Markets of Tomorrow* (Harvard Business School Press, Boston, 1994), page 97.

4. For more information about the National Retail Federation, call (202) 783-7971 or surf www.nrf.com.

5. Maurice Mascaren, as a U.S. management consultant, who died in 1995, frequently used this expression in teaching TEC (The Executive Committee) Groups throughout North America. The expression is courtesy of Doug Bouey, a TEC chairman of Catalyst Strategic Consultants in Calgary, Alberta, (403) 777-1144.

6. "Fear of Technology is Phobia of the 90's; Computer Habits, Attitudes Determine 'Techno-Type'," Dell Computer Corporation, July 26, 1993.

7. *Time*, "Wake-up call," July 17, 1995, page 49.

8. David Gagie, Marketing Director, Auriemma Consulting Group. Contact (516) 333-4800.

9. Bruce Brittain of Brittain Associates. Contact (404) 636-6155.

10. Michael Auriemma of Auriemma Consulting Group, a credit-card consulting firm. Contact (516) 333-4800.

11. MasterCard reports on annual card usage for 1996. Average classic card holder charges $2,024 annually without cash dispersements, while the average gold card holder charges $3,799. Contact James Accomando, Accomando Consulting at (203) 367-3306 or acificon@aol.com

12. Bruce Brittain of Brittain Associates. Contact (404) 636-6155.

13. Figures from the RAM research group, www.ramresearch.com.

14. A 1.000 batter—pronounced one thousand—will hit the ball 1,000 times out of 1,000 times at bat. A .250 batter will hit the ball 250 times out of 1,000 times at bat.

15. Hamel and Prahalad, *Competing*, page 238.

16. Francis Vincent's a speech at Fairfield University, "Education and Baseball" reported in *America*, April 6, 1991, pages 372–373.

17. Jan Carlzon, *Moments of Truth* (Harper & Row, New York, 1987), page 3.

18. For an excellent study of this trend, read Don Peppers' and Martha Rogers' *The One to One Future* (Currency Doubleday, New York, 1993).

CHAPTER 10: THE NEW IT PARADIGM

1. Don Tapscott and Art Caston, *Paradigm Shift: The New Promise of Information Technology* (McGraw-Hill, New York, 1993), page 97.

2. Wal-Mart 1997 Annual Report, page 3.

3. Peter Senge, *The Fifth Discipline: The Art & Practice of the Learning Organization* (Doubleday/Currency, New York, 1990).

4. Page 77 of the *Digital Economy*. Call 1-800-522-8656 to confirm figures, details. Substantial is mild. Tom Panlas tpanelas@eb.com.

5. Other processes that foster creativity an innovation include Edward de Bono's *Six Thinking Hats* or *Lateral Thinking*. For information call MICA at (416) 366-6422 or 1-800-668-8298.

6. *Time* special issue, "Age of the Road Warrior," Spring 1995, page 39.

7. Douglas Coupland's *Microserfs* is a great read.

8. Tapscott and Caston, *Paradigm Shift*, page 129.

9. Ibid.

10. Interview with Ken Nickerson, Director of Technical Services, Microsoft.

11. Christos Cotsakos, President and CEO of e*trade, "Chaos and Uncertainty Please . . ." in *Entrepriser*, Vol 4, Fall 1996. For full article surf http://www.etrade.com/news/cc12097.html.

12. *The Economist*, "The Birth of a New Species," Software Industry Survey, May 25, 1996, page 1.

13. Ibid, page 4.

14. Don Tapscott, *The Digital Economy: Promise and Peril in the Age of Networked Intelligence* (McGraw-Hill, New York, 1996), page 62.

CHAPTER 11: THE INTERNET REVOLUTION

1. From September 1994 to September 1995, the US Post Service Office delivered 96.3 billion first-class letters, 10.2 billion second-class and 800 million international pieces of mail, for a total of 107.3 billion letters. (This does not include advertising mail, or unaddressed junk mail, which totaled 71.1 billion pieces.) According to *Electronic Mail and Messaging Systems*, the industry publication dedicated to the phenomenon of e-mail, in 1996 e-mail boxes worldwide exceeded 120 million while in North America over 82 million people have e-mail boxes. These 82 million e-mail users need to receive only 3.6 messages a day for the year (for both business and personal) to have e-mail volume exceed postal volumes. Internal use of e-mail is booming in Sun Microsystems, Intel, Microsoft and Netscape, where it runs as high as 120 per person per day. So, in 1996, for the first time in the history of the world, e-mails have exceeded letters carried by the postal service. This creates fundamental changes in the way organizations work.

2. International Data Corporation (IDC) www.idc.com.

3. Erwin Blane, Mary A. Modahl and Jesse Johnson, *Business Trade & Technology Strategies*, Vol. 1, No. 1 (Forrester Research, July 1997), www.forrester.com.

4. International Data Corporation (IDC) www.idc.com.

5. *Computer Dealer News*, "Cold Hard e-cash" by Jerry Zeidenberg, March 7, 1996, page 23.

6. *Fast Company*, "Are You Fast Enough? Are You Hungry Enough? Are You Tough Enough to Work, Live, Compete in Netscape Time?" Premier issue, page 96. (An awesome article!)

7. Steve Hamm, "The Long Shadow of Bill Gates," *Business Week*, Aug. 18, 1997, page 85.

8. Blane, Modahl and Johnson, *Business,* Vol. 1, No. 1.

9. *Fortune,* "Could the Very Best PC Maker be Dell Computer?" April 14, 1997, page 26.

10. *Fortune,* "Could," page 26.

11. "World Internet Telephony Products," 1997 $49M; 1998 $122M; 1999 $305M; and 2001 $1.89B

12. "Internet Telephony Poised for Growth" *Information Week*, reporting on the PC Expo in New York in June 1997. Four panelists—Allen Lutz, senior VP of Compaq Computer; Tom Evslin, VP of AT&T WorldNet Services; Frank Gill, executive VP of Intel; and Elon Ganor, VocalTec CEO, concurred that within the next 10 years, and as soon as five years, at least 50 percent of telephone traffic will go over IP networks rather than circuit switched networks.

13. Brian Swimme and Thomas Berry, *The Universe Story* (Harper Collins, New York, 1992) pages 11–12.

14. *Toronto Star,* "A Question of Copyright" by K.K. Campbell, Jan. 18, 1996, page H1 & H5.

15. http://www.aol.com/corp/news/press/more/970807.html.

16. http://world.compuserve.com/corporate/stockholder/quarter/index.asp.

17. Tapscott, *The Digital Economy,* page 16.

18. *Toronto Star,* "PC Powerhouses Brew up a Standard" by Robert Wright, Jan. 18, 1996, page H2.

19. Figures from 1997 Banking Systems and Technology: Retail Delivery and Branch Automation study by Mentis Corporation May 2, 1997. Mentis is the leading international research firm specializing in evaluating information and communications technology within the financial services sector. Visit http://www.mentis.com.

CHAPTER 12: BUSINESS AND THE ENVIRONMENT

1. Dr. Janet Lapp is the author of *Plant Your Feet Firmly in Mid-Air* and *Dancing with Tigers.* She hosts the CBS affiliate TV series *Keep Well.* To find out more, visit www.lapp.com.

2. Richard Dennis being quoted by Jack D Schwager, *Market Wizards* (Harper Business, New York, 1993), page 110.

3. Contact the Rocky Mountain Institute at (970)927-3851.

4. Amory Lovins and William Browning, "Negawatts for Buildings," *Urban Land,* July 1992.

5. *MacLean's,* April 1996, page 41.

APPENDIX: KANBAN: FLEXIBLE MANUFACTURING

1. Mikel Harry, *The Vision of Six Sigma*

Bibliography

Allan, Robyn. *Quest for Prosperity: The Dance of Success.* Vancouver: Blue Feather Publishing (A Division of CYF Consulting), 1995.

American Management Association. *Blueprints for Service Quality: The Federal Express Approach.* AMA Briefing, 1991.

Bardwick, Judith. *Danger in the Comfort Zone.* New York: American Management Association, 1991.

———— . *The Plateauing Trap.* New York: Bantam, 1988.

Barker, Joel Arthur. *Paradigms: The Business of Discovering the Future.* New York: HarperBusiness, 1993.

Beck, Nuala. *Shifting Gears: Thriving in the New Economy.* Toronto: HarperCollins, 1992.

Blanchard, Ken and Sheldon Bowles. *Raving Fans.* New York: William Morrow & Co., 1993.

Carlzon, Jan. *Moments of Truth.* New York: Harper & Row, 1987.

Carnegie, Dale. *How to Win Friends and Influence People.* New York: Pocket Books, 1936.

Carson, Patrick, and Julia Moulden. *Green Is Gold.* Toronto: HarperBusiness, 1991.

Champy, James. *Reengineering Management: The Mandate for New Leadership.* New York: HarperBusiness, 1995.

Cerf, Christopher, and Victor Navasky. *The Experts Speak.* New York: Pantheon, 1984.

Chilton, David. *The Wealthy Barber.* Toronto: Stoddart, 1989.

Covey, Stephen. *The 7 Habits of Highly Effective People.* New York: Fireside, 1989.

————. *Principle Centered Leadership.* New York: Summit Books, 1990.

————. *How to Succeed with People.* Salt Lake City: Deseret Book Company, 1971.

Csikszentmihalyi, Mihaly. *Flow: The Psychology of Optimal Experience.* New York: Harper & Row, 1990.

Cusumano, Michael A., and Richard W. Selby *Microsoft Secrets: How the World's Most Powerful Software Company Creates Technology, Shapes Markets and Manages People.* New York: Free Press (Simon & Schuster), 1995.

de Geus, Arie. *The Living Company.* Boston: Harvard Business School Press, 1997.

————. "Planning as Learning." *Harvard Business Review,* Mar./Apr. 1988.

Deming, W. Edwards. *Out of Crisis.* Cambridge, Mass: MIT Center for Advanced Engineering Study, 1982.

Fisher, Roger, and William Ury. *Getting to Yes: Negotiating Agreement Without Giving In.* New York: Penguin, 1981.

Fitz-Enz, Jac. *Benchmarking Staff Performance.* San Francisco: Jossey-Bass, 1993.

————. *Human Value Management.* San Francisco: Jossey-Bass, 1990.

Foot, David with Daniel Stoffman. *Boom, Bust & Echo.* Toronto: Macfarlane Walter & Ross, 1996.

Gates, Bill. *The Road Ahead.* New York: Viking (Penguin Books) 1995.

Grove, Andrew. *Only the Paranoid Survive.* New York: Bantam Doubleday Dell, 1996.

All wisdom is plagiarism; only stupidity is original.

Hugh Kerr, Preacher

Hamel, Gary, and C.K. Prahalad. *Competing for the Future: Breakthrough Strategies for Seizing Control of Your Industry and Creating the Markets of Tomorrow.* Boston: Harvard Business School Press, 1994.

Hammer, Michael. *Reengineering Work: Don't Automate, Obliterate. Harvard Business Review,* July/Aug. 1990.

———, and James Champy. *Reengineering the Corporation: A Manifesto for Business Revolution.* New York: HarperBusiness, 1993.

Harris, Jim. *The Leadership Challenge,* 1990.

———. *The New IT Paradigm: EDI or DIE,* 1991.

———. *The New Training Paradigm,* 1990.

———. *Customer Retention: Exceed Expectations,* 1990.

Herzberg, Frederick. "One More Time: How Do You Motivate Employees?" *Harvard Business Review,* Jan./Feb. 1968.

Innes, Eva, Lyon, Jim, and Harris, Jim. *The 100 Best Companies to Work for in Canada.* Toronto: HarperCollins, 1990.

Kanter, Rosabeth Moss. *When Giants Learn to Dance.* New York: Simon & Schuster, 1989.

Kuhn, Thomas S. *The Structure of Scientific Revolutions.* Chicago: University of Chicago Press, 1970.

Levering, Robert. *A Great Place to Work: What Makes Some Employers So Good (and Most So Bad).* New York: Random House, 1985.

———, and Milton Moskowitz. *The 100 Best Companies to Work for in America.* New York: Doubleday/Currency, 1993.

Lynch, Dudley, and Paul L. Kordis. *Strategy of the Dolphin.* New York: Ballantine, 1988.

Negroponte, Nicholas. *being digital.* New York: Alfred A. Knopf, 1995.

Osborne, David and Ted Gaebler. *Reinventing Government.* Reading, Addison-Wesley, 1992.

O'Toole, James. *Leading Change: The Argument for Values-Based Leadership.* New York: Random House, 1995.

Peck, M. Scott. *The Road Less Traveled.* New York: Simon & Schuster, 1978.

Peppers, Don and Martha Rogers. *The One to One Future.* New York: Currency Doubleday, 1993.

Reichheld, Frederick F. *The Loyalty Effect: The Hidden Force Behind Growth, Profits, and Lasting Value.* Boston: Harvard Business School Press, 1996.

Reynolds, Bob. *The 100 Best Companies to Work for in the U.K.* London: Fontana, 1989.

Roberts, Wayne, and Susan Brandum. *Get a Life: How to Make a Good Buck, Dance Around the Dinosaurs and Save the World While You're at it. Get a Life.* Publishing House, October 1995.

Senge, Peter. *The Fifth Discipline: The Art and Practice of the Learning Organization.* New York: Doubleday/Currency, 1990.

Swanson, Richard A., and Deane B. Gradous. *Forecasting Financial Benefits of Human Resource Development.* San Francisco: Jossey-Bass, 1988.

Semler, Ricardo. *Maverick.* New York: Warner Books, 1993.

Souque, Jean-Pascal. *Training & Development Practices, Expenditures and Trends.* Conference Board of Canada, 1996.

Many times I realize how much of my own outer and inner life is built upon the labors of my fellowmen, both living and dead and how earnestly I must exert myself in order to give in return as much as I have received.

Albert Einstein, physicist

Tapscott, Don, and Art Caston. *Paradigm Shift: The New Promise of Information Technology.* New York: McGraw-Hill, 1993.

————. *The Digital Economy: Promise and Peril in the Age of Networked Intelligence.* New York: McGraw-Hill, 1996.

Toffler, Alvin. *The Third Wave.* New York: Bantam Books, 1981.

Treacy, Michael, and Fred Wiersema. *The Discipline of Market Leaders.* Reading, Mass: Addison-Wesley, 1995.

Wallace, James, and Jim Erickson *Hard Drive: Bill Gates and the Making of the Microsoft Empire.* New York: HarperBusiness, 1992.

Wheatley, Margaret J. *Leadership and the New Science: Learning About Organization from an Orderly Universe.* San Francisco: Berrett-Koehler Publishers, 1992.

Acknowledgments

This work began in 1989 after I wrote *The 100 Best Companies to Work for in Canada*. I began to ask, "How do individuals and organizations create greater security?" This material evolved in working with clients over eight years. It has been tested by thousands of executives, managers, frontline staff, parents and community group volunteers who participated in seminars. Their insights, questions, critiques and feedback have shaped the material. I am grateful to them for their wisdom.

I owe special thanks to the entire team at Macmillan Canada: Alison Maclean whose willingness to explore new ideas and vision for this book attracted me to Macmillan, Jill Lambert, my editor (who has been a delight to work with), Shannon Potts who shepherded the book through production, Meghan Brousseau for her marketing acumen and excitement, Alison Besse, the preeminent publicist, Marla Krisko, who works with national accounts, Anna Stancer for coordinating the editing changes and David McWhirter.

A few people played a key role: Andrew McMurtry for his faith, Lionel Robins for his encouragement, Tom Burney for his urging, Kathleen Seaver for her feedback, Judy Bell and Ian Melanson for their insights and Fraser McAllan and Rick Spence for their exceptional eye to detail.

I wish to thank my clients. They are my best teachers. Their encouragement and feedback on this journey has been the ultimate reward. So many individuals have enthusiastically embraced this work. Seeing the principles applied has given me tremendous satisfaction. Over 25,000 copies of The Learning Paradox were printed and ordered prior to this edition, which means the book was a national bestseller many times over before it was ever available in a bookstore. Thanks to all my friends, colleagues and clients who have greatly enriched the text through their insights: Robyn Allan, Everett Anstey, Christopher Ash, Colum Bastable, Ralph Beslin, Jeremy Boudreau, Rick Broadhead, Eli Bay, Ruth Brothers, Donna Burn, Peter Buchanan, Ken Clarke, Jim Clubine, Patrick Carson, Carol Cox, David Cox, Phyllis Downing, Diane Eisele, Jim Evans, Catherine Fels-Smith, Brian Foley, Wayne Fiander, Bill Foster, Theresa Gill, Margo Gordon, Arlynn Greenbaum, David Hardy, Sharon Harvey-Smith, Pat Henderson, Chuck Hoffman, Richard Jensen, Bill Johnston, Susan Jurow, John Kempster, Wayne Kempton, Debra Kerby, Ray Lancashire, Donald Languedoc, Daphne Lavers, Irene Lum, D'Arcy Mackenzie, Ginette Maklo, Stephen Marks, Barbara Marshall, Brian McConnell, Sheree McGarrity, David McIntyre, Susan McLarty, Ian Melanson,

> If the lenses of our perception were cleansed we would see everything as it is — infinite.
> William Blake, poet

Catherine Middleton, Nancy Myers, David McIntyre, Sheree McGarrity, Suzanne McGee, Susan McLarty, John Mowat, John Kempster, Barbara Marshall, James Mitchell, Gail Palkovich, Randy Parkin, Ian Percy, Farah Perelmuter, Jim Poirier, David Power, Glori Rosato-Sararus, Richard Searns, Kelly Smith, Arthur Soler, Jody Stevens, Chris Stoate, Nat Stoddard, Nick Truyens, Ravi Vijh, Pat Vincent, Chantal Vlachos, Debi Whistlecraft, Bob Willard, Bill Wilson, Warner Woodley, Hugh Zochling and Ken Zoschke.

Between 1994–1997 I worked with a series of editors developing this book through seven editions: Meg Taylor, Paddy Kamen, JoAnne Sommers on the third and fourth, Andrea Kuch, Eric Mills, Barbara Frances and Janice McNally. Fredrik Carlberg and his team at Boomerang Art + Design designed editions 4–7.

Chapter 5, "Creating Sustainable Enterprises," is a collaborative effort. The primary contributor is Randy Parkin of Key Consulting in Calgary, Alberta, with input from Robert Craddock, Ron Koper and Don Beeken. Fred and Kate McLean of Fusion Consulting in London, Ontario, also contributed insights. We have created the *Leadership Alliance: Canada*, sharing a commitment to principle-based consulting—working with clients to increase individual and organizational effectiveness.

I am *truly grateful* to my agents, the gang at Can*Speak: Linda Davidson, Tina Boudreau, Sheree McGarrity, Phyllis Downing, Belinda Miller-Foey, Lesley Rizvi, Laurie Peck and Christine Christianson. Life is short so it had better be fun, and the team certainly has made it fun. They are a joy to work with!

A special group of people in North America have popularized this work by convincing organizations to apply it. They are the people at the speakers bureaus that represent me and this material: Perry Goldsmith, Theresa Gill, Michael Downes, Lisa Kemper, Lynda Kuiack, Leslie Gould, Sandra Vieira, Tanya Hamilton, Megan Gordon, Susanne Foord, Monica Lueg, Lorraine Trott, Signy Freyseng and Claudine Smith at National Speakers Bureau;

Nancy and Bill Lauterbach, James Bauchum, Anne Bayless, Nancy Culbertson, Carol Durham, Steve Gardner, Beth Hawley, Kathy Morris, Frank Pileggi, Joleen Sauer, Dianne Driver, Tricia Fielder, Sue Green, Christa Haub, Kristy Schubert, Fran Sims, Wallace Wilson, Diane Eisele and Carla Maloney at Five Star Speakers and Trainers Bureau. And Brad and Karen Plum, Barbara Byrnes and Susan Young who have joined Five Star from North American Speaker Bureau.

Mark French, Matthew Jones, Jim Garner, Tony Berardo, Jacqueline Pindat, Bobbi Sauls, Anya Pardue, David Jay, Marina Forstmann, Meridith Wagner, Kathleen Fahey, Katy Anderson, Steve Moynihan, Tonia Cleland, Suzy Gourdie, Helena Antoniades, Bobbi Sauls, Rainey Foster, Anne Richardson, David Blevins, Kevin Kelly, Edna Kirk, Carolyn Miller,

Theresa Page, Robin Reeder, Nicki Tsakonas and Colby McGrael at Leading Authorities;

Christine Moss and Karen and Sharon Boyce at Idea Connection; Ruth MacLean at Professional Speakers Bureau; Grant and Christine Doyle at Pinnacle Mountain Speakers Bureau; Andrea Norris at Laura M. Ferrier and Associates; Arlynn Greenbaum at Authors Unlimited.

Finally, I want to thank my literary agents, Perry Goldsmith and Robert Mackwood of Contemporary Communications, who are diligent, professional, skilled and delightful to work with.

Jim Harris

Jim Harris is the principal of Strategic Advantage, a management consulting firm providing strategic planning and leadership development to leading organizations. In 1990, Mr. Harris co-authored the second edition of *The Financial Post's* Canadian bestseller, *The 100 Best Companies to Work for in Canada*. And between 1992 and 1996 he represented the Covey Leadership Center of Utah in Canada by teaching Dr. Stephen Covey's work *The 7 Habits of Highly Effective People*.

Presentations by Jim Harris
Passionate, inspirational, fun, describe Jim Harris. He speaks at over 70 conference presentations a year internationally on issues of most concern to executives:

- Change Leadership
- Information Technology
- Creativity & Innovation
- Customer Intimacy
- Time Management

Interactive Workshops on:
- Strategic Planning
- Mission & Vision
- Teamwork

International clients representing all industries
Arthur Andersen • Association of College and Research Libraries • Barclays Bank • Bell Canada International • CSAE • Connaught Laboratories & Pasteur Mérieux • Credit Union Executives Society • CXY Chemicals • Deloitte & Touche • Ernst & Young • The Executive Committee (TEC) • European Snack Food Association • General Motors • George Weston • Glaxo-Welcome • IBM • IABC • International Council of Shopping Centers • International Meeting Planners & Incentive Travel • LEGO • Mackenzie Financial • MPI • NEC Computer Systems • North American Life • Royal LePage Commercial Real Estate • SHL Systemhouse • US Snack Food Association • Society of Management Accountants • Society of Professional Engineers • Sun Life • Sybase • Vermont State Employees Credit Union

To Book Jim Harris call 1-800-561-3591 or 1-800-665-7376

Jim Harris' presentations have a powerful impact.
Here's what clients say:

"Our partners and managers rated your workshop the highest."
— Megan Frigon, Specialty Consulting, Arthur Andersen & Co.

"The content applied to everyone's professional and personal lives. Your immense popularity was indicated by the audience's response and our survey. We can unequivocally recommend Jim Harris."
— Pete Peters, Quality Resource Center, General Motors of Canada

"As if the enthusiastic response wasn't enough, our survey was conclusive: You were a major hit! The response of 2,000 delegates: the content was on target, the presentation superlative."
— Phil Cunningham, President, Mackenzie Financial

"Thank you for kicking off our executive workshop in such an inspiring, entertaining and thought-provoking manner."
— Kathleen Seaver, Director, Worldwide Reengineering, Pasteur Mérieux

"You went beyond the standard 'shelf talk' and linked your ideas to the interests and experiences of the audience."
— Marvin Morrison, Senior VP, Intn'l Council of Shopping Centers

"The obvious extra efforts in listening to the other two keynote speakers paid huge dividends. Your presentation linked our theme and their presentations. You left our audience positively pumped."
— Al Doran, Past President, Canadian H.R. Systems Professionals

"Congratulations on completely captivating your audience! Our event planner says you won the 'most fun speaker to work with.'"
— Julie Charles, Editor, *Meetings & Incentive Travel*

"Your research, spending time with the group the night before your presentation, clearly shows you are committed to your audience."
— John Keizer, Director Corporate Affairs, Sobeys Inc.

"In the course of my work with CEOs of growth-oriented companies, I have experienced many first-class presentations. Without a doubt, yours ranks among the most insightful. Your special ability to bridge the theoretical and practical realms made a very strong impact. Many left with actionable concepts that will really help them build their organizations."
— Peter Buchanan, CEO, Network of the 50 Best Managed Private Cos.

"Jim Harris delivered one of the best training messages I've heard at Meeting Professionals International (MPI)."
— Marjorie Hamilton, Past International President, MPI

"The audience was riveted. What thought-provoking material!"
— Gilbert Cordell, Intn'l Conference on Horizontal Well Drilling

Bulk Orders
Volume Discount Schedule

"A great book for enlightened leaders to give to all their staff."
Susan Jurow, Executive Director,
College & University Personnel Association

Many organizations have purchased *The Learning Paradox* in bulk, giving a copy of the book or audio tape(s) to every executive, manager and employee. Some companies are giving these to clients as marketing and promotion premiums. The aggressive discount schedule below makes this possible. Books can only be purchased in 100+ quantities by special order, otherwise buy them from your local bookstore. Companies buying 5,000+ books can have a custom-designed cover and a full-color advertisement on the back cover at no extra cost. Call for a quote to purchase 10,000+ copies.

Price per item in $Canadian

# items ordered @ once	% Discount	Single Audio	3 Tape Audio Set
1+	-	14.95	44.95
5+	20	12.00	36.00
10+	30	10.50	31.50
25+	40	9.00	27.00
50+	46	8.10	24.30
100+	50	7.50	22.50
200+	56	6.60	19.80
500+	61	5.85	17.55
1,500+	65	5.25	15.75
2,500+	70	4.50	13.50
5,000+	71	4.35	13.05

Prices are in $Canadian. Deduct 25 per cent for U.S. orders in $US. Taxes & shipping excluded. You can mix and match—i.e., when buying 500 units—100 books, 300 single audios and 100 of the three tape sets—you get the 61 percent discount on all items. Companies hiring Jim to speak at a conference and buying a product for every delegate get one deeper discount level (i.e., when buying 300 items, see 500-unit level to calculate the discount). **To order, call 1-800-561-3591 or 1-800-665-7376.**